UNIVERSITY CASEBOOK SERIES

2017 SUPPLEMENT TO

FAMILY LAW

CASES AND MATERIALS

UNABRIDGED AND CONCISE SIXTH EDITIONS

JUDITH AREEN
Paul Regis Dean Professor of Law
Georgetown University Law Center

MARC SPINDELMAN
Isadore and Ida Topper Professor of Law
Michael E. Moritz College of Law
The Ohio State University

PHILOMILA TSOUKALA
Professor of Law
Georgetown University Law Center

SUPPLEMENT

by

MARC SPINDELMAN
PHILOMILA TSOUKALA

FOUNDATION
PRESS

University Casebook Series is a trademark registered in the U.S. Patent and Trademark Office.

© 2015, 2016 LEG, Inc. d/b/a West Academic
© 2017 LEG, Inc. d/b/a West Academic
     444 Cedar Street, Suite 700
     St. Paul, MN 55101
     1-877-888-1330

Printed in the United States of America

ISBN: 978-1-64020-159-0

PREFACE

Thanks to Alex Al-Doory, Susan Azyndar, Brooks Boron, Kori Brady, Sabrina Brown, Susan Edwards, Katherine Gullo, Brookes Hammock, Allyson Hennelly, Mycheala Holley, Marilyn Raisch, Syane Roy, Gretchen Rutz, Alexander Sonsev, James Talbert, Ethan Weber, and Molly Werhan, for various forms of assistance in preparing these materials.

MARC SPINDELMAN
PHILOMILA TSOUKALA

July 2017

TABLE OF CONTENTS

TABLE OF CASES

The principal cases are in bold type.

UNIVERSITY CASEBOOK SERIES®

2017 SUPPLEMENT TO

FAMILY LAW

CASES AND MATERIALS

**UNABRIDGED AND CONCISE
SIXTH EDITIONS**

CHAPTER 2

MARRYING

A. RESTRICTIONS ON WHO MAY MARRY

1. TRADITIONAL RESTRICTIONS

d. SAME-SEX MARRIAGE

Page 87, Unabridged (Page 60, Concise). Replace the materials in this section with the following cases and notes.

United States v. Windsor

Supreme Court of the United States, 2013.
570 U.S. ___, 133 S.Ct. 2675, 186 L.Ed.2d 808.

■ JUSTICE KENNEDY delivered the opinion of the Court.

. . .

I

In 1996, as some States were beginning to consider the concept of same-sex marriage, and before any State had acted to permit it, Congress enacted the Defense of Marriage Act (DOMA), 110 Stat. 2419. DOMA contains two operative sections[.] . . .

Section 3 is at issue here. It amends the Dictionary Act in Title 1, § 7, of the United States Code to provide a federal definition of "marriage" and "spouse." Section 3 of DOMA provides as follows:

"In determining the meaning of any Act of Congress, or of any ruling, regulation, or interpretation of the various administrative bureaus and agencies of the United States, the word 'marriage' means only a legal union between one man and one woman as husband and wife, and the word 'spouse' refers only to a person of the opposite sex who is a husband or a wife." 1 U.S.C. § 7.

The definitional provision does not . . . forbid States from enacting laws permitting same-sex marriages or civil unions or providing state benefits to residents in that status. The enactment's comprehensive definition of marriage for purposes of all federal statutes and other regulations or directives covered by its terms, however, does control over 1,000 federal laws in which marital or spousal status is addressed as a matter of federal law.

Edith Windsor and Thea Spyer met in New York City in 1963 and began a long-term relationship. . . . Concerned about Spyer's health, the couple made [a] . . . 2007 trip to Canada [to be married] . . . , but they continued to reside in New York City. The State of New York deems their Ontario marriage to be a valid one.

Spyer died in February 2009, and left her entire estate to Windsor. Because DOMA denies federal recognition to same-sex spouses, Windsor did not qualify for the marital exemption from the federal estate tax, which excludes from taxation "any interest in property which passes or has passed from the decedent to his surviving spouse." 26 U.S.C. § 2056(a). Windsor paid $363,053 in estate taxes and sought a refund. The Internal Revenue Service denied the refund, concluding that, under DOMA, Windsor was not a "surviving spouse." Windsor commenced this refund suit[.]

While the tax refund suit was pending, the Attorney General of the United States notified the Speaker of the House of Representatives, pursuant to 28 U.S.C. § 530D, that the Department of Justice would no longer defend the constitutionality of DOMA's § 3. . . . [T]he Attorney General informed Congress that "the President has concluded that given a number of factors, including a documented history of discrimination, classifications based on sexual orientation should be subject to a heightened standard of scrutiny." . . .

Although "the President . . . instructed the Department not to defend the statute in *Windsor*," he also decided "that Section 3 will continue to be enforced by the Executive Branch" and that the United States had an "interest in providing Congress a full and fair opportunity to participate in the litigation of those cases." The stated rationale for this dual-track procedure (determination of unconstitutionality coupled with ongoing enforcement) was to "recogniz[e] the judiciary as the final arbiter of the constitutional claims raised."

In response to the notice from the Attorney General, the Bipartisan Legal Advisory Group (BLAG) of the House of Representatives voted to intervene in the litigation to defend the constitutionality of § 3 of DOMA. The Department of Justice did not oppose limited intervention by BLAG. The District Court denied BLAG's motion to enter the suit as of right, on the rationale that the United States already was represented by the Department of Justice. The District Court, however, did grant intervention by BLAG as an interested party. See Fed. Rule Civ. Proc. 24(a)(2).

. . .

III

. . . [U]ntil recent years, many citizens had not even considered the possibility that two persons of the same sex might aspire to occupy the same status and dignity as that of a man and woman in lawful marriage. For marriage between a man and a woman no doubt had been thought of by most people as essential to the very definition of that term and to its role and function throughout the history of civilization. That belief, for many who long have held it, became even more urgent, more cherished when challenged. For others, however, came the beginnings of a new perspective, a new insight. Accordingly some States concluded that same-sex marriage ought to be given recognition and validity in the law for those same-sex couples who wish to define themselves by their commitment to each other. The limitation of lawful marriage to heterosexual couples, which for centuries had been deemed both necessary and fundamental, came to be seen in New York and certain other States as an unjust exclusion.

. . . New York, in common with, as of this writing, 11 other States and the District of Columbia, [ultimately] decided that same-sex couples should have the right to marry and so live with pride in themselves and their union and in a status of equality with all other married persons. . . .

Against this background of lawful same-sex marriage in some States, the design, purpose, and effect of DOMA should be considered as the beginning point in deciding whether it is valid under the Constitution. By history and tradition[,] the definition and regulation of marriage . . . has been treated as being within the authority and realm of the separate States. Yet it is further established that Congress, in enacting discrete statutes, can make determinations that bear on marital rights and privileges. . . .

. . .

In order to assess the validity of [Section 3 of DOMA] . . . it is necessary to discuss the extent of the state power and authority over marriage as a matter of history and tradition. . . . [S]ubject to [constitutional] . . . guarantees, "regulation of domestic relations" is "an area that has long been regarded as a virtually exclusive province of the States." *Sosna v. Iowa*, 419 U.S. 393, 404 (1975).

The recognition of civil marriages is central to state domestic relations law applicable to its residents and citizens. The definition of marriage is the foundation of the State's broader authority to regulate the subject of domestic relations[.] . . . "[T]he states, at the time of the adoption of the Constitution, possessed full power over the subject of marriage and divorce . . . [and] the Constitution delegated no authority to the Government of the United States on the subject of marriage and divorce." *Haddock v. Haddock*, 201 U.S. 562, 575 (1906).

Consistent with this allocation of authority, the Federal Government, through our history, has deferred to state-law policy decisions with respect to domestic relations. . . .

. . .

. . . DOMA rejects the long-established precept that the incidents, benefits, and obligations of marriage are uniform for all married couples within each State, though they may vary, subject to constitutional guarantees, from one State to the next. Despite these considerations, it is unnecessary to decide whether this federal intrusion on state power is a violation of the Constitution because it disrupts the federal balance.

The State's power in defining the marital relation is of central relevance in this case quite apart from principles of federalism. Here the State's decision to give this class of persons the right to marry conferred upon them a dignity and status of immense import. When the State used its historic and essential authority to define the marital relation in this way, its role and its power in making the decision enhanced the recognition, dignity, and protection of the class in their own community. DOMA, because of its reach and extent, departs from this history and tradition of reliance on state law to define marriage. " '[D]iscriminations of an unusual character especially suggest careful consideration to determine whether they are obnoxious to the constitutional provision.' " *Romer v. Evans*, 517 U.S. 620, 633 (1996).

The Federal Government uses this state-defined class for the opposite purpose—to impose restrictions and disabilities. That result requires this Court now to address whether the resulting injury and indignity is a deprivation of an essential part of the liberty protected by the Fifth Amendment. What the State of New York treats as alike the federal law deems unlike by a law designed to injure the same class the State seeks to protect.

. . .

IV

DOMA seeks to injure the very class New York seeks to protect. By doing so it violates basic due process and equal protection principles applicable to the Federal Government. The Constitution's guarantee of equality "must at the very least mean that a bare congressional desire to harm a politically unpopular group cannot" justify disparate treatment of that group. *Department of Agriculture v. Moreno*, 413 U.S. 528, 534–535 (1973). In determining whether a law is motived by an improper animus or purpose, " '[d]iscriminations of an unusual character' " especially require careful consideration. DOMA cannot survive under these principles. . . . DOMA's unusual deviation from the usual tradition of recognizing and accepting state definitions of marriage here operates to deprive same-sex couples of the benefits and responsibilities that come with the federal recognition of their marriages. This is strong evidence of a law having the purpose and effect of disapproval of that class. The avowed purpose and practical effect of the law here in question are to impose a disadvantage, a separate status, and so a stigma upon all who enter into same-sex marriages made lawful by the unquestioned authority of the States.

The history of DOMA's enactment and its own text demonstrate that interference with the equal dignity of same-sex marriages, a dignity conferred by the States in the exercise of their sovereign power, was more than an incidental effect of the federal statute. It was its essence. The House Report announced its conclusion that "it is both appropriate and necessary for Congress to do what it can to defend the institution of traditional heterosexual marriage. . . . H.R. 3396 is appropriately entitled the 'Defense of Marriage Act.' The effort to redefine 'marriage' to extend to homosexual couples is a truly radical proposal that would fundamentally alter the institution of marriage." H.R. Rep. No. 104–664, pp. 12–13 (1996). The House concluded that DOMA expresses "both moral disapproval of homosexuality, and a moral conviction that heterosexuality better comports with traditional (especially Judeo-Christian) morality." *Id.*, at 16 (footnote deleted). The stated purpose of the law was to promote an "interest in protecting the traditional moral teachings reflected in heterosexual-only marriage laws." *Ibid.* Were there any doubt of this far-reaching purpose, the title of the Act confirms it: The Defense of Marriage.

The arguments put forward by BLAG are just as candid about the congressional purpose to influence or interfere with state sovereign choices about who may be married. As the title and dynamics of the bill indicate, its purpose is to discourage enactment of state same-sex marriage laws and to restrict the freedom and choice of couples married under those laws if they are enacted. The congressional goal was "to put a thumb on the scales and influence a state's decision as to how to shape its own marriage laws." *Mass. v. U.S. Dept. of Health and Human Servs.*, 682 F.3d 1, 12–13 (1st Cir. 2012). The Act's demonstrated purpose is to ensure that if any State decides to recognize same-sex marriages, those unions will be treated as second-class marriages for purposes of federal law. This raises a most serious question under the Constitution's Fifth Amendment.

DOMA's operation in practice confirms this purpose. When New York adopted a law to permit same-sex marriage, it sought to eliminate inequality; but DOMA frustrates that objective through a system-wide enactment with no identified connection to any particular area of federal law. DOMA writes inequality into the entire United States Code. The particular case at hand concerns the estate tax, but DOMA is more than a simple determination of what should or should not be allowed as an estate tax refund. Among the over 1,000 statutes and numerous federal regulations that DOMA controls are laws pertaining to Social Security, housing, taxes, criminal sanctions, copyright, and veterans' benefits.

DOMA's principal effect is to identify a subset of state-sanctioned marriages and make them unequal. The principal purpose is to impose inequality, not for other reasons like governmental efficiency. Responsibilities, as well as rights, enhance the dignity and integrity of the person. And DOMA contrives to deprive some couples married under the laws of their State, but not other couples, of both rights and responsibilities. By creating two contradictory marriage regimes within the same State, DOMA forces same-sex couples to live as married for the purpose of state law but unmarried for the purpose of federal law, thus diminishing the stability and predictability of basic personal relations the State has found it proper to acknowledge and protect. By this dynamic DOMA undermines both the public and private significance of state-sanctioned same-sex marriages; for it tells those couples, and all the world, that their otherwise valid marriages are unworthy of federal recognition. This places same-sex couples in an unstable position of being in a second-tier marriage. The differentiation demeans the couple, whose moral and sexual choices the Constitution protects, see *Lawrence* [*v. Texas*], 539 U.S. 558 [(2003)], and whose relationship the State has sought to dignify. And it humiliates tens of thousands of children now being raised by same-sex couples. The law in question makes it even more difficult for the children to understand the integrity and closeness of their own family and its concord with other families in their community and in their daily lives.

Under DOMA, same-sex married couples have their lives burdened, by reason of government decree, in visible and public ways. By its great reach, DOMA touches many aspects of married and family life, from the mundane to the profound. It prevents same-sex married couples from obtaining government healthcare benefits they would otherwise receive. It deprives them of the Bankruptcy Code's special protections for domestic-support obligations. It forces them to follow a complicated procedure to file their state and federal taxes jointly. It prohibits them from being buried together in veterans' cemeteries.

For certain married couples, DOMA's unequal effects are even more serious. The federal penal code makes it a crime to "assaul[t], kidna[p], or murde[r] . . . a member of the immediate family" of "a United States official, a United States judge, [or] a Federal law enforcement officer," 18 U.S.C. § 115(a)(1)(A), with the intent to influence or retaliate against that official, § 115(a)(1). Although a "spouse" qualifies as a member of the officer's "immediate family," § 115(c)(2), DOMA makes this protection inapplicable to same-sex spouses.

DOMA also brings financial harm to children of same-sex couples. It raises the cost of health care for families by taxing health benefits provided by employers to their workers' same-sex spouses. And it denies or reduces benefits allowed to families upon the loss of a spouse and parent, benefits that are an integral part of family security.

DOMA divests married same-sex couples of the duties and responsibilities that are an essential part of married life and that they in most cases would be honored to accept were DOMA not in force. For instance, because it is expected that spouses will support each other as they pursue educational opportunities, federal law takes into consideration a spouse's income in calculating a student's federal financial aid eligibility. Same-sex married couples are exempt from this requirement. The same is true with respect to federal ethics rules. Federal executive and agency officials are prohibited from "participat[ing] personally and substantially" in matters as to which they or their spouses have a financial interest. A similar statute prohibits Senators, Senate employees, and their spouses from accepting high-value gifts from certain sources, and another mandates detailed financial disclosures by numerous high-ranking officials and their spouses. Under DOMA, however, these Government-integrity rules do not apply to same-sex spouses.

. . .

What has been explained to this point should more than suffice to establish that the principal purpose and the necessary effect of this law are to demean those persons who are in a lawful same-sex marriage. This requires the Court to hold, as it now does, that DOMA is unconstitutional as a deprivation of the liberty of the person protected by the Fifth Amendment of the Constitution.

The liberty protected by the Fifth Amendment's Due Process Clause contains within it the prohibition against denying to any person the equal protection of the laws. See *Bolling* [*v. Sharpe*, 347 U.S. 497,] 499–500 [(1954)]. While the Fifth Amendment itself withdraws from Government the power to degrade or demean in the way this law does, the equal protection guarantee of the Fourteenth Amendment makes that Fifth Amendment right all the more specific and all the better understood and preserved.

The class to which DOMA directs its restrictions and restraints are those persons who are joined in same-sex marriages made lawful by the State. DOMA singles out a class of persons deemed by a State entitled to recognition and protection to enhance their own liberty. It imposes a disability on the class by refusing to acknowledge a status the State finds to be dignified and proper. DOMA instructs all federal officials, and indeed all persons with whom same-sex couples interact, including their own children, that their marriage is less worthy than the marriages of others. The federal statute is invalid, for no legitimate purpose overcomes the purpose and effect to disparage and to injure those whom the State, by its marriage laws, sought to protect in personhood and dignity. By seeking to displace this protection and treating those persons as living in marriages less respected than others, the federal statute is in violation of the Fifth Amendment. This opinion and its holding are confined to those lawful marriages.

. . .

■ CHIEF JUSTICE ROBERTS, dissenting.

. . . On the merits of the constitutional dispute the Court decides to decide, I . . . agree with JUSTICE SCALIA that Congress acted constitutionally in passing the Defense of Marriage Act (DOMA). Interests in uniformity and stability amply justified Congress's decision to retain the definition of marriage that, at that point, had been adopted by every State in our Nation, and every nation in the world.

The majority sees a more sinister motive, pointing out that the Federal Government has generally (though not uniformly) deferred to state definitions of marriage in the past. That is true, of course, but none of those prior state-by-state variations had involved differences over something—as the majority puts it—"thought of by most people as essential to the very definition of [marriage] and to its role and function throughout the history of civilization." That the Federal Government treated this fundamental question differently than it treated variations over consanguinity or minimum age is hardly surprising—and hardly enough to support a conclusion that the "principal purpose," of the 342 Representatives and 85 Senators who voted for it, and the President who signed it, was a bare desire to harm. Nor do the snippets of legislative history and the banal title of the Act to which the majority points suffice to make such a showing. At least without some more convincing evidence that the Act's principal purpose was to codify malice, and that it furthered *no* legitimate government interests, I would not tar the political branches with the brush of bigotry.

But while I disagree with the result to which the majority's analysis leads it in this case, I think it more important to point out that its analysis leads no further. The Court does not have before it, and the logic of its opinion does not decide, the distinct question whether the States, in the exercise of their "historic and essential authority to define the marital relation," may continue to utilize the traditional definition of marriage.

The majority goes out of its way to make this explicit in the penultimate sentence of its opinion. It states that "[t]his opinion and its holding are confined to those lawful marriages"—referring to same-sex marriages that a State has already recognized as a result of the local "community's considered perspective on the historical roots of the institution of marriage and its evolving understanding of the meaning of equality." JUSTICE SCALIA believes this is a "'bald, unreasoned disclaime[r].'" In my view, though, the disclaimer is a logical and necessary consequence of the argument the majority has chosen to adopt. The dominant theme of the majority opinion is that the Federal Government's intrusion into an area "central to state domestic relations law applicable to its residents and citizens" is sufficiently "unusual" to set off alarm bells. I think the majority goes off course, as I have said, but it is undeniable that its judgment is based on federalism.

The majority extensively chronicles DOMA's departure from the normal allocation of responsibility between State and Federal Governments, emphasizing that DOMA "rejects the long-established precept that the incidents, benefits, and obligations of marriage are uniform for all married couples within each State." But there is no such departure when one State adopts or keeps a definition of marriage that differs from that of its neighbor, for it is entirely expected that state definitions would "vary, subject to constitutional guarantees, from one State to the next." Thus, while "[t]he State's power in defining the marital relation is of central relevance" to the majority's decision to strike down DOMA here, that power will come into play on the other side of the board in future cases about the constitutionality of state marriage definitions.

So too will the concerns for state diversity and sovereignty that weigh against DOMA's constitutionality in this case.

It is not just this central feature of the majority's analysis that is unique to DOMA, but many considerations on the periphery as well. For example, the majority focuses on the legislative history and title of this particular Act; those statute-specific considerations will, of course, be irrelevant in future cases about different statutes. The majority emphasizes that DOMA was a "systemwide enactment with no identified connection to any particular area of federal law," but a State's definition of marriage "is the foundation of the State's broader authority to regulate the subject of domestic relations with respect to the '[p]rotection of offspring, property interests, and the enforcement of marital responsibilities.'" And the federal decision undermined (in the majority's view) the "dignity [already] conferred by the States in the exercise of their sovereign power," whereas a State's decision whether to expand the definition of marriage from its traditional contours involves no similar concern.

We may in the future have to resolve challenges to state marriage definitions affecting same-sex couples. That issue, however, is not before us in this case[.] . . . I write only to highlight the limits of the majority's holding and reasoning today, lest its opinion be taken to resolve not only a question that I believe is not properly before us—DOMA's constitutionality—but also a question that all agree, and the Court explicitly acknowledges, is not at issue.

■ JUSTICE SCALIA, with whom JUSTICE THOMAS joins[.]*

. . .

II

. . .

A

There are many remarkable things about the majority's merits holding. The first is how rootless and shifting its justifications are. For example, the opinion starts with seven full pages about the traditional power of States to define domestic relations—initially fooling many readers, I am sure, into thinking that this is a federalism opinion. But we are eventually told that "it is unnecessary to decide whether this federal intrusion on state power is a violation of the Constitution," and that "[t]he State's power in defining the marital relation is of central relevance in this case quite apart from principles of federalism" because "the State's decision to give this class of persons the right to marry conferred upon them a dignity and status of immense import." But no one questions the power of the States to define marriage (with the concomitant conferral of dignity and status), so what is the point of

---

*   Ed.: Chief Justice Roberts joined in Part I of this opinion, omitted here, dealing with jurisdictional questions involved in the case.

devoting seven pages to describing how long and well established that power is? Even after the opinion has formally disclaimed reliance upon principles of federalism, mentions of "the usual tradition of recognizing and accepting state definitions of marriage" continue. What to make of this? The opinion never explains. My guess is that the majority, while reluctant to suggest that defining the meaning of "marriage" in federal statutes is unsupported by any of the Federal Government's enumerated powers, nonetheless needs some rhetorical basis to support its pretense that today's prohibition of laws excluding same-sex marriage is confined to the Federal Government (leaving the second, state-law shoe to be dropped later . . .). But I am only guessing.

Equally perplexing are the opinion's references to "the Constitution's guarantee of equality." . . .

. . . [I]f this is meant to be an equal-protection opinion, it is a confusing one. The opinion does not resolve and indeed does not even mention what had been the central question in this litigation: whether, under the Equal Protection Clause, laws restricting marriage to a man and a woman are reviewed for more than mere rationality. . . . In accord with my previously expressed skepticism about the Court's "tiers of scrutiny" approach, I would review this classification only for its rationality. As nearly as I can tell, the Court agrees with that; its opinion does not apply strict scrutiny, and its central propositions are taken from rational-basis cases. . . . But the Court certainly does not *apply* anything that resembles that deferential framework.

The majority opinion need not get into the strict-vs.-rational-basis scrutiny question, and need not justify its holding under either, because it says that DOMA is unconstitutional as "a deprivation of the liberty of the person protected by the Fifth Amendment of the Constitution"; that it violates "basic due process" principles; and that it inflicts an "injury and indignity" of a kind that denies "an essential part of the liberty protected by the Fifth Amendment[.]" The majority never utters the dread words "substantive due process," . . . but that is what those statements mean. Yet the opinion does not argue that same-sex marriage is "deeply rooted in this Nation's history and tradition," *Washington v. Glucksberg*, 521 U.S. 702, 720–721 (1997), a claim that would of course be quite absurd. So would the further suggestion (also necessary, under our substantive-due-process precedents) that a world in which DOMA exists is one bereft of " 'ordered liberty.' " *Id.*, at 721 (quoting *Palko v. Connecticut*, 302 U.S. 319, 325 (1937)).

. . . The sum of all the Court's nonspecific hand-waving is that this law is invalid (maybe on equal-protection grounds, maybe on substantive-due-process grounds, and perhaps with some amorphous federalism component playing a role) because it is motivated by a " 'bare . . . desire to harm' " couples in same-sex marriages. It is this proposition with which I will therefore engage.

B

As I have observed before, the Constitution does not forbid the government to enforce traditional moral and sexual norms. See *Lawrence v. Texas*, 539 U.S. 558, 599 (2003) (Scalia, J., dissenting). I will not swell the U.S. Reports with restatements of that point. It is enough to say that the Constitution neither requires nor forbids our society to approve of same-sex marriage, much as it neither requires nor forbids us to approve of no-fault divorce, polygamy, or the consumption of alcohol.

However, even setting aside traditional moral disapproval of same-sex marriage (or indeed same-sex sex), there are many perfectly valid—indeed, downright boring—justifying rationales for this legislation. Their existence ought to be the end of this case. For they give the lie to the Court's conclusion that only those with hateful hearts could have voted "aye" on this Act. And more importantly, they serve to make the contents of the legislators' hearts quite irrelevant: "It is a familiar principle of constitutional law that this Court will not strike down an otherwise constitutional statute on the basis of an alleged illicit legislative motive." *United States v. O'Brien*, 391 U.S. 367, 383 (1968). Or at least it *was* a familiar principle. By holding to the contrary, the majority has declared open season on any law that (in the opinion of the law's opponents and any panel of like-minded federal judges) can be characterized as mean-spirited.

The majority concludes that the only motive for this Act was the "bare . . . desire to harm a politically unpopular group." Bear in mind that the object of this condemnation is not the legislature of some once-Confederate Southern state (familiar objects of the Court's scorn, see, *e.g.*, *Edwards v. Aguillard*, 482 U.S. 578 (1987)), but our respected coordinate branches, the Congress and Presidency of the United States. Laying such a charge against them should require the most extraordinary evidence, and I would have thought that every attempt would be made to indulge a more anodyne explanation for the statute. The majority does the opposite—affirmatively concealing from the reader the arguments that exist in justification. It makes only a passing mention of the "arguments put forward" by the Act's defenders, and does not even trouble to paraphrase or describe them. I imagine that this is because it is harder to maintain the illusion of the Act's supporters as unhinged members of a wild-eyed lynch mob when one first describes their views as *they* see them.

To choose just one of these defenders' arguments, DOMA avoids difficult choice-of-law issues that will now arise absent a uniform federal definition of marriage. Imagine a pair of women who marry in Albany and then move to Alabama, which does not "recognize as valid any marriage of parties of the same sex." Ala. Code § 30–1–19(e) (2011). When the couple files their next federal tax return, may it be a joint one? Which State's law controls, for federal-law purposes: their State of celebration (which recognizes the marriage) or their State of domicile (which does not)? (Does the answer depend on whether they were just visiting in Albany?) Are these questions to be answered as a matter of federal common law, or perhaps by borrowing a State's choice-of-law rules? If so, *which* State's? And what about States where the status of an out-of-state same-sex marriage is an unsettled question under local law? See *Godfrey v. Spano*, 920 N.E.2d 328 ([N.Y.] 2009). DOMA avoided all of this uncertainty by specifying which marriages would be recognized for federal purposes. That is a classic purpose for a definitional provision.

Further, DOMA preserves the intended effects of prior legislation against then-unforeseen changes in circumstance. When Congress provided (for example) that a special estate-tax exemption would exist for spouses, this exemption reached only *opposite-sex* spouses—those being the only sort that were recognized in *any* State at the time of DOMA's passage. When it became clear that changes in state law might one day alter that balance, DOMA's definitional section was enacted to ensure that state-level experimentation did not automatically alter the basic operation of federal law, unless and until Congress made the further judgment to do so on its own. That is not animus—just stabilizing prudence. Congress has hardly demonstrated itself unwilling to make such further, revising judgments upon due deliberation. See, *e.g.*, Don't Ask, Don't Tell Repeal Act of 2010, 124 Stat. 3515.

The Court mentions none of this. Instead, it accuses the Congress that enacted this law and the President who signed it of something much worse than, for example, having acted in excess of enumerated federal powers—or even having drawn distinctions that prove to be irrational. Those legal errors may be made in good faith, errors though they are. But the majority says that the supporters of this Act acted with *malice*—with *the "purpose"* "to disparage and to injure" same-sex couples. It says that the motivation for DOMA was to "demean"; to "impose inequality"; to "impose . . . a stigma"; to deny people "equal dignity"; to brand gay people as "unworthy"; and to "*humiliat*[*e*]" their children.

I am sure these accusations are quite untrue. To be sure . . . , the legislation is called the Defense of Marriage Act. But to defend traditional marriage is not to condemn, demean, or humiliate those who would prefer other arrangements, any more than to defend the Constitution of the United States is to condemn, demean, or humiliate other constitutions. To hurl such accusations so casually demeans *this institution*. In the majority's judgment, any resistance to its holding is beyond the pale of reasoned disagreement. To question its high-handed invalidation of a presumptively valid statute is to act (the majority is sure) with *the purpose* to "disparage," "injure," "degrade," "demean," and "humiliate" our fellow human beings, our fellow citizens, who are homosexual. All that, simply for supporting an Act that did no more than codify an aspect of marriage that had been unquestioned in our society for most of its existence—indeed, had been unquestioned in virtually all societies for virtually all of human history. It is one thing for a society to elect change; it is another for a court of law to impose change by adjudging those who oppose it . . . enemies of the human race.

* * *

The penultimate sentence of the majority's opinion is a naked declaration that "[t]his opinion and its holding are confined" to those couples "joined in same-sex marriages made lawful by the State." I have heard such "bald, unreasoned disclaimer[s]" before. *Lawrence*, 539 U.S., at 604 [(Scalia, J., dissenting)]. When the Court declared a constitutional right to homosexual sodomy, we were assured that the case had nothing, nothing at all to do with "whether the government must give formal recognition to any relationship that homosexual persons seek to enter." *Id.*, at 578. Now we are told that DOMA is invalid because it "demeans the couple, whose moral and sexual choices the Constitution protects"— with an accompanying citation of *Lawrence*. It takes real cheek for today's majority to assure us . . . that a constitutional requirement to give formal recognition to same-sex marriage is not at issue here—when what has preceded that assurance is a lecture on how superior the majority's moral judgment in favor of same-sex marriage is to the Congress's hateful moral judgment against it. I promise you this: The only thing that will "confine" the Court's holding is its sense of what it can get away with.

I do not mean to suggest disagreement with THE CHIEF JUSTICE's view, that lower federal courts and state courts can distinguish today's case when the issue before them is state denial of marital status to same-sex couples—or even that this Court could *theoretically* do so. Lord, an opinion with such scatter-shot rationales as this one (federalism noises among them) can be distinguished in many ways. And deserves to be. State and lower federal courts should take the Court at its word and distinguish away.

In my opinion, however, the view that *this* Court will take of state prohibition of same-sex marriage is indicated beyond mistaking by today's opinion. As I have said, the real rationale of today's opinion, whatever disappearing trail of its legalistic argle-bargle one chooses to follow, is that DOMA is motivated by " 'bare . . . desire to harm' " couples in same-sex marriages. How easy it is, indeed how inevitable, to reach the same conclusion with regard to state laws denying same-sex couples marital status. . . . [T]hat Court which finds it so horrific that Congress irrationally and hatefully robbed same-sex couples of the "personhood and dignity" which state legislatures conferred upon them, will of a certitude be similarly appalled by state legislatures' irrational and hateful failure to acknowledge that "personhood and dignity" in the first place. As far as this Court is concerned, no one should be fooled; it is just a matter of listening and waiting for the other shoe.

By formally declaring anyone opposed to same-sex marriage an enemy of human decency, the majority arms well every challenger to a state law restricting marriage to its traditional definition. Henceforth those challengers will lead with this Court's declaration that there is "no legitimate purpose" served by such a law, and will claim that the traditional definition has "the purpose and effect to disparage and to injure" the "personhood and dignity" of same-sex couples. The majority's limiting assurance will be meaningless in the face of language like that, as the majority well knows. That is why the language is there. The result will be a judicial distortion of our society's debate over marriage—a debate that can seem in need of our clumsy "help" only to a member of this institution.

As to that debate: Few public controversies touch an institution so central to the lives of so many, and few inspire such attendant passion by good people on all sides. Few public controversies will ever demonstrate so vividly the beauty of what our Framers gave us, a gift the Court pawns today to buy its stolen moment in the spotlight: a system of government that permits us to rule *ourselves*. Since DOMA's passage, citizens on all sides of the question have seen victories and they have seen defeats. There have been plebiscites, legislation, persuasion, and loud voices—in other words, democracy. . . .

In the majority's telling, this story is black-and-white: Hate your neighbor or come along with us. The truth is more complicated. It is hard to admit that one's political opponents are not monsters, especially in a struggle like this one, and the challenge in the end proves more than today's Court can handle. Too bad. A reminder that disagreement over something so fundamental as marriage can still be politically legitimate would have been a fit task for what in earlier times was called the judicial temperament. We might have covered ourselves with honor today, by promising all sides of this debate that it was theirs to settle and that we would respect their resolution. We might have let the People decide.

But that the majority will not do. Some will rejoice in today's decision, and some will despair at it; that is the nature of a controversy that matters so much to so many. But the Court has cheated both sides, robbing the winners of an honest victory, and the losers of the peace that comes from a fair defeat. We owed both of them better. I dissent.

■ JUSTICE ALITO, with whom JUSTICE THOMAS joins as to Parts II and III, dissenting.

Our Nation is engaged in a heated debate about same-sex marriage. That debate is, at bottom, about the nature of the institution of marriage. . . .

. . .

II

. . .

Same-sex marriage presents a highly emotional and important question of public policy—but not a difficult question of constitutional law. The Constitution does not guarantee the right to enter into a same-sex marriage. Indeed, no provision of the Constitution speaks to the issue.

[T]he Court's holding that "DOMA is unconstitutional as a deprivation of the liberty of the person protected by the Fifth Amendment of the Constitution" suggests that substantive due process may partially underlie the Court's decision today. . . .

It is beyond dispute that the right to same-sex marriage is not deeply rooted in this Nation's history and tradition. In this country, no State permitted same-sex marriage until the Massachusetts Supreme Judicial Court held in 2003 that limiting marriage to opposite-sex couples violated the State Constitution. See *Goodridge v. Department of Public Health*, 798 N.E.2d 941 [(Mass. 2003)]. Nor is the right to same-sex marriage deeply rooted in the traditions of other nations. No country allowed same-sex couples to marry until the Netherlands did so in 2000.

What Windsor and the United States seek, therefore, is not the protection of a deeply rooted right but the recognition of a very new right, and they seek this innovation not from a legislative body elected by the people, but from unelected judges. Faced with such a request, judges have cause for both caution and humility.

The family is an ancient and universal human institution. Family structure reflects the characteristics of a civilization, and changes in family structure and in the popular understanding of marriage and the family can have profound effects. Past changes in the understanding of marriage—for example, the gradual ascendance of the idea that romantic love is a prerequisite to marriage—have had far-reaching consequences. But the process by which such consequences come about is complex, involving the interaction of numerous factors, and tends to occur over an extended period of time.

We can expect something similar to take place if same-sex marriage becomes widely accepted. The long-term consequences of this change are not now known and are unlikely to be ascertainable for some time to come. . . .

At present, no one—including social scientists, philosophers, and historians—can predict with any certainty what the long-term ramifications of widespread acceptance of same-sex marriage will be. And judges are certainly not equipped to make such an assessment. The Members of this Court have the authority and the responsibility to interpret and apply the Constitution. Thus, if the Constitution contained a provision guaranteeing the right to marry a person of the same sex, it would be our duty to enforce that right. But the Constitution simply does not speak to the issue of same-sex marriage. In our system of government, ultimate sovereignty rests with the people, and the people have the right to control their own destiny. Any change on a question so fundamental should be made by the people through their elected officials.

III

Perhaps because they cannot show that same-sex marriage is a fundamental right under our Constitution, Windsor and the United States couch their arguments in equal protection terms. . . .

. . .

. . . Acceptance of the [equal protection] argument would cast all those who cling to traditional beliefs about the nature of marriage in the role of bigots or superstitious fools.

By asking the Court to strike down DOMA as not satisfying some form of heightened scrutiny, Windsor and the United States are really seeking to have the Court resolve a debate between two competing views of marriage.

The first and older view, which I will call the "traditional" or "conjugal" view, sees marriage as an intrinsically opposite-sex institution. . . . [One idea animating this view is] . . . that the institution of marriage was created for the purpose of channeling heterosexual intercourse into a structure that supports child rearing. Others explain the basis for the institution . . . argu[ing] that marriage is essentially the solemnizing of a comprehensive, exclusive, permanent union that is intrinsically ordered to producing new life, even if it does not always do so. While modern cultural changes have weakened the link between marriage and procreation in the popular mind, . . . throughout human history and across many cultures, marriage has been viewed as an exclusively opposite-sex institution and as one inextricably linked to procreation and biological kinship.

The other, newer view is what I will call the "consent-based" vision of marriage, a vision that primarily defines marriage as the solemnization of mutual commitment—marked by strong emotional attachment and sexual attraction—between two persons. . . . [O]ur popular culture is infused with this understanding of marriage. Proponents of same-sex marriage argue that because gender differentiation is not relevant to this vision, the exclusion of same-sex couples from the institution of marriage is rank discrimination.

The Constitution does not codify either of these views of marriage[.] . . . Because our constitutional order assigns the resolution of questions of this nature to the people, I would not presume to enshrine either vision of marriage in our constitutional jurisprudence.

. . .

Rather than fully embracing the arguments made by Windsor and the United States, the Court strikes down § 3 of DOMA as a classification not properly supported by its objectives. The Court reaches this conclusion in part because it believes that § 3 encroaches upon the States' sovereign prerogative to define marriage. Indeed, the Court's ultimate conclusion is that DOMA falls afoul of the Fifth Amendment because it "singles out a class of persons deemed *by a State* entitled to recognition and protection to enhance their own liberty" and "imposes a disability on the class by refusing to acknowledge a status *the State finds* to be dignified and proper."

To the extent that the Court takes the position that the question of same-sex marriage should be resolved primarily at the state level, I wholeheartedly agree. I hope that the Court will ultimately permit the people of each State to decide this question for themselves. Unless the Court is willing to allow this to occur, the whiffs of federalism in the today's opinion of the Court will soon be scattered to the wind.

In any event, § 3 of DOMA, in my view, does not encroach on the prerogatives of the States, assuming of course that the many federal statutes affected by DOMA have not already done so. Section 3 does not prevent any State from recognizing same-sex marriage or from extending to same-sex couples any right, privilege, benefit, or obligation stemming from state law. All that § 3 does is to define a class of persons to whom federal law extends certain special benefits and upon whom federal law imposes certain special burdens. In these provisions, Congress used marital status as a way of defining this class—in part, I assume, because it viewed marriage as a valuable institution to be fostered and in part because it viewed married couples as comprising a unique type of economic unit that merits special regulatory treatment. Assuming that Congress has the power under the Constitution to enact the laws affected by § 3, Congress has the power to define the category of persons to whom those laws apply.

* * *

For these reasons, I would hold that § 3 of DOMA does not violate the Fifth Amendment. I respectfully dissent.

NOTE

1. In a companion case decided the same day as *Windsor*, the Supreme Court declined to explain whether its ruling on the merits in *Windsor* applied to a state-level limitation on same-sex marriage. *Hollingsworth v. Perry*, 133 S.Ct. 2652 (2013) (involving the constitutionality of California's Proposition 8). In *Perry*, the Court ruled on constitutional procedural grounds that the defendant-intervenors in the case, who helped get Proposition 8 on the ballot in California, did not have standing to appeal the trial court decision declaring Proposition 8 unconstitutional. *Id.* at 2662. According to the Court, they did not have a "direct stake," and hence a personalized injury, that differentiated them for federal constitutional purposes from other Californians unhappy with the trial court's decision. *Id.* ("[P]etitioners [have] no 'direct stake' in the outcome of their appeal. Their only interest in having the District Court order reversed [is] to vindicate the constitutional validity of a generally applicable California law. . . . [S]uch a 'generalized grievance' . . . is insufficient to confer standing."). Among the Justices who dissented on this point, Justice Kennedy wrote a separate opinion in *Perry* suggesting that

the defendant-intervenors did have standing to appeal the trial court's decision as a matter of federal constitutional law. *Id.* at 2668 (Kennedy, J., dissenting). Among other things, Justice Kennedy expressed the view that the Court's failure to recognize defendant-intervenors' standing in the case failed to respect California's direct democracy, voter-initiative process. *Id.* at 2670–71. Very quickly on the heels of the Supreme Court's decision in *Perry*, the Ninth Circuit dissolved a stay that it had imposed on the effectuation of the trial court's order in the case. *Perry v. Brown*, 725 F.3d 968, 970 (9th Cir. 2013), *application to vacate order denied*, No. 13A18 (U.S. June 30, 2013) (Kennedy, J.). The effect of lifting this stay, which Justice Kennedy, as Circuit Justice, refused to halt, was to allow same-sex weddings to begin virtually immediately in the state of California. Jess Bravin, *Gay-Marriage Opponents Lose Bid to Stop California Ceremonies*, WALL ST. J. (June 30, 2013), http://www.wsj.com/articles/SB100014241278873232975045785776 10486721152. Subsequent efforts to try to "revive California's Proposition 8" are reported in Howard Mintz, *Gay Marriage Foes Try Again to Revive California's Proposition 8*, SAN JOSE MERCURY NEWS (July 12, 2013), http://www.mercurynews.com/ci_23648882/gay-marriage-foes-try-again-revive-californias-proposition; Howard Mintz, *Gay Marriage Foes Lose State Supreme Court Plea to Halt Weddings*, SAN JOSE MERCURY NEWS (July 16, 2013), http://www.mercurynews.com/news/ci_23664796/gay-marriage-foes-lose-state-supreme; Howard Mintz, *California Supreme Court Won't Halt Same-Sex Marriages*, SAN JOSE MERCURY NEWS (July 24, 2013), http://www.mercurynews.com/breaking-news/ci_23718908/california-supreme-court-wont-halt-same-sex-marriages.

Obergefell v. Hodges[*]

Supreme Court of the United States, 2015.
576 U.S. ___, 135 S.Ct. 2584, 192 L.Ed.2d 609.

■ JUSTICE KENNEDY delivered the opinion of the Court.

The Constitution promises liberty to all within its reach, a liberty that includes certain specific rights that allow persons, within a lawful realm, to define and express their identity. The petitioners in these cases seek to find that liberty by marrying someone of the same sex and having their marriages deemed lawful on the same terms and conditions as marriages between persons of the opposite sex.

I

These cases come from Michigan, Kentucky, Ohio, and Tennessee, States that define marriage as a union between one man and one woman. The petitioners are 14 same-sex couples and two men whose same-sex partners are deceased. The respondents are state officials responsible for enforcing the laws in question. The petitioners claim the respondents violate the Fourteenth Amendment by denying them the right to marry

---

[*] Together with No. 14–562, *Tanco et al. v. Haslam, Governor of Tennessee, et al.*, No. 14–571, *DeBoer et al. v. Snyder, Governor of Michigan, et al.*, and No. 14–574, *Bourke et al. v. Beshear, Governor of Kentucky*, also on certiorari to the same court.

or to have their marriages, lawfully performed in another State, given full recognition.

. . .

. . . This Court granted review, limited to two questions. The first, presented by the cases from Michigan and Kentucky, is whether the Fourteenth Amendment requires a State to license a marriage between two people of the same sex. The second, presented by the cases from Ohio, Tennessee, and, again, Kentucky, is whether the Fourteenth Amendment requires a State to recognize a same-sex marriage licensed and performed in a State which does grant that right.

II

. . .

A

From their beginning to their most recent page, the annals of human history reveal the transcendent importance of marriage. The lifelong union of a man and a woman always has promised nobility and dignity to all persons[.] . . . Marriage is sacred to those who live by their religions and offers unique fulfillment to those who find meaning in the secular realm. Its dynamic allows two people to find a life that could not be found alone, for a marriage becomes greater than just the two persons. Rising from the most basic human needs, marriage is essential to our most profound hopes and aspirations.

The centrality of marriage to the human condition makes it unsurprising that the institution [defined as "a union between two persons of the opposite sex"] has existed for millennia and across civilizations. . . .

. . .

B

The ancient origins of marriage confirm its centrality, but . . . [t]hat institution—even as confined to opposite-sex relations—has evolved over time.

For example, . . . [u]nder the centuries-old doctrine of coverture, a married man and woman were treated by the State as a single, male-dominated legal entity. As women gained legal, political, and property rights, and as society began to understand that women have their own equal dignity, the law of coverture was abandoned. These and other developments in the institution of marriage over the past centuries were not mere superficial changes. Rather, they worked deep transformations in its structure, affecting aspects of marriage long viewed by many as essential.

These new insights have strengthened, not weakened, the institution of marriage. Indeed, changed understandings of marriage are characteristic of a Nation where new dimensions of freedom become apparent to new generations, often through perspectives that begin in pleas or protests and then are considered in the political sphere and the judicial process.

This dynamic can be seen in the Nation's experiences with the rights of gays and lesbians. Until the mid-20th century, same-sex intimacy long had been condemned as immoral by the state itself in most Western nations, a belief often embodied in the criminal law. . . .

. . .

In the late 20th century, . . . same-sex couples began to lead more open and public lives and to establish families. This development was followed by a quite extensive discussion of the issue in both governmental and private sectors and by a shift in public attitudes toward greater tolerance. As a result, questions about the rights of gays and lesbians soon reached the courts, where the issue could be discussed in the formal discourse of the law.

This Court first gave detailed consideration to the legal status of homosexuals in *Bowers v. Hardwick*, 478 U.S. 186 (1986). There it upheld the constitutionality of a Georgia law deemed to criminalize certain homosexual acts. Ten years later, in *Romer v. Evans*, 517 U.S. 620 (1996), the Court invalidated an amendment to Colorado's Constitution that sought to foreclose any branch or political subdivision of the State from protecting persons against discrimination based on sexual orientation. Then, in 2003, the Court overruled *Bowers*, holding that laws making same-sex intimacy a crime "demea[n] the lives of homosexual persons." *Lawrence v. Texas*, 539 U.S. 558, 575 [(2003)].

. . . [I]n 1996, Congress passed the Defense of Marriage Act (DOMA), 110 Stat. 2419, defining marriage for all federal-law purposes as "only a legal union between one man and one woman as husband and wife." 1 U.S.C. § 7.

. . . Two Terms ago, in *United States v. Windsor*, 570 U.S. ___ (2013), this Court invalidated DOMA to the extent it barred the Federal Government from treating same-sex marriages as valid even when they were lawful in the State where they were licensed. . . .

. . .

After years of litigation, legislation, referenda, and the discussions that attended these public acts, the States are now divided on the issue of same-sex marriage.

III

. . . The fundamental liberties protected by [the Due Process Clause of the Fourteenth Amendment] . . . extend to certain personal choices central to individual dignity and autonomy, including intimate choices that define personal identity and beliefs. See, *e.g.*, *Eisenstadt v. Baird*, 405 U.S. 438, 453 (1972); *Griswold v. Connecticut*, 381 U.S. 479, 484–486 (1965).

The identification and protection of fundamental rights . . . "has not been reduced to any formula." *Poe v. Ullman*, 367 U.S. 497, 542 (1961) (Harlan, J., dissenting). Rather, it requires courts to exercise reasoned judgment in identifying interests of the person so fundamental that the State must accord them its respect. See *ibid.* . . . History and tradition guide and discipline this inquiry but do not set its outer boundaries. See *Lawrence, supra*, at 572. . . .

The nature of injustice is that we may not always see it in our own times. The generations that wrote and ratified the Bill of Rights and the Fourteenth Amendment did not presume to know the extent of freedom in all of its dimensions, and so they entrusted to future generations a charter protecting the right of all persons to enjoy liberty as we learn its meaning. . . .

. . . [T]he Court has long held the right to marry is protected by the Constitution. In *Loving v. Virginia*, 388 U.S. 1, 12 (1967), which invalidated bans on interracial unions, a unanimous Court held marriage is "one of the vital personal rights essential to the orderly pursuit of happiness by free men." The Court reaffirmed that holding in *Zablocki v. Redhail*, 434 U.S. 374, 384 (1978), which held the right to marry was burdened by a law prohibiting fathers who were behind on child support from marrying. The Court again applied this principle in *Turner v. Safley*, 482 U.S. 78, 95 (1987), which held the right to marry was abridged by regulations limiting the privilege of prison inmates to marry. Over time and in other contexts, the Court has reiterated that the right to marry is fundamental under the Due Process Clause.

. . . [T]his Court's cases describing the right to marry presumed a relationship involving opposite-sex partners. The Court, like many institutions, has made assumptions defined by the world and time of which it is a part. This was evident in *Baker v. Nelson*, 409 U.S. 810 [(1972)], a one-line summary decision issued in 1972, holding the exclusion of same-sex couples from marriage did not present a substantial federal question.

Still, there are other, more instructive precedents. This Court's cases have expressed constitutional principles of broader reach. In defining the right to marry these cases have identified essential attributes of that right based in history, tradition, and other constitutional liberties inherent in this intimate bond. See, *e.g., Lawrence*, 539 U.S., at 574; *Turner, supra*, at 95; *Zablocki, supra*, at 384; *Loving, supra*, at 12; *Griswold, supra*, at 486. And in assessing whether the force and rationale of its cases apply to same-sex couples, the Court must respect the basic reasons why the right to marry has been long protected. See, *e.g., Eisenstadt, supra*, at 453–454; *Poe, supra*, at 542–553 (Harlan, J., dissenting).

This analysis compels the conclusion that same-sex couples may exercise the right to marry. The four principles and traditions to be discussed demonstrate that the reasons marriage is fundamental under the Constitution apply with equal force to same-sex couples.

A first premise of the Court's relevant precedents is that the right to personal choice regarding marriage is inherent in the concept of individual autonomy. . . . Like choices concerning contraception, family relationships, procreation, and childrearing, all of which are protected by the Constitution, decisions concerning marriage are among the most intimate that an individual can make. . . .

Choices about marriage shape an individual's destiny. As the Supreme Judicial Court of Massachusetts has explained, . . . " . . . the decision whether and whom to marry is among life's momentous acts of self-definition." *Goodridge* [*v. Department of Public Health*], 798 N.E.2d [941], 955 [(Mass. 2003)].

The nature of marriage is that, through its enduring bond, two persons together can find other freedoms, such as expression, intimacy, and spirituality. This is true for all persons, whatever their sexual orientation. There is dignity in the bond between two men or two women who seek to marry and in their autonomy to make such profound choices.

A second principle in this Court's jurisprudence is that the right to marry is fundamental because it supports a two-person union unlike any other in its importance to the committed individuals. This point was central to *Griswold v. Connecticut*, which held the Constitution protects the right of married couples to use contraception. 381 U.S., at 485. . . . And in *Turner*, the Court again acknowledged the intimate association protected by this right, holding prisoners could not be denied the right to marry because their committed relationships satisfied the basic reasons why marriage is a fundamental right. See 482 U.S., at 95–96. The right to marry thus dignifies couples who "wish to define themselves by their commitment to each other." *Windsor*, *supra*, at ___ (slip op., at 14). Marriage responds to the universal fear that a lonely person might call out only to find no one there. It offers the hope of companionship and understanding and assurance that while both still live there will be someone to care for the other.

As this Court held in *Lawrence*, same-sex couples have the same right as opposite-sex couples to enjoy intimate association. . . . But while *Lawrence* confirmed a dimension of freedom that allows individuals to engage in intimate association without criminal liability, it does not follow that freedom stops there. Outlaw to outcast may be a step forward, but it does not achieve the full promise of liberty.

A third basis for protecting the right to marry is that it safeguards children and families and thus draws meaning from related rights of childrearing, procreation, and education. See *Pierce v. Society of Sisters*, 268 U.S. 510 (1925); *Meyer* [*v. Nebraska*], 262 U.S. [390], 399 [(1923)]. The Court has recognized these connections by describing the varied rights as a unified whole: "[T]he right to 'marry, establish a home and bring up children' is a central part of the liberty protected by the Due Process Clause." *Zablocki*, 434 U.S., at 384 (quoting *Meyer, supra,* at 399). Under the laws of the several States, some of marriage's protections for children and families are material. But marriage also confers more profound benefits. By giving recognition and legal structure to their parents' relationship, marriage allows children "to understand the integrity and closeness of their own family and its concord with other families in their community and in their daily lives." *Windsor, supra,* at ___ (slip op., at 23). Marriage also affords the permanency and stability important to children's best interests.

As all parties agree, many same-sex couples provide loving and nurturing homes to their children, whether biological or adopted. And hundreds of thousands of children are presently being raised by such couples. Most States have allowed gays and lesbians to adopt, either as individuals or as couples, and many adopted and foster children have same-sex parents. This provides powerful confirmation from the law itself that gays and lesbians can create loving, supportive families.

Excluding same-sex couples from marriage thus conflicts with a central premise of the right to marry. Without the recognition, stability, and predictability marriage offers, their children suffer the stigma of knowing their families are somehow lesser. They also suffer the significant material costs of being raised by unmarried parents, relegated through no fault of their own to a more difficult and uncertain family life. The marriage laws at issue here thus harm and humiliate the children of same-sex couples.

That is not to say the right to marry is less meaningful for those who do not or cannot have children. . . . In light of precedent protecting the right of a married couple not to procreate, it cannot be said the Court or the States have conditioned the right to marry on the capacity or commitment to procreate. The constitutional marriage right has many aspects, of which childbearing is only one.

Fourth and finally, this Court's cases and the Nation's traditions make clear that marriage is a keystone of our social order. . . . In *Maynard v. Hill*, 125 U.S. 190, 211 (1888), the Court . . . explain[ed] that marriage is "the foundation of the family and of society, without which there would be neither civilization nor progress." Marriage, the *Maynard* Court said, has long been " 'a great public institution, giving character to our whole civil polity.' " *Id.*, at 213. This idea has been reiterated even as the institution has evolved in substantial ways over time, superseding rules related to parental consent, gender, and race once thought by many to be essential. . . .

For that reason, just as a couple vows to support each other, so does society pledge to support the couple, offering symbolic recognition and material benefits to protect and nourish the union. Indeed, while the States are in general free to vary the benefits they confer on all married couples, they have throughout our history made marriage the basis for an expanding list of governmental rights, benefits, and responsibilities. . . . Valid marriage under state law is also a significant status for over a thousand provisions of federal law. The States have contributed to the fundamental character of the marriage right by placing that institution at the center of so many facets of the legal and social order.

There is no difference between same-[sex] and opposite-sex couples with respect to this principle. Yet by virtue of their exclusion from that institution, same-sex couples are denied the constellation of benefits that the States have linked to marriage. This harm results in more than just material burdens. Same-sex couples are consigned to an instability many opposite-sex couples would deem intolerable in their own lives. As the State itself makes marriage all the more precious by the significance it attaches to it, exclusion from that status has the effect of teaching that gays and lesbians are unequal in important respects. It demeans gays and lesbians for the State to lock them out of a central institution of the Nation's society. Same-sex couples, too, may aspire to the transcendent purposes of marriage and seek fulfillment in its highest meaning.

The limitation of marriage to opposite-sex couples may long have seemed natural and just, but its inconsistency with the central meaning of the fundamental right to marry is now manifest. With that knowledge must come the recognition that laws excluding same-sex couples from the marriage right impose stigma and injury of the kind prohibited by our basic charter.

Objecting . . . , the respondents refer to *Washington v. Glucksberg*, 521 U.S. 702, 721 (1997), which called for a " 'careful description' " of fundamental rights. They assert the petitioners do not seek to exercise the right to marry but rather a new and nonexistent "right to same-sex marriage." Brief for Respondent in No. 14–556, p. 8. *Glucksberg* did insist that liberty under the Due Process Clause must be defined in a most circumscribed manner, with central reference to specific historical practices. Yet while that approach may have been appropriate for the asserted right there involved (physician-assisted suicide), it is inconsistent with the approach this Court has used in discussing other fundamental rights, including marriage and intimacy. *Loving* did not ask about a "right to interracial marriage"; *Turner* did not ask about a "right of inmates to marry"; and *Zablocki* did not ask about a "right of fathers with unpaid child support duties to marry." Rather, each case inquired about the right to marry in its comprehensive sense, asking if there was a sufficient justification for excluding the relevant class from the right.

That principle applies here. If rights were defined by who exercised them in the past, then received practices could serve as their own continued justification and new groups could not invoke rights once denied. This Court has rejected that approach, both with respect to the right to marry and the rights of gays and lesbians. See *Loving*, 388 U.S., at 12; *Lawrence*, 539 U.S., at 566–567.

The right to marry is fundamental as a matter of history and tradition, but rights come not from ancient sources alone. They rise, too, from a better informed understanding of how constitutional imperatives define a liberty that remains urgent in our own era. Many who deem same-sex marriage to be wrong reach that conclusion based on decent and honorable religious or philosophical premises, and neither they nor their beliefs are disparaged here. But when that sincere, personal opposition becomes enacted law and public policy, the necessary consequence is to put the imprimatur of the State itself on an exclusion that soon demeans or stigmatizes those whose own liberty is then denied. Under the Constitution, same-sex couples seek in marriage the same legal treatment as opposite-sex couples, and it would disparage their choices and diminish their personhood to deny them this right.

The right of same-sex couples to marry that is part of the liberty promised by the Fourteenth Amendment is derived, too, from that Amendment's guarantee of the equal protection of the laws. The Due Process Clause and the Equal Protection Clause are connected in a profound way, though they set forth independent principles. Rights implicit in liberty and rights secured by equal protection may rest on different precepts and are not always co-extensive, yet in some instances each may be instructive as to the meaning and reach of the other. In any particular case one Clause may be thought to capture the essence of the right in a more accurate and comprehensive way, even as the two Clauses may converge in the identification and definition of the right. This interrelation of the two principles furthers our understanding of what freedom is and must become.

The Court's cases touching upon the right to marry reflect this dynamic. In *Loving* the Court invalidated a prohibition on interracial marriage under both the Equal Protection Clause and the Due Process Clause. The Court first declared the prohibition invalid because of its un-equal treatment of interracial couples. . . . 388 U.S., at 12. With this link to equal protection[,] the Court proceeded to hold the prohibition offended central precepts of liberty[.] . . . *Ibid.* The reasons why marriage is a fundamental right became more clear and compelling from a full awareness and understanding of the hurt that resulted from laws barring interracial unions.

The synergy between the two protections is illustrated further in *Zablocki*. There the Court invoked the Equal Protection Clause as its basis for invalidating the challenged law, which, as already noted, barred fathers who were behind on child-support payments from marrying without judicial approval. The equal protection analysis depended in central part on the Court's holding that the law burdened a right "of fundamental importance." 434 U.S., at 383. It was the essential nature of the marriage right, discussed at length in *Zablocki*, see *id.*, at 383–387, that made apparent the law's incompatibility with requirements of equality. Each concept—liberty and equal protection—leads to a stronger understanding of the other.

. . .

Other cases confirm this relation between liberty and equality. . . .

. . .

This dynamic also applies to same-sex marriage. It is now clear that the challenged laws burden the liberty of same-sex couples, and it must be further acknowledged that they abridge central precepts of equality. Here the marriage laws enforced by the respondents are in essence unequal: same-sex couples are denied all the benefits afforded to opposite-sex couples and are barred from exercising a fundamental right. Especially against a long history of disapproval of their relationships, this denial to same-sex couples of the right to marry works a grave and continuing harm. The imposition of this disability on gays and lesbians serves to disrespect and subordinate them. And the Equal Protection Clause, like the Due Process Clause, prohibits this unjustified infringement of the fundamental right to marry. See, *e.g.*, *Zablocki*, *supra*, at 383–388.

These considerations lead to the conclusion that the right to marry is a fundamental right inherent in the liberty of the person, and under the Due Process and Equal Protection Clauses of the Fourteenth Amendment couples of the same-sex may not be deprived of that right and that liberty. The Court now holds that same-sex couples may exercise the fundamental right to marry. No longer may this liberty be denied to them. *Baker v. Nelson* must be and now is overruled, and the State laws challenged by Petitioners in these cases are now held invalid to the extent they exclude same-sex couples from civil marriage on the same terms and conditions as opposite-sex couples.

IV

There may be an initial inclination in these cases to proceed with caution—to await further legislation, litigation, and debate. The respondents warn there has been insufficient democratic discourse before deciding an issue so basic as the definition of marriage. . . .

Yet there has been far more deliberation than this argument acknowledges. There have been referenda, legislative debates, and grassroots campaigns, as well as countless studies, papers, books, and other popular and scholarly writings. There has been extensive litigation in state and federal courts. Judicial opinions addressing the issue have been informed by the contentions of parties and counsel, which, in turn, reflect the more general, societal discussion of same-sex marriage and its meaning that has occurred over the past decades. As more than 100 *amici* make clear in their filings, many of the central institutions in American life—state and local governments, the military, large and small businesses, labor unions, religious organizations, law enforcement, civic groups, professional organizations, and universities—have devoted substantial attention to the question. This has led to an enhanced understanding of the issue—an understanding reflected in the arguments now presented for resolution as a matter of constitutional law.

Of course, the Constitution contemplates that democracy is the appropriate process for change, so long as that process does not abridge fundamental rights. . . . Thus, when the rights of persons are violated, "the Constitution requires redress by the courts," notwithstanding the more general value of democratic decisionmaking. [*Schuette v. BAMN*, 572 U.S. ___, ___ (2014)] (slip op., at 17). This holds true even when protecting individual rights affects issues of the utmost importance and sensitivity.

. . .

. . . Properly presented with the petitioners' cases, the Court has a duty to address these claims and answer these questions.

. . . Were the Court to uphold the challenged laws as constitutional, it would teach the Nation that these laws are in accord with our society's most basic compact. Were the Court to stay its hand to allow slower, case-by-case determination of the required availability of specific public benefits to same-sex couples, it still would deny gays and lesbians many rights and responsibilities intertwined with marriage.

The respondents also argue allowing same-sex couples to wed will harm marriage as an institution by leading to fewer opposite-sex marriages. This may occur, the respondents contend, because licensing same-sex marriage severs the connection between natural procreation and marriage. That argument, however, rests on a counterintuitive view[.] . . . [I]t is unrealistic to conclude that an opposite-sex couple would choose not to marry simply because same-sex couples may do so. The respondents have not shown a foundation for the conclusion that allowing same-sex marriage will cause the harmful outcomes they describe. . . . [T]hese cases involve only the rights of two consenting adults whose marriages would pose no risk of harm to themselves or third parties.

Finally, . . . religions, and those who adhere to religious doctrines, may continue to advocate with utmost, sincere conviction that, by divine precepts, same-sex marriage should not be condoned. The First Amendment ensures that religious organizations and persons are given proper protection as they seek to teach the principles that are so fulfilling and so central to their lives and faiths, and to their own deep aspirations to continue the family structure they have long revered. The same is true of those who oppose same-sex marriage for other reasons. In turn, those who believe allowing same-sex marriage is proper or indeed essential, whether as a matter of religious conviction or secular belief, may engage those who disagree with their view in an open and searching debate. The Constitution, however, does not permit the State to bar same-sex couples from marriage on the same terms as accorded to couples of the opposite sex.

V

. . .

As counsel for the respondents acknowledged at argument, if States are required by the Constitution to issue marriage licenses to same-sex couples, the justifications for refusing to recognize those marriages performed elsewhere are undermined. The Court, in this decision, holds same-sex couples may exercise the fundamental right to marry in all States. It follows that the Court also must hold—and it now does hold—that there is no lawful basis for a State to refuse to recognize a lawful same-sex marriage performed in another State on the ground of its same-sex character.

* * *

No union is more profound than marriage, for it embodies the highest ideals of love, fidelity, devotion, sacrifice, and family. In forming a marital union, two people become something greater than once they were. As some of the petitioners in these cases demonstrate, marriage embodies a love that may endure even past death. It would misunderstand these men and women to say they disrespect the idea of marriage. Their plea is that they do respect it, respect it so deeply that they seek to find its fulfillment for themselves. Their hope is not to be condemned to live in loneliness, excluded from one of civilization's oldest institutions. They ask for equal dignity in the eyes of the law. The Constitution grants them that right.

The judgment of the Court of Appeals for the Sixth Circuit is reversed.

It is so ordered.

■ CHIEF JUSTICE ROBERTS, with whom JUSTICE SCALIA and JUSTICE THOMAS join, dissenting.

. . .

I

. . . There is no serious dispute that, under our precedents, the Constitution protects a right to marry and requires States to apply their marriage laws equally. The real question in these cases is what constitutes "marriage," or—more precisely—*who decides* what constitutes "marriage"?

The majority largely ignores these questions, relegating ages of human experience with marriage to a paragraph or two. Even if history and precedent are not "the end" of these cases, I would not "sweep away what has so long been settled" without showing greater respect for all that preceded us. *Town of Greece v. Galloway*, 572 U.S. ___, ___ (2014) (slip op., at 8).

A

As the majority acknowledges, marriage "has existed for millennia and across civilizations." For all those millennia, across all those civilizations, "marriage" referred to only one relationship: the union of a man and a woman. . . .

This universal definition of marriage as the union of a man and a woman is no historical coincidence. Marriage . . . arose in the nature of things to meet a vital need: ensuring that children are conceived by a mother and father committed to raising them in the stable conditions of a lifelong relationship. See G. QUALE, A HISTORY OF MARRIAGE SYSTEMS 2 (1988).

The premises supporting this concept of marriage are so fundamental that they rarely require articulation. The human race must procreate to survive. Procreation occurs through sexual relations between a man and a woman. When sexual relations result in the conception of a child, that child's prospects are generally better if the mother and father stay together[.] . . . Therefore, for the good of children and society, sexual relations that can lead to procreation should occur only between a man and a woman committed to a lasting bond.

Society has recognized that bond as marriage. And by bestowing a respected status and material benefits on married couples, society encourages men and women to conduct sexual relations within marriage rather than without. . . .

This singular understanding of marriage has prevailed in the United States throughout our history. . . .

The Constitution itself says nothing about marriage, and the Framers thereby entrusted the States with "[t]he whole subject of the domestic relations of husband and wife." [*United States v.*] *Windsor*, 570 U.S., at ___ [(2013)] (slip op., at 17) (quoting *In re Burrus*, 136 U.S. 586, 593–594 (1890)). There is no dispute that every State at the founding— and every State throughout our history until a dozen years ago—defined marriage in the traditional, biologically rooted way. . . .

. . .

This Court's precedents have repeatedly described marriage in ways that are consistent only with its traditional meaning. Early cases on the subject referred to marriage as "the union for life of one man and one woman," *Murphy v. Ramsey*, 114 U.S. 15, 45 (1885), which forms "the foundation of the family and of society, without which there would be neither civilization nor progress," *Maynard v. Hill*, 125 U.S. 190, 211 (1888). We later described marriage as "fundamental to our very existence and survival," an understanding that necessarily implies a procreative component. *Loving v. Virginia*, 388 U.S. 1, 12 (1967). More recent cases have directly connected the right to marry with the "right to procreate." *Zablocki v. Redhail*, 434 U.S. 374, 386 (1978).

As the majority notes, some aspects of marriage have changed over time. Arranged marriages have largely given way to pairings based on romantic love. States have replaced coverture, the doctrine by which a married man and woman became a single legal entity, with laws that respect each participant's separate status. Racial restrictions on marriage, which "arose as an incident to slavery" to promote "White Supremacy," were repealed by many States and ultimately struck down by this Court. *Loving*, 388 U.S., at 6–7.

The majority observes that these developments "were not mere superficial changes" in marriage, but rather "worked deep transformations in its structure." They did not, however, work any transformation in the core structure of marriage as the union between a man and a woman. . . . The majority may be right that the "history of marriage is one of both continuity and change," but the core meaning of marriage has endured.

. . .

II

Petitioners first contend that the marriage laws of their States violate the Due Process Clause. . . .

The majority purports to identify four "principles and traditions" in this Court's due process precedents that support a fundamental right for same-sex couples to marry. . . . Stripped of its shiny rhetorical gloss, the majority's argument is that the Due Process Clause gives same-sex couples a fundamental right to marry because it will be good for them and for society. . . .

A

Petitioners' "fundamental right" claim [is an argument] . . . that the [State] laws [at issue in the case] violate a right *implied* by the Fourteenth Amendment's requirement that "liberty" may not be deprived without "due process of law."

This Court has interpreted the Due Process Clause to include a "substantive" component that protects certain liberty interests against state deprivation "no matter what process is provided." *Reno v. Flores*, 507 U.S. 292, 302 (1993). The theory is that some liberties are "so rooted in the traditions and conscience of our people as to be ranked as fundamental," and therefore cannot be deprived without compelling justification. *Snyder v. Massachusetts*, 291 U.S. 97, 105 (1934).

Allowing unelected federal judges to select which unenumerated rights rank as "fundamental"—and to strike down state laws on the basis of that determination—raises obvious concerns about the judicial role. Our precedents have accordingly insisted that judges "exercise the utmost care" in identifying implied fundamental rights, "lest the liberty protected by the Due Process Clause be subtly transformed into the policy preferences of the Members of this Court." *Washington v. Glucksberg*, 521 U.S. 702, 720 (1997) (internal quotation marks omitted).

. . .

B

. . .

1

The majority's driving themes are that marriage is desirable and petitioners desire it. The opinion describes the "transcendent importance" of marriage and repeatedly insists that petitioners do not seek to "demean," "devalue," "denigrate," or "disrespect" the institution. Nobody disputes those points. . . . As a matter of constitutional law, however, the sincerity of petitioners' wishes is not relevant.

When the majority turns to the law, it relies primarily on precedents discussing the fundamental "right to marry." *Turner v. Safley*, 482 U.S. 78, 95 (1987); *Zablocki*, 434 U.S., at 383; see *Loving*, 388 U.S., at 12. These cases do not hold, of course, that anyone who wants to get married has a constitutional right to do so. They instead require a State to justify barriers to marriage as that institution has always been understood. In *Loving*, the Court held that racial restrictions on the right to marry lacked a compelling justification. In *Zablocki*, restrictions based on child support debts did not suffice. In *Turner*, restrictions based on status as a prisoner were deemed impermissible.

None of the laws at issue in those cases purported to change the core definition of marriage as the union of a man and a woman. . . . As the majority admits, the institution of "marriage" discussed in every one of these cases "presumed a relationship involving opposite-sex partners."

In short, the "right to marry" cases stand for the important but limited proposition that particular restrictions on access to marriage *as traditionally defined* violate due process. These precedents say nothing at all about a right to make a State change its definition of marriage, which is the right petitioners actually seek here. Neither petitioners nor the majority cites a single case or other legal source providing any basis for such a constitutional right. None exists, and that is enough to foreclose their claim.

2

The majority suggests that "there are other, more instructive precedents" informing the right to marry. Although not entirely clear, this reference seems to correspond to a line of cases discussing an implied fundamental "right of privacy." *Griswold* [*v. Connecticut*], 381 U.S. [479,] 486 [(1965)]. . . .

The Court also invoked the right to privacy in *Lawrence v. Texas*, 539 U.S. 558 (2003), which struck down a Texas statute criminalizing homosexual sodomy. *Lawrence* relied on the position that criminal sodomy laws . . . invaded privacy by inviting "unwarranted government intrusions" that "touc[h] upon the most private human conduct, sexual behavior . . . in the most private of places, the home." *Id.*, at 562, 567.

Neither *Lawrence* nor any other precedent in the privacy line of cases supports the right that petitioners assert here. . . . [T]he marriage laws at issue here involve no government intrusion. They create no crime and impose no punishment. Same-sex couples remain free to live together, to engage in intimate conduct, and to raise their families as they see fit. No one is "condemned to live in loneliness" by the laws challenged in these cases—no one. At the same time, the laws in no way interfere with the "right to be let alone."

. . .

. . . [T]he privacy cases provide no support for the majority's position, because petitioners do not seek privacy. Quite the opposite, they seek public recognition of their relationships, along with corresponding government benefits. Our cases have consistently refused to allow litigants to convert the shield provided by constitutional liberties into a sword to demand positive entitlements from the State. See *DeShaney v. Winnebago County Dept. of Social Servs.*, 489 U.S. 189, 196 (1989); *San Antonio Independent School Dist. v. Rodriguez*, 411 U.S. 1, 35–37 (1973). Thus, although the right to privacy recognized by our precedents certainly plays a role in protecting the intimate conduct of same-sex couples, it provides no affirmative right to redefine marriage and no basis for striking down the laws at issue here.

3

. . .

Ultimately, only one precedent offers any support for the majority's methodology: *Lochner v. New York*, 198 U.S. 45 [(1905)]. The majority opens its opinion by announcing petitioners' right to "define and express their identity." The majority later explains that "the right to personal choice regarding marriage is inherent in the concept of individual autonomy." This freewheeling notion of individual autonomy echoes nothing so much as "the general right of an individual to be *free in his person* and in his power to contract in relation to his own labor." *Lochner*, 198 U.S., at 58 (emphasis added).

To be fair, the majority does not suggest that its individual autonomy right is entirely unconstrained. The constraints it sets are precisely those that accord with its own "reasoned judgment," informed by its "new insight" into the "nature of injustice," which was invisible to all who came before but has become clear "as we learn [the] meaning" of liberty. The truth is that today's decision rests on nothing more than the majority's own conviction that same-sex couples should be allowed to marry because they want to, and that "it would disparage their choices and diminish their personhood to deny them this right." Whatever force that belief may have as a matter of moral philosophy, it has no more basis in the

Constitution than did the naked policy preferences adopted [by the Court] in *Lochner*.

The majority recognizes that today's cases do not mark "the first time the Court has been asked to adopt a cautious approach to recognizing and protecting fundamental rights." On that much, we agree. The Court was "asked"—and it agreed—to "adopt a cautious approach" to implying fundamental rights after the debacle of the *Lochner* era. Today, the majority casts caution aside and revives the grave errors of that period.

One immediate question invited by the majority's position is whether States may retain the definition of marriage as a union of two people. Although the majority randomly inserts the adjective "two" in various places, it offers no reason at all why the two-person element of the core definition of marriage may be preserved while the man-woman element may not. Indeed, from the standpoint of history and tradition, a leap from opposite-sex marriage to same-sex marriage is much greater than one from a two-person union to plural unions, which have deep roots in some cultures around the world. If the majority is willing to take the big leap, it is hard to see how it can say no to the shorter one.

It is striking how much of the majority's reasoning would apply with equal force to the claim of a fundamental right to plural marriage. If "[t]here is dignity in the bond between two men or two women who seek to marry and in their autonomy to make such profound choices," why would there be any less dignity in the bond between three people who, in exercising their autonomy, seek to make the profound choice to marry? If a same-sex couple has the constitutional right to marry because their children would otherwise "suffer the stigma of knowing their families are somehow lesser," why wouldn't the same reasoning apply to a family of three or more persons raising children? If not having the opportunity to marry "serves to disrespect and subordinate" gay and lesbian couples, why wouldn't the same "imposition of this disability," serve to disrespect and subordinate people who find fulfillment in polyamorous relationships?

I do not mean to equate marriage between same-sex couples with plural marriages in all respects. There may well be relevant differences that compel different legal analysis. But if there are, petitioners have not pointed to any. . . .

4

Near the end of its opinion, the majority offers perhaps the clearest insight into its decision. Expanding marriage to include same-sex couples, the majority insists, would "pose no risk of harm to themselves or third parties." . . .

. . . [T]his assertion of the "harm principle" sounds more in philosophy than law. The elevation of the fullest individual self-realization over the constraints that society has expressed in law may or may not be attractive moral philosophy. But a Justice's commission does not confer any special moral, philosophical, or social insight sufficient to justify imposing those perceptions on fellow citizens under the pretense of "due process." There is indeed a process due the people on issues of this sort—the democratic process. Respecting that understanding requires the Court to be guided by law, not any particular school of social thought. . . . [T]he Fourteenth Amendment . . . certainly does not enact any one concept of marriage.

The majority's understanding of due process lays out a tantalizing vision of the future for Members of this Court: If an unvarying social institution enduring over all of recorded history cannot inhibit judicial policymaking, what can? But this approach is dangerous for the rule of law. The purpose of insisting that implied fundamental rights have roots in the history and tradition of our people is to ensure that when unelected judges strike down democratically enacted laws, they do so based on something more than their own beliefs. The Court today not only overlooks our country's entire history and tradition but actively repudiates it, preferring to live only in the heady days of the here and now. I agree with the majority that the "nature of injustice is that we may not always see it in our own times." As petitioners put it, "times can blind." But to blind yourself to history is both prideful and unwise. . . .

III

In addition to their due process argument, petitioners contend that the Equal Protection Clause requires their States to license and recognize same-sex marriages. . . . The central point [of the majority's discussion of this claim] seems to be that there is a "synergy between" the Equal Protection Clause and the Due Process Clause, and that some precedents relying on one Clause have also relied on the other. . . .

The majority . . . assert[s] . . . that the Equal Protection Clause provides an alternative basis for its holding. Yet the majority fails to provide even a single sentence explaining how the Equal Protection Clause supplies independent weight for its position, nor does it attempt to justify its gratuitous violation of the canon against unnecessarily resolving constitutional questions. In any event, the marriage laws at issue here do not violate the Equal Protection Clause, because distinguishing between opposite-sex and same-sex couples is rationally related to the States' "legitimate state interest" in "preserving the traditional institution of marriage." *Lawrence*, 539 U.S., at 585 (O'Connor, J., concurring in judgment).

. . . The equal protection analysis might be different, in my view, if we were confronted with a more focused challenge to the denial of certain tangible benefits [associated with marriage]. Of course, those more selective claims will not arise now that the Court has taken the drastic step of requiring every State to license and recognize marriages between same-sex couples.

IV

The legitimacy of this Court ultimately rests "upon the respect accorded to its judgments." *Republican Party of Minn. v. White*, 536 U.S. 765, 793 (2002) (Kennedy, J., concurring). That respect flows from the perception—and reality—that we exercise humility and restraint in deciding cases according to the Constitution and law. The role of the Court envisioned by the majority today, however, is anything but humble or restrained. Over and over, the majority exalts the role of the judiciary in delivering social change. In the majority's telling, it is the courts, not the people, who are responsible for making "new dimensions of freedom . . . apparent to new generations," for providing "formal discourse" on social issues, and for ensuring "neutral discussions, without scornful or disparaging commentary."

. . .

Those who founded our country would not recognize the majority's conception of the judicial role. They after all risked their lives and fortunes for the precious right to govern themselves. They would never have imagined yielding that right on a question of social policy to unaccountable and unelected judges. And they certainly would not have been satisfied by a system empowering judges to override policy judgments so long as they do so after "a quite extensive discussion." In our democracy, debate about the content of the law is not an exhaustion requirement to be checked off before courts can impose their will. . . .

. . .

. . . There will be consequences to shutting down the political process on an issue of such profound public significance. Closing debate tends to close minds. People denied a voice are less likely to accept the ruling of a court on an issue that does not seem to be the sort of thing courts usually decide. . . . Indeed, however heartened the proponents of same-sex marriage might be on this day, it is worth acknowledging what they have lost, and lost forever: the opportunity to win the true acceptance that comes from persuading their fellow citizens of the justice of their cause. . . .

Federal courts are blunt instruments when it comes to creating rights. They . . . do not have the flexibility of legislatures to address concerns of parties not before the court or to anticipate problems that may arise from the exercise of a new right. . . .

Respect for sincere religious conviction has led voters and legislators in every State that has adopted same-sex marriage democratically to include accommodations for religious practice. The majority's decision imposing same-sex marriage cannot, of course, create any such accommodations. The majority graciously suggests that religious believers may continue to "advocate" and "teach" their views of marriage. The First Amendment guarantees, however, the freedom to *"exercise"* religion. Ominously, that is not a word the majority uses.

Hard questions arise when people of faith exercise religion in ways that may be seen to conflict with the new right to same-sex marriage—when, for example, a religious college provides married student housing only to opposite-sex married couples, or a religious adoption agency declines to place children with same-sex married couples. Indeed, the Solicitor General candidly acknowledged that the tax exemptions of some religious institutions would be in question if they opposed same-sex marriage. There is little doubt that these and similar questions will soon be before this Court. Unfortunately, people of faith can take no comfort in the treatment they receive from the majority today.

Perhaps the most discouraging aspect of today's decision is the extent to which the majority feels compelled to sully those on the other side of the debate. The majority offers a cursory assurance that it does not intend to disparage people who, as a matter of conscience, cannot accept same-sex marriage. That disclaimer is hard to square with the very next sentence, in which the majority explains that "the necessary consequence" of laws codifying the traditional definition of marriage is to "demea[n] or stigmatiz[e]" same-sex couples. The majority reiterates such characterizations over and over. . . . These apparent assaults on the character of fairminded people will have an effect, in society and in court. . . . It is one thing for the majority to conclude that the Constitution protects a right to same-sex marriage; it is something else to portray everyone who does not share the majority's "better informed understanding" as bigoted.

In the face of all this, a much different view of the Court's role is possible. That view is more modest and restrained. It is more skeptical that the legal abilities of judges also reflect insight into moral and philosophical issues. It is more sensitive to the fact that judges are unelected and unaccountable, and that the legitimacy of their power depends on confining it to the exercise of legal judgment. It is more attuned to the lessons of history, and what it has meant for the country and Court when Justices have exceeded their proper bounds. And it is less pretentious than to suppose that while people around the world have viewed an institution in a particular way for thousands of years, the present generation and the present Court are the ones chosen to burst the bonds of that history and tradition.

* * *

If you are among the many Americans—of whatever sexual orientation—who favor expanding same-sex marriage, by all means celebrate today's decision. Celebrate the achievement of a desired goal. Celebrate the opportunity for a new expression of commitment to a partner. Celebrate the availability of new benefits. But do not celebrate the Constitution. It had nothing to do with it.

I respectfully dissent.

■ JUSTICE SCALIA, with whom JUSTICE THOMAS joins, dissenting.

. . .

The substance of today's decree is not of immense personal importance to me. The law can recognize as marriage whatever sexual attachments and living arrangements it wishes, and can accord them favorable civil consequences[.] . . . It is of overwhelming importance, however, who it is that rules me. Today's decree says that my Ruler, and the Ruler of 320 million Americans coast-to-coast, is a majority of the nine lawyers on the Supreme Court. The opinion in these cases is the furthest extension in fact—and the furthest extension one can even imagine—of the Court's claimed power to create "liberties" that the Constitution and its Amendments neglect to mention. This practice of constitutional revision by an unelected committee of nine, always accompanied . . . by extravagant praise of liberty, robs the People of the most important liberty they asserted in the Declaration of Independence and won in the Revolution of 1776: the freedom to govern themselves.

I

Until the courts put a stop to it, public debate over same-sex marriage displayed American democracy at its best. Individuals on both sides of the issue passionately, but respectfully, attempted to persuade their fellow citizens to accept their views. Americans considered the arguments and put the question to a vote. The electorates of 11 States, either directly or through their representatives, chose to expand the traditional definition of marriage. Many more decided not to. Win or lose, advocates for both sides continued pressing their cases, secure in the knowledge that an electoral loss can be negated by a later electoral win. That is exactly how our system of government is supposed to work.

The Constitution places some constraints on self-rule—constraints adopted *by the People themselves* when they ratified the Constitution and its Amendments. . . . Aside from these limitations, those powers "reserved to the States respectively, or to the people[,]" [U.S. CONST. amend. X,] can be exercised as the States or the People desire. These cases ask us to decide whether the Fourteenth Amendment contains a limitation that requires the States to license and recognize marriages between two people of the same sex. Does it remove *that* issue from the political process?

Of course not. . . . When the Fourteenth Amendment was ratified in 1868, every State limited marriage to one man and one woman, and no one doubted the constitutionality of doing so. That resolves these cases. . . . We have no basis for striking down a practice that is not expressly prohibited by the Fourteenth Amendment's text, and that bears the endorsement of a long tradition of open, widespread, and unchallenged use dating back to the Amendment's ratification. Since there is no doubt whatever that the People never decided to prohibit the limitation of marriage to opposite-sex couples, the public debate over same-sex marriage must be allowed to continue.

But the Court ends this debate, in an opinion lacking even a thin veneer of law. Buried beneath the mummeries and straining-to-be-memorable passages of the opinion is a candid and startling assertion: No matter *what* it was the People ratified, the Fourteenth Amendment protects those rights that the Judiciary, in its "reasoned judgment," thinks the Fourteenth Amendment ought to protect. . . . Thus, rather than focusing on *the People's* understanding of "liberty"—at the time of ratification or even today—the majority focuses on four "principles and traditions" that, *in the majority's view*, prohibit States from defining marriage as an institution consisting of one man and one woman.

This is a naked judicial claim to legislative—indeed, *super*-legislative—power; a claim fundamentally at odds with our system of government. Except as limited by a constitutional prohibition agreed to by the People, the States are free to adopt whatever laws they like[.] . . . A system of government that makes the People subordinate to a committee of nine unelected lawyers does not deserve to be called a democracy.

. . . [T]o allow the policy question of same-sex marriage to be considered and resolved by a select, patrician, highly unrepresentative panel of nine is to violate a principle even more fundamental than no taxation without representation: no social transformation without representation.

II

But what really astounds is the hubris reflected in today's judicial Putsch. The five Justices who compose today's majority are entirely comfortable concluding that every State violated the Constitution for all of the 135 years between the Fourteenth Amendment's ratification and Massachusetts' permitting of same-sex marriages in 2003. [*Goodridge v. Department of Public Health*, 798 N.E.2d 941 (Mass. 2003).] They have discovered in the Fourteenth Amendment a "fundamental right" overlooked by every person alive at the time of ratification, and almost everyone else in the time since. . . . They are certain that the People ratified the Fourteenth Amendment to bestow on them the power to remove questions from the democratic process when that is called for by their "reasoned judgment." These Justices *know* that limiting marriage to one man and one woman is contrary to reason; they *know* that an institution as old as government itself, and accepted by every nation in history until 15 years ago, cannot possibly be supported by anything other than ignorance or bigotry. And they are willing to say that any citizen who does not agree with that, who adheres to what was, until 15 years ago, the unanimous judgment of all generations and all societies, stands against the Constitution.

The opinion is couched in a style that is as pretentious as its content is egotistic. It is one thing for separate concurring or dissenting opinions to contain extravagances, even silly extravagances, of thought and expression; it is something else for the official opinion of the Court to do so.[22] Of course the opinion's showy profundities are often profoundly incoherent. "The nature of marriage is that, through its enduring bond, two persons together can find other freedoms, such as expression, intimacy, and spirituality." (Really? Who ever thought that intimacy and spirituality [whatever that means] were freedoms? And if intimacy is, one would think Freedom of Intimacy is abridged rather than expanded by marriage. Ask the nearest hippie. Expression, sure enough, *is* a freedom, but anyone in a long-lasting marriage will attest that that happy state constricts, rather than expands, what one can prudently say.) Rights, we are told, can "rise ... from a better informed understanding of how constitutional imperatives define a liberty that remains urgent in our own era." (Huh? How can a better informed understanding of how constitutional imperatives [whatever that means] define [whatever that means] an urgent liberty [never mind], give birth to a right?) And we are told that, "[i]n any particular case," either the Equal Protection or Due Process Clause "may be thought to capture the essence of [a] right in a more accurate and comprehensive way," than the other, "even as the two Clauses may converge in the identification and definition of the right." (What say? What possible "essence" does substantive due process "capture" in an "accurate and comprehensive way"? It stands for nothing whatever, except those freedoms and entitlements that this Court *really* likes. And the Equal Protection Clause, as employed today, identifies nothing except a difference in treatment that this Court *really* dislikes. Hardly a distillation of essence. If the opinion is correct that the two clauses "converge in the identification and definition of [a] right," that is only because the majority's likes and dislikes are predictably compatible.) I could go on. The world does not expect logic and precision in poetry or inspirational pop-philosophy; it demands them in the law. The stuff contained in today's opinion has to diminish this Court's reputation for clear thinking and sober analysis.

* * *

Hubris is sometimes defined as o'erweening pride; and pride, we know, goeth before a fall. . . . The Judiciary is the "least dangerous" of the federal branches because it has "neither Force nor Will, but merely judgment; and must ultimately depend upon the aid of the executive arm" and the States, "even for the efficacy of its judgments." [THE

---

[22] If, even as the price to be paid for a fifth vote, I ever joined an opinion for the Court that began: "The Constitution promises liberty to all within its reach, a liberty that includes certain specific rights that allow persons, within a lawful realm, to define and express their identity," I would hide my head in a bag. The Supreme Court of the United States has descended from the disciplined legal reasoning of John Marshall and Joseph Story to the mystical aphorisms of the fortune cookie.

FEDERALIST NO. 78, pp. 522, 523 (J. Cooke ed. 1961) (A. Hamilton).] With each decision of ours that takes from the People a question properly left to them—with each decision that is unabashedly based not on law, but on the "reasoned judgment" of a bare majority of this Court—we move one step closer to being reminded of our impotence.

■ JUSTICE THOMAS, with whom JUSTICE SCALIA joins, dissenting.

. . .

I

The majority's decision today will require States to issue marriage licenses to same-sex couples and to recognize same-sex marriages entered in other States largely based on a constitutional provision guaranteeing "due process" before a person is deprived of his "life, liberty, or property." I have elsewhere explained the dangerous fiction of treating the Due Process Clause as a font of substantive rights. *McDonald v. Chicago*, 561 U.S. 742, 811–812 (2010) (Thomas, J., concurring in part and concurring in judgment). It distorts the constitutional text, which guarantees only whatever "process" is "due" before a person is deprived of life, liberty, and property. U.S. CONST. [amend. XIV,] § 1. Worse, it invites judges to do exactly what the majority has done here—" 'roa[m] at large in the constitutional field' guided only by their personal views" as to the " 'fundamental rights' " protected by that document. *Planned Parenthood of Southeastern Pa. v. Casey*, 505 U.S. 833, 953, 965 (1992) (Rehnquist, C.J., concurring in judgment in part and dissenting in part) (quoting *Griswold v. Connecticut*, 381 U.S. 479, 502 (1965) (Harlan, J., concurring in judgment)).

By straying from the text of the Constitution, substantive due process exalts judges at the expense of the People from whom they derive their authority. . . . That a "bare majority" of this Court is able to . . . wip[e] out with a stroke of the keyboard the results of the political process in over 30 States, based on a provision that guarantees only "due process" is but further evidence of the danger of substantive due process.[1]

II

Even if the doctrine of substantive due process were somehow defensible—it is not—petitioners still would not have a claim. To invoke the protection of the Due Process Clause at all—whether under a theory of "substantive" or "procedural" due process—a party must first identify a deprivation of "life, liberty, or property." The majority claims these state laws deprive petitioners of "liberty," but the concept of "liberty" it

---

[1] The majority states that the right it believes is "part of the liberty promised by the Fourteenth Amendment is derived, too, from that Amendment's guarantee of the equal protection of the laws." Despite the "synergy" it finds "between th[ese] two protections," the majority clearly uses equal protection only to shore up its substantive due process analysis, an analysis both based on an imaginary constitutional protection and revisionist view of our history and tradition.

conjures up bears no resemblance to any plausible meaning of that word as it is used in the Due Process Clauses.

A

1

As used in the Due Process Clauses, "liberty" most likely refers to "the power of locomotion, of changing situation, or removing one's person to whatsoever place one's own inclination may direct; without imprisonment or restraint, unless by due course of law." 1 W. BLACKSTONE, COMMENTARIES ON THE LAWS OF ENGLAND 130 (1769) (Blackstone). That definition is drawn from the historical roots of the Clauses and is consistent with our Constitution's text and structure.

. . .

. . . That the Court appears to have lost its way in more recent years does not justify deviating from the original meaning of the Clauses.

2

Even assuming that the "liberty" in those Clauses encompasses something more than freedom from physical restraint, it would not include the types of rights claimed by the majority. In the American legal tradition, liberty has long been understood as individual freedom *from* governmental action, not as a right *to* a particular governmental entitlement.

. . .

B

Whether we define "liberty" as locomotion or freedom from governmental action more broadly, petitioners have in no way been deprived of it.

Petitioners cannot claim, under the most plausible definition of "liberty," that they have been imprisoned or physically restrained by the States for participating in same-sex relationships. . . . Far from being incarcerated or physically restrained, petitioners have been left alone to order their lives as they see fit.

Nor, under the broader definition, can they claim that the States have restricted their ability to go about their daily lives as they would be able to absent governmental restrictions. Petitioners do not ask this Court to order the States to stop restricting their ability to enter same-sex relationships, to engage in intimate behavior, to make vows to their partners in public ceremonies, to engage in religious wedding ceremonies, to hold themselves out as married, or to raise children. The States have imposed no such restrictions. Nor have the States prevented petitioners from approximating a number of incidents of marriage through private legal means, such as wills, trusts, and powers of attorney.

Instead, the States have refused to grant them governmental entitlements. Petitioners claim that as a matter of "liberty," they are entitled to access privileges and benefits that exist solely *because of* the government. They want, for example, to receive the State's *imprimatur* on their marriages—on state issued marriage licenses, death certificates, or other official forms. And they want to receive various monetary benefits, including reduced inheritance taxes upon the death of a spouse, compensation if a spouse dies as a result of a work-related injury, or loss of consortium damages in tort suits. But receiving governmental recognition and benefits has nothing to do with any understanding of "liberty" that the Framers would have recognized.

To the extent that the Framers would have recognized a natural right to marriage that fell within the broader definition of liberty, it would not have included a right to governmental recognition and benefits. Instead, it would have included a right to engage in the very same activities that petitioners have been left free to engage in—making vows, holding religious ceremonies celebrating those vows, raising children, and otherwise enjoying the society of one's spouse—without governmental interference. At the founding, such conduct was understood to predate government, not to flow from it. . . . Petitioners misunderstand the institution of marriage when they say that it would "mean little" absent governmental recognition. Brief for Petitioners in No. 14–556, p. 33.

Petitioners' misconception of liberty carries over into their discussion of our precedents identifying a right to marry, not one of which has expanded the concept of "liberty" beyond the concept of negative liberty. Those precedents all involved absolute prohibitions on private actions associated with marriage. *Loving v. Virginia*, 388 U.S. 1 (1967), for example, involved a couple who was criminally prosecuted for marrying in the District of Columbia and cohabiting in Virginia, *id.*, at 2–3.[5] They were each sentenced to a year of imprisonment, suspended for a term of 25 years on the condition that they not reenter the Commonwealth together during that time. *Id.*, at 3. In a similar vein, *Zablocki v. Redhail*, 434 U.S. 374 (1978), involved a man who was prohibited, on pain of criminal penalty, from "marry[ing] in Wisconsin or

---

[5] The suggestion . . . that antimiscegenation laws are akin to laws defining marriage as between one man and one woman is both offensive and inaccurate. "America's earliest laws against interracial sex and marriage were spawned by slavery." P. PASCOE, WHAT COMES NATURALLY: MISCEGENATION LAW AND THE MAKING OF RACE IN AMERICA 19 (2009). . . .

Laws defining marriage as between one man and one woman do not share this sordid history. The traditional definition of marriage has prevailed in every society that has recognized marriage throughout history. Brief for Scholars of History and Related Disciplines as *Amici Curiae* 1. It arose not out of a desire to shore up an invidious institution like slavery, but out of a desire "to increase the likelihood that children will be born and raised in stable and enduring family units by both the mothers and the fathers who brought them into this world." *Id.*, at 8. And it has existed in civilizations containing all manner of views on homosexuality. See Brief for Ryan T. Anderson as *Amicus Curiae* 11–12 (explaining that several famous ancient Greeks wrote approvingly of the traditional definition of marriage, though same-sex sexual relations were common in Greece at the time).

elsewhere" because of his outstanding child-support obligations, *id.*, at 387; see *id.*, at 377–378. And *Turner v. Safley*, 482 U.S. 78 (1987), involved state inmates who were prohibited from entering marriages without the permission of the superintendent of the prison, permission that could not be granted absent compelling reasons, *id.*, at 82. In *none* of those cases were individuals denied solely governmental recognition and benefits associated with marriage.

In a concession to petitioners' misconception of liberty, the majority characterizes petitioners' suit as a quest to "find . . . liberty by marrying someone of the same sex and having their marriages deemed lawful on the same terms and conditions as marriages between persons of the opposite sex." But "liberty" is not lost, nor can it be found in the way petitioners seek. As a philosophical matter, liberty is only freedom from governmental action, not an entitlement to governmental benefits. And as a constitutional matter, it is likely even narrower than that, encompassing only freedom from physical restraint and imprisonment. The majority's "better informed understanding of how constitutional imperatives define . . . liberty"—better informed, we must assume, than that of the people who ratified the Fourteenth Amendment—runs headlong into the reality that our Constitution is a "collection of 'Thou shalt nots,'" *Reid v. Covert*, 354 U.S. 1, 9 (1957) (plurality opinion), not "Thou shalt provides."

III

The majority's inversion of the original meaning of liberty will likely cause collateral damage to other aspects of our constitutional order that protect liberty.

A

The majority apparently disregards the political process as a protection for liberty. . . .

That process has been honored here. The definition of marriage has been the subject of heated debate in the States. Legislatures have repeatedly taken up the matter on behalf of the People, and 35 States have put the question to the People themselves. In 32 of those 35 States, the People have opted to retain the traditional definition of marriage. That petitioners disagree with the result of that process does not make it any less legitimate. Their civil liberty has been vindicated.

B

Aside from undermining the political processes that protect our liberty, the majority's decision threatens the religious liberty our Nation has long sought to protect.

. . .

Numerous *amici*—even some not supporting the States—have cautioned the Court that its decision here will "have unavoidable and wide-ranging implications for religious liberty." Brief for General

Conference of Seventh-Day Adventists et al. as *Amici Curiae* 5. In our society, marriage is not simply a governmental institution; it is a religious institution as well. . . . It appears all but inevitable that the two will come into conflict, particularly as individuals and churches are confronted with demands to participate in and endorse civil marriages between same-sex couples.

. . .

Although our Constitution provides some protection against such governmental restrictions on religious practices, the People have long elected to afford broader protections than this Court's constitutional precedents mandate. Had the majority allowed the definition of marriage to be left to the political process—as the Constitution requires—the People could have considered the religious liberty implications of deviating from the traditional definition as part of their deliberative process. Instead, the majority's decision short-circuits that process, with potentially ruinous consequences for religious liberty.

IV

. . . [T]he majority goes to great lengths to assert that its decision will advance the "dignity" of same-sex couples.[8] The flaw in that reasoning, of course, is that the Constitution contains no "dignity" Clause, and even if it did, the government would be incapable of bestowing dignity.

Human dignity has long been understood in this country to be innate. When the Framers proclaimed in the Declaration of Independence that "all men are created equal" and "endowed by their Creator with certain unalienable Rights," they referred to a vision of mankind in which all humans are created in the image of God and therefore of inherent worth. That vision is the foundation upon which this Nation was built.

The corollary of that principle is that human dignity cannot be taken away by the government. Slaves did not lose their dignity (any more than they lost their humanity) because the government allowed them to be enslaved. Those held in internment camps did not lose their dignity because the government confined them. And those denied governmental benefits certainly do not lose their dignity because the government denies them those benefits. The government cannot bestow dignity, and it cannot take it away.

The majority's musings are thus deeply misguided, but at least those musings can have no effect on the dignity of the persons the majority demeans. Its mischaracterization of the arguments presented by the States and their *amici* can have no effect on the dignity of those litigants.

---

[8]   The majority also suggests that marriage confers "nobility" on individuals. I am unsure what that means. People may choose to marry or not to marry. The decision to do so does not make one person more "noble" than another. And the suggestion that Americans who choose not to marry are inferior to those who decide to enter such relationships is specious.

Its rejection of laws preserving the traditional definition of marriage can have no effect on the dignity of the people who voted for them. Its invalidation of those laws can have no effect on the dignity of the people who continue to adhere to the traditional definition of marriage. And its disdain for the understandings of liberty and dignity upon which this Nation was founded can have no effect on the dignity of Americans who continue to believe in them.

* * *

. . . I respectfully dissent.

■ JUSTICE ALITO, with whom JUSTICE SCALIA and JUSTICE THOMAS join, dissenting.

. . .

I

. . .

To prevent five unelected Justices from imposing their personal vision of liberty upon the American people, the Court has held that "liberty" under the Due Process Clause should be understood to protect only those rights that are " 'deeply rooted in this Nation's history and tradition.' " *Washington v. Glucksberg*, 521 U.S. 701, 720–721 (1997). And it is beyond dispute that the right to same-sex marriage is not among those rights. See *United States v. Windsor*, 570 U.S. ___, ___ (2013) (Alito, J., dissenting) (slip op., at 7). . . .

For today's majority, it does not matter that the right to same-sex marriage lacks deep roots or even that it is contrary to long-established tradition. The Justices in the majority claim the authority to confer constitutional protection upon that right simply because they believe that it is fundamental.

II

. . .

. . . For millennia, marriage was inextricably linked to the one thing that only an opposite-sex couple can do: procreate.

Adherents to different schools of philosophy use different terms to explain why society should formalize marriage and attach special benefits and obligations to persons who marry. Here, the States defending their adherence to the traditional understanding of marriage have explained . . . that [they] formalize and promote marriage, unlike other fulfilling human relationships, in order to encourage potentially procreative conduct to take place within a lasting unit that has long been thought to provide the best atmosphere for raising children. They thus argue that there are reasonable secular grounds for restricting marriage to opposite-sex couples.

. . .

. . . It is far beyond the outer reaches of this Court's authority to say that a State may not adhere to the understanding of marriage that has long prevailed, not just in this country and others with similar cultural roots, but also in a great variety of countries and cultures all around the globe.

. . .

III

Today's decision usurps the constitutional right of the people to decide whether to keep or alter the traditional understanding of marriage. The decision will also have other important consequences.

It will be used to vilify Americans who are unwilling to assent to the new orthodoxy. In the course of its opinion, the majority compares traditional marriage laws to laws that denied equal treatment for African-Americans and women. The implications of this analogy will be exploited by those who are determined to stamp out every vestige of dissent.

. . . [T]he majority attempts . . . to reassure those who oppose same-sex marriage that their rights of conscience will be protected. We will soon see whether this proves to be true. I assume that those who cling to old beliefs will be able to whisper their thoughts in the recesses of their homes, but if they repeat those views in public, they will risk being labeled as bigots and treated as such by governments, employers, and schools.

The system of federalism established by our Constitution provides a way for people with different beliefs to live together in a single nation. If the issue of same-sex marriage had been left to the people of the States, it is likely that some States would recognize same-sex marriage and others would not. It is also possible that some States would tie recognition to protection for conscience rights. The majority today makes that impossible. By imposing its own views on the entire country, the majority facilitates the marginalization of the many Americans who have traditional ideas. Recalling the harsh treatment of gays and lesbians in the past, some may think that turnabout is fair play. But if that sentiment prevails, the Nation will experience bitter and lasting wounds.

Today's decision will also have a fundamental effect on this Court and its ability to uphold the rule of law. If a bare majority of Justices can invent a new right and impose that right on the rest of the country, the only real limit on what future majorities will be able to do is their own sense of what those with political power and cultural influence are willing to tolerate. Even enthusiastic supporters of same-sex marriage should worry about the scope of the power that today's majority claims.

Today's decision shows that decades of attempts to restrain this Court's abuse of its authority have failed. A lesson that some will take from today's decision is that preaching about the proper method of interpreting the Constitution or the virtues of judicial self-restraint and humility cannot compete with the temptation to achieve what is viewed as a noble end by any practicable means. I do not doubt that my colleagues in the majority sincerely see in the Constitution a vision of liberty that happens to coincide with their own. But this sincerity is cause for concern, not comfort. What it evidences is the deep and perhaps irremediable corruption of our legal culture's conception of constitutional interpretation.

Most Americans—understandably—will cheer or lament today's decision because of their views on the issue of same-sex marriage. But all Americans, whatever their thinking on that issue, should worry about what the majority's claim of power portends.

NOTES

1. The majority opinion in *Obergefell* underscores that its ruling rests on both Fourteenth Amendment Due Process and Equal Protection grounds. While it is clear enough that the Court's Due Process "right to marry" ruling spells the end to traditional bans on same-sex marriage, what function, exactly, does the Court's Equal Protection holding serve? Does it, as Justice Thomas's dissent maintains, serve "only to shore up [the majority's] substantive due process analysis"? Or does it also operate to guarantee lesbians, gay men, and same-sex couples equal protection and treatment under law in the context of marriage, family law, and perhaps more generally? An important answer is suggested by the Supreme Court's post-*Obergefell* decision in *Pavan v. Smith*, 582 U.S. ___, 2017 WL 2722472 (June 26, 2017) (*see infra*, p. 153). *See also, e.g., Campaign for S. Equal. v. Miss. Dep't Hum. Servs.*, 175 F.Supp.3d 691 (S.D. Miss. 2016) (*see infra*, p. 136).

2. Chief Justice Roberts ends his dissent by recognizing that "many Americans"—not all—will welcome the majority opinion with a spirit of celebration. However, he then goes on to cap off that recognition with an important qualification:

> If you are among the many Americans—of whatever sexual orientation—who favor expanding same-sex marriage, by all means celebrate today's decision. Celebrate the achievement of a desired goal. Celebrate the opportunity for a new expression of commitment to a partner. Celebrate the availability of new benefits. But do not celebrate the Constitution. It had nothing to do with it.

Obergefell v. Hodges, 135 S.Ct. 2584, 2626 (2015) (Roberts, C.J., dissenting). What does the dissent mean when it says "the Constitution . . . had nothing to do with it"? As a matter of principle, what are the implications of this idea for the cases that the majority opinion cites along the way to its conclusion, including *Lawrence v. Texas* and *United States v. Windsor*? Does Chief Justice Roberts's dissent assume or undermine their continuing validity? Both? (In answering these questions, you might consider *Pavan v. Smith*, *supra* note 1.)

3. Does Justice Thomas's dissenting opinion effectively announce that the "liberty" protected by the Due Process Clauses of the Fifth and Fourteenth Amendments does not include any protection for a fundamental right to marry "as state recognition" at all—whether for same-sex *or* cross-sex couples? Consider Michael C. Dorf, *In Defense of Justice Kennedy's Soaring Language*, SCOTUSBLOG (June 27, 2015, 5:08 PM), http://www.scotusblog .com/2015/06/symposium-in-defense-of-justice-kennedys-soaring-language/:

> To the extent that Justice Thomas would allow any substantive due process it would be for the liberty of movement only, and failing that, for no more than negative liberties. Marriage, as state recognition, would not be a fundamental right for anyone. Recognizing that, taken at face value, his view would require overruling *Loving* [*v. Virginia*] (in its fundamental rights aspect), *Zablocki v. Redhail*, and *Turner v. Safley*, he elevates the happenstance that those cases involved criminal prohibitions into central features, concluding that "in *none* of those cases were individuals denied solely governmental recognition and benefits associated with marriage."

4. The *Obergefell* dissenters are unpersuaded that the majority opinion does not threaten the religious freedoms guaranteed by the First Amendment, except perhaps the freedom to enter into plural marriages, which may have been given a boost, in their view, by the principles of the Court's ruling. Are the dissenters merely predicting the future course of events, imagining how religious liberty may in time come to be diminished by *Obergefell*? Or do their concerns also entail a claim, firmly grounded in the present tense, that *Obergefell* diminishes the sphere for the political operation of traditional moral values—at least respecting same-sex relationships—in the context of marriage and family law? *Cf.* CBS News/AP, *County Court Clerks Rebel Against Same-sex Marriage Ruling*, CBS NEWS (July 6, 2015), http://www.cbsnews.com/news/county-court-house-clerks-rebel-against-same-sex-marriage-ruling/; Chris Geidner, *Federal Judge Criticizes Mississippi Recusal Law, Will Expand Injunction*, BUZZFEED NEWS (June 27, 2016), https://www.buzzfeed.com/chrisgeidner/federal-judge-criticizes-mississippi-recusal-law-will-expand?utm_term=.pbvvzRwdY#.awBnrZ9le; Jacob Gershman, *After Gay-Marriage Ruling, Tensions, Questions Ripple in States with Bans*, WALL ST. J.: L. BLOG (July 9, 2015, 7:07 PM), http://blogs.wsj.com/law/2015/07/09/after-gay-marriage-ruling-tensions-questions-ripple-in-states-with-bans/. Some answers may soon be forthcoming in *Masterpiece Cakeshop, Ltd. v. Colo. Civ. Rights Comm'n*, 370 P.3d 272 (Colo. App. 2015), *cert. granted*, 85 U.S.L.W. 3600 (U.S. June 26, 2017).

5. What sorts of effects might *Obergefell* have in the longer term on the legal availability of non-marital relationship forms, such as civil unions and domestic partnerships? Do you think *Obergefell* is more consistent with the preservation and even the expansion of these non-marital relationship forms? Or is it more consistent with their elimination? *Cf. Jiwungkul v. Dir., Div. of Taxation*, No. 009346-2015, 2016 WL 2996871 (N.J. Tax Ct. May 11, 2016).

6. The Maryland Attorney General has issued a legal opinion that builds on *Obergefell* to explain that Maryland's adultery law applies to same-sex married couples. According to the opinion:

> Given that same-sex couples have the right to marry on equal terms with opposite-sex couples, it makes little sense to say that same-sex infidelity does not constitute a breach of the marriage vow. It makes even less sense to conclude that same-sex infidelity does not constitute adultery for purposes of [Maryland's divorce law] when that interpretation would make it nearly impossible for same-sex couples to qualify for divorce on that ground.

Divorce—Whether Same-Sex Marital Infidelity Can Qualify as Adultery for Purposes of Family Law Provisions Governing Divorce, 100 Op. Md. Att'y Gen. (July 24, 2015). Consistent with *Obergefell*, could a State properly treat adultery differently based on whether it is committed by a spouse in a cross-sex or a same-sex marriage? Even before *Obergefell*, Professor Peter Nicolas expressed the view that:

> [T]he same equality principles that have resulted in the extension of the right to marry to same sex-couples likewise require the application of adultery laws and related doctrines to same-sex couples and same-sex conduct. Indeed, a failure to apply them in those contexts devalues same-sex relationships and perpetuates antiquated, negative stereotypes about gay people[.] . . . As ironic as it seems, despite decades of litigation to get the government out of the bedrooms of gays and lesbians, . . . principles of equality on the bases of gender and sexual orientation require that the private sexual conduct of gays and lesbians be intruded upon to the same extent as their heterosexual counterparts.

Peter Nicolas, *The Lavender Letter: Applying the Law of Adultery to Same-Sex Couples and Same-Sex Conduct*, 63 FLA. L. REV. 97, 99–100 (2011). Do you agree or disagree? Why? Assuming that *Obergefell's* principles do require cross-sex and same-sex adultery to be treated the same for legal purposes, how exactly should adultery be treated? Consider Edward Stein, Marriage and Sexual Fidelity at the Midyear AALS Conference on Shifting Foundations in Family Law (June 23, 2015).

B. RESTRICTIONS ON THE PROCEDURE FOR MARRYING

Page 165, Unabridged (Page 111, Concise). Insert the following case and notes after the notes following *Rappaport v. Katz*.

Jones v. Perry

U.S. District Court, E.D. Kentucky, October 18, 2016.
215 F.Supp.3d 563.

■ GREGORY F. VAN TATENHOVE, U.S. DISTRICT JUDGE.

OPINION & ORDER

Bradley Jones and Kathryn Brooke Sauer simply want to get married. Defendant Sue Carole Perry, the Shelby County Clerk, refuses to issue them a marriage license. She insists that Kentucky law prohibits her from doing so unless both Jones and Sauer physically appear at the clerk's office to apply for a license. Sauer happens to be a prisoner at the Kentucky Correctional Institution for Women, so she cannot travel to the clerk's office for this purpose.

Although Perry believes that Kentucky law compels her to prevent Jones and Sauer from exercising their fundamental right to marry, the relevant statutes tell a different story. In fact, these statutes make no mention of Perry's in-person requirement, nor do they otherwise discuss the significance of a marriage applicant's presence at the clerk's office. The blanket in-person requirement is a contrivance of Perry and other government officials of this Commonwealth. It is also unconstitutional. For that reason, the Court will now permanently enjoin Perry from enforcing this requirement against Jones in the future.

I

Jones and Sauer were only teenagers when they first met at Westport Middle School in 1994. They dated for about a month, after which Sauer moved away from Louisville with her family. Jones never forgot about her. He spent a lot of time "in and out of juvenile institutions and prison for a variety of non-violent charges" over the next ten years, and he and Sauer lost touch. When he finally exited the prison system, Jones began looking for her. . . . Years passed without any luck. Then, in 2014, he ran into an old middle school classmate who was still friends with Sauer. She told him that Sauer had experienced her own share of legal trouble over the years, and that she was currently serving a long-term prison sentence.

Given his history, Jones "understood how much it means to an incarcerated person to talk to people on the outside." He and Sauer began exchanging letters and talking on the phone. What started "as a rekindled friendship eventually led to a rekindled romantic relationship." Jones then obtained approval to visit her at the Kentucky Correctional Institution for Women ("KCIW"). At their first in-person encounter since middle school, he proposed marriage. She said yes. He has continued to visit her "twice a week nearly every week since then."

Sauer is not eligible for parole until June of 2026. Because of his religious beliefs, Jones does not believe he can "or should wait until then to solidify their bond before God and the Commonwealth of Kentucky." But state officials have consistently thwarted the couple's attempts to marry. Jones reports that he has contacted "numerous county clerks" throughout the Commonwealth and "not one [will] agree to grant [the couple] a marriage license."

One of these clerks is Defendant Sue Carole Perry. She is the clerk of Shelby County, Kentucky, where KCIW is located. When Jones sought a marriage license from Perry in July 2016, she told him that "her office interprets Kentucky law as saying both parties must be present to issue a marriage license." Jones informed her that his fiancée could not appear at the clerk's office because she was in prison, "but [Perry] still refused to issue a license." Prison officials at KCIW also offered no help; in a letter sent to Jones that same month, Warden Janet Conover informed him that she had "no objection to the marriage," but that "both parties must be present [at the clerk's office] to obtain a license and [the prison does] not transport inmates for this reason."

Jones later asked Perry to identify what "Kentucky law" prevented her from issuing the couple a license. Rather than cite a Kentucky statute, Perry supplied a memo that she received from the Kentucky Department for Libraries & Archives ("KDLA") in 2008. This memo noted that marriage license applications have "signature places for both the bride and groom." And because KRS § 402.110 states that clerks must "see to it that every blank space required to be filled by the applicant is so filled before delivering" a marriage license, the KDLA determined that "the county clerk in each county must have both parties sign the application and both must be present at that time." The department also claimed to have reached this conclusion "after consulting with" Kentucky's Attorney General.

In 2009, however, the Office of the Attorney General ("OAG") expressed a very different opinion. The OAG issued a letter in response to a question from the Education and Workforce Development Cabinet (which houses the KDLA) about "the inability of incarcerated persons to obtain a marriage license because they cannot present themselves to the county clerk." The office declined to issue a formal opinion "because litigation [was] being contemplated," but did note that the in-person requirement likely interfered with a prisoner's fundamental right to marry. The OAG affirmed that "public officials cannot sit on their hands and frustrate an incarcerated person's right to marry," and advised the state to adopt "procedures ... to assist incarcerated persons in exercising" that right.

Seven years after the OAG warned public officials not "to sit on their hands and frustrate an incarcerated person's right to marry," Jones walked into the Shelby County Clerk's Office. Perry refused to issue him a marriage license. He then filed a Motion for Preliminary Injunction in this Court, arguing that Perry's in-person requirement violates his "fundamental right to marry . . . which is guaranteed by the Due Process Clause of the Fourteenth Amendment to the United States Constitution."

II

A

i

Before reaching the substance of Jones's request, the Court must first decide whether to treat his motion as one for a preliminary or permanent injunction. Ordinarily, courts should not convert a motion for a preliminary injunction into one for a permanent injunction without first holding an evidentiary hearing. *Moltan Co. v. Eagle-Picher Indus., Inc.*, 55 F.3d 1171, 1174 (6th Cir. 1995). But no hearing is required when the dispute concerns a "purely legal question" and there are "no triable issues of fact." *United States v. McGee*, 714 F.2d 607, 613 (6th Cir. 1983).

. . .

. . . In the absence of any legitimate dispute, the Court will treat Jones's motion as one for a permanent injunction.

ii

To obtain a permanent injunction, a plaintiff "must first establish that [he has] suffered a constitutional violation." *Women's Med. Prof'l Corp. v. Baird*, 438 F.3d 595, 602 (6th Cir. 2006). And even if the Court finds that a violation occurred, the plaintiff must also "demonstrate: (1) that [he] has suffered an irreparable injury; (2) that remedies available at law, such as monetary damages, are inadequate to compensate for that injury; (3) that, considering the balance of hardships between the plaintiff and defendant, a remedy in equity is warranted; and (4) that the public interest would not be disserved by a permanent injunction." *eBay Inc. v. MercExchange, L.L.C.*, 547 U.S. 388, 391 (2006).

B

i

The constitutional right at issue here is plain. The right to marry "has long been recognized as one of the vital personal rights essential to the orderly pursuit of happiness by free men" and women. *Loving v. Virginia*, 388 U.S. 1, 12 (1967). This freedom "is one of the most basic civil rights of every [human being], fundamental to our very existence and survival." *Id.* (internal quotations and citation omitted). Through this commitment our collective rights deepen, and "two persons together . . . find other freedoms, such as expression, intimacy, and spirituality." *Obergefell v. Hodges*, [576] U.S. ___, 135 S.Ct. 2584, 2599 (2015). Many, like Jones, consider "the commitment of marriage [to] be an exercise of religious faith as well as an expression of personal dedication." *Turner v. Safley*, 482 U.S. 78, 95–96 (1987).

For all these reasons, courts will apply strict scrutiny to any law or policy that places a "direct and substantial burden" on the right to marry. *Vaughn v. Lawrenceburg Power Sys.*, 269 F.3d 703, 710 (6th Cir. 2001). This means the rule "cannot be upheld unless it is supported by sufficiently important state interests and is closely tailored to effectuate only those interests." *Zablocki v. Redhail*, 434 U.S. 374, 388 (1978). A state policy places a "direct and substantial burden" on this right when "a large portion of those affected by the rule are absolutely or largely prevented from marrying, or whe[n] those affected by the rule are absolutely or largely prevented from marrying a large portion of the otherwise eligible population of spouses." *Vaughn*, 269 F.3d at 710. But if the policy does not "directly and substantially interfere with the fundamental right to marry," courts will only subject the rule to rational basis review. *Wright v. MetroHealth Med. Ctr.*, 58 F.3d 1130, 1135 (6th Cir. 1995). This forgiving test requires the Court to find only that the policy is "rationally related to legitimate government interests." *Johnson v. Bredesen*, 624 F.3d 742, 746 (6th Cir. 2010).

ii

Perry, of course, argues that the Court should apply rational basis review to the in-person requirement. She cites *Toms v. Taft*, 338 F.3d 519, 525 (6th Cir. 2003), for the proposition that "a prisoner's right to marry may be restricted where the restriction is reasonably related to a legitimate penological interest." *Toms v. Taft*, 338 F.3d 519, 525 (6th Cir. 2003) (citing *Turner*, 482 U.S. at 96–97). . . . But *Toms* does not apply to this case. . . . Perry does not manage a prison. She cannot lean on any penological interests to rescue this policy.

. . .

At oral argument, Perry . . . announced that she "would like to . . . plant the question [in the Court's mind] as to why the county clerk is the one [being sued] if the warden is also responsible for interpreting the statute." The KCIW Warden is not a defendant in this suit. Whether the prison's refusal to transport Sauer is "reasonably related to a legitimate penological interest" is not at issue in this case. But the Court does note that the Warden's policy—which need only satisfy rational basis review—is more likely constitutional than Perry's, which deserves strict scrutiny. For the purposes of this order, it is enough to say that the KCIW Warden expressly stated she will "not transport inmates" to the clerk's office to obtain a marriage license. That fact, coupled with Perry's refusal to issue a license, absolutely prevents Jones from marrying Sauer.

Perry's next argument is that her policy does not impose a "direct and substantial burden" because Jones and Sauer remain free "to marry anybody they want[,] just not each other." In support, she cites a case of this Circuit, *Vaughn*, 269 F.3d 703. In *Vaughn*, the plaintiffs—a married couple who previously worked together in state government—challenged a state employer's policy "requir[ing] the resignation of one spouse in the event two employees marry." *Id.* at 706. The court found that this policy did not place a "direct and substantial burden" on the couple because "it did not bar [them] from getting married, nor did it prevent them [from] marrying a large portion of population," but "only made it economically burdensome to marry a small number of those eligible individuals, their fellow employees at [the office where they worked]." *Id.* at 712. The court added that "[o]nce [the couple] decided to marry *one another*, [the] policy became onerous for them, but *ex ante*, it did not greatly restrict their freedom to marry or whom to marry." *Id.* (emphasis in original).

The holding in *Vaughn* does not control this case for at least three reasons. First, the relevant facts in *Vaughn* are facially distinguishable from those at issue here. The *Vaughn* court's decision rested on an obvious fact that is not present in this case: the disputed policy "did not bar [the couple] from getting married," but "only made it economically burdensome" to do so. *Id.* The plaintiffs in *Vaughn* were already married by the time they filed suit. *Id.* at 708. . . . The [*Vaughn*] court's rather dismissive treatment of this *ex post* burden need not extend to the policy in dispute here, which absolutely prohibits Jones from marrying Sauer.

Second, to the extent that *Vaughn* counsels against applying strict scrutiny in all cases where a policy "only" burdens the applicants' right to marry "one another," this aspect of the court's holding is no longer good law. That is especially true where, as here, the petitioner mounts an as-applied challenge to a policy that absolutely erases his right to marry the individual of his choice. Fourteen years after *Vaughn*, the Supreme Court announced that "the decision whether *and whom* to marry is among life's momentous acts of self-definition." *Obergefell*, 135 S.Ct. at 2599 (emphasis added) (internal quotations and citation omitted). The Court cannot recognize this principle without also honoring Jones's constitutional right to marry *this woman*, the woman he freely chose. Loved ones are not fungible commodities.

Third, *Vaughn*'s holding also rested on the fact that the employer's policy "did [not] prevent [the couple from] marrying a large portion of population," but "only made it economically burdensome to marry a small number of those eligible individuals, their fellow employees at [the office where they worked]." *Id.* at 712. Here, by contrast, the in-person requirement absolutely prevents Jones from marrying any person who (1) happens to be in prison and (2) cannot travel to the clerk's office.[5] If we lived in any other country in the world, Perry might plausibly argue that prisoners do not constitute a sizeable portion of the population. But the United States has the largest prison population on earth.[6] And Kentucky is one reason why.

---

[5] In truth, the policy prohibits Jones from marrying anyone who cannot travel to the clerk's office, incarcerated or otherwise. That would also include, for example, an invalid or a diagnosed agoraphobic.

[6] *Highest to Lowest—Prison Population Total*, WORLD PRISON BRIEF, http://www.prison studies.org/highest-to-lowest/prison-population-total?field_region_taxonomy_tid=All&=Apply (last visited Sept. 28, 2016).

A recent study found that "[i]f each U.S. state were its own country, Kentucky would have the seventh-highest incarceration rate in the world."[7] Our state jails and prisons currently house over 23,000 people.[8] Our federal facilities have roughly 7,000 prisoners.[9] And the problem is especially bad in Shelby County. As of September 2016, the Shelby County Correctional Center housed 351 inmates.[10] KCIW, located in Shelby County, had 683 prisoners.[11] According to the last census, only around 42,000 people live in Shelby County.[12] That means the prison population of KCIW alone amounts to 1–2 percent of the county's total population. By comparison, the federal government reported in 2014 that "1.6 percent of adults [in the United States] self-identify as gay or lesbian."[13] At the very least, then, the in-person requirement prohibits Jones from marrying a significant percentage of Shelby County residents.

These facts support one conclusion: the in-person requirement absolutely prevents Jones from marrying Sauer, and absolutely prevents him from marrying a large portion of the population. The policy thus imposes a "direct and substantial burden" on Jones's fundamental right to marry, and it "cannot be upheld unless it is supported by sufficiently important state interests and is closely tailored to effectuate only those interests." *Zablocki*, 434 U.S. at 388, 98 S.Ct. 673.

iii

Perry's rationale for imposing the in-person requirement collapses under strict scrutiny. She first argues that her policy serves the "important state interest" of ensuring that both applicants are legally eligible to marry. The Court will accept that verifying the eligibility of marriage applicants is a "sufficiently important state interest." *Zablocki*, 434 U.S. at 388, 98 S.Ct. 673. But the in-person requirement is not "closely tailored to effectuate only" that interest. *Id.*

At oral argument, the Court repeatedly asked Perry's counsel to explain how the in-person requirement actually promotes the state's interest in verifying the eligibility of marriage applicants. Counsel never

---

[7]   *Kentucky's Incarceration Rate Ranks 7th in the World*, WFPL NEWS (Nov. 12, 1015), http://wfpl.org/if-it-were-a-country-kentuckys-prison-rate-would-rank-7th-in-the-world/.

[8]   *Inmate Profiles*, KENTUCKY DEPARTMENT OF CORRECTIONS (Sept. 15, 2016), http://corrections.ky.gov/about/Documents/Research%20and%20Statistics/Monthly%20Reports/Inmate%20Profile/2016/Inmate%20Profile%2009–2016.pdf (last visited Sept. 28, 2016).

[9]   *Generate Inmate Population Reports*, FEDERAL BUREAU OF PRISONS, https://www.bop.gov/about/statisticspopulation_statistics.jsp (search "All Kentucky Facilities;" then click "Generate Report") (last visited Sept. 28, 2016).

[10]   *Inmates*, SHELBY COUNTY DETENTION CENTER, http://www.shelbycountydetention.com/SCDC_inmatelist.html (last visited Sept. 28, 2016).

[11]   *About KCIW*, KENTUCKY DEPARTMENT OF CORRECTIONS, http://corrections.ky.gov/depts/AI/KCIW/Pages/AboutKCIW.aspx (last visited Sept. 28, 2016).

[12]   *Quick Facts: Shelby County*, UNITED STATES CENSUS BUREAU, http://www.census.gov/quickfacts/table/PST045215/21211,00 (last visited Sept. 28, 2016).

[13]   *Health survey gives government its first large-scale data on gay, bisexual population*, THE WASHINGTON POST (July 15, 2014), https://www.washingtonpost.com/national/health-science/health-survey-gives-government-its-first-large-scale-data-on-gay-bisexual-population/2014/07/14/2db9f4b0-092f-11e4-bbf1-cc51275e7f8f_story.html.

fully answered this question. Without much guidance from Perry, the Court will summarize a few reasons why her policy might plausibly advance this interest. First, the in-person requirement could encourage applicants to provide thorough and honest answers to the clerk's questions about their eligibility. Some find it easier to lie on paper than in face-to-face communication. Second, observing an applicant's demeanor in person might make it easier to evaluate the applicant's credibility. The subtleties of a facial expression are lost in a documentary exchange. Third, an applicant might have some disqualifying characteristics that are readily observable in person. A pregnant minor, for example, would have difficulty obtaining a license at the clerk's office.

Even though Perry's chosen policy may serve the interest at stake, many alternative methods could just as easily effectuate that interest. Most evidently, Perry or one of her deputies could drive up the road to KCIW and watch Sauer sign the marriage license. That would take about twenty-five minutes. Or she could do what the clerk did in *Toms* and arrange to "deputize an employee of the 'central office' of the [prison] (specifically, an Assistant Attorney General) as a clerk to issue the marriage license" to Sauer at the prison itself. *Toms*, 338 F.3d at 522–23. Both of these alternatives would allow the state to preserve the benefits of observing an applicant in person.

Another alternative appears in *Amos v. Higgins*, 996 F.Supp.2d 810 (W.D. Mo. 2014). In *Amos*, the court confronted a Missouri statute that "required each applicant for a marriage [to] sign the application 'in the presence of the recorder of deeds or their deputy.'" *Id.* at 811. The court held that this requirement was unconstitutional as applied to both prisoners and their fiancées[.] . . . As an alternative procedure, the court ordered the clerk to permit each prisoner to (1) submit "all fees and other documents required for the issuance of a marriage license under the laws of the [state]," and (2) submit an "affidavit or sworn statement," verified by both "the warden or the warden's designee and . . . a notary public," that identified the "names of both applicants" and stated that "the applicant [was] unable to appear in the presence of the recorder of deeds due to [her] incarceration." *Id.* at 814–15.

Admittedly, the *Amos* procedure addressed the clerk's concern about verifying the *identity* of marriage applicants. Perry's expressed concern is about the *eligibility* of applicants. In Kentucky, however, prison wardens are already required to verify the eligibility of prisoners before they obtain a marriage license. Kentucky's official corrections policy requires a warden to approve a marriage application in advance. This approval process directs the warden to ensure that there are no "legal restriction[s]" to the marriage and that the "inmate making the request is not . . . incompetent." This additional step, coupled with the procedure established in *Amos*, would likely resolve any questions about the prisoner's eligibility.

The Court adds that here, unlike in *Amos*, no state law actually obligates Perry to enforce the in-person requirement. . . . [T]he provision relied upon by the KDLA, KRS § 402.110, provides only that "[t]he clerk shall see to it that every blank space required to be filled by the applicants is so filled before delivering it to the licensee." Perry could comply with these requirements by adopting any one of the procedures outlined above.[17]

iv

Because Perry's policy is unconstitutional as applied to Jones, the remaining elements of the permanent injunction standard can be resolved easily. The "irreparable harm" to Jones flows naturally from Perry's constitutional violation. *See Overstreet v. Lexington-Fayette Urban Cnty. Gov't*, 305 F.3d 566, 578 (6th Cir. 2002). The Court cannot remedy this harm through monetary damages alone; no amount of compensation will substitute for the exercise of "one of the vital personal rights essential to the orderly pursuit of happiness by free men" and women. *Loving*, 388 U.S. at 12, 87 S.Ct. 1817.

The balance of the harms also tips in Jones's favor. As explained above, Perry can satisfy her statutory duties through a range of readily available alternatives to the in-person requirement. The harm she might suffer from, for example, driving to KCIW—or perhaps asking one of her deputies to make the short trip—is minimal. And most importantly, the public has a powerful interest in vindicating "one of the most basic civil rights of every [human being], fundamental to our very existence and survival." *Id.*

III

When state officials disrupt the free exercise of fundamental rights, courts will scrutinize their conduct with unusual precision and care. Perry's in-person requirement cannot survive that scrutiny. The Court does recognize, however, that Perry is best situated to choose from among the available alternatives to her current policy. *See Howe v. City of Akron*, 801 F.3d 718, 754 (6th Cir. 2015). Accordingly, the Court **HEREBY ORDERS** as follows:

(1) Jones's motion for injunctive relief is **GRANTED**;

(2) Defendant Sue Carole Perry is **PERMANENTLY ENJOINED** from requiring Sauer to appear at the Shelby County Clerk's Office prior to issuing Jones a marriage license; and

---

[17] Perry also briefly argued that "to open the door for these individual exceptions without any formal protocol is simply opening up Pandora's Box, and [she] shouldn't be forced to do that." The Court is not asking Perry to make a special exception for Jones. The Court is ordering Perry to comply with the Constitution. If Perry enforced the in-person requirement against another individual who absolutely could not appear at the clerk's office—for example, someone who was terminally ill and could not safely leave her home—that would also likely be unconstitutional. Needless to say, the likelihood that Perry's policy may be unconstitutional in other circumstances does not preclude the Court from also finding it unconstitutional here.

(3) Perry shall have up to and including **Friday, November 4, 2016**, to adopt and perform a procedure that will permit Jones and Sauer to obtain a marriage license without physically appearing at the Shelby County Clerk's Office.

NOTES

1.　According to Aaron J. Bentley, who helped represent Bradley Jones in *Jones v. Perry*:

> After the Court's decision, the Shelby County Clerk agreed to accept a notarized form signed by the incarcerated person to fulfill the requirements to obtain a marriage license. Brad and Brooke received a license, and married on November 10, 2016. The ceremony was a deserved ending to Brad's long, determined fight to marry his childhood sweetheart. After contacting nearly every Kentucky county clerk, unsuccessfully trying to hire several lawyers, researching laws of other states and countries regarding proxy marriages, and even turning down an early settlement offer that included a marriage license but no prospective change in policy, Brad secured a federal court judgment vindicating his constitutional right to marry.
>
> Since Brad's case, some Kentucky clerks have adopted procedures to permit incarcerated Kentuckians to marry; however, the large majority have not. . . .

Email from Aaron J. Bentley, Craig Henry, to Marc Spindelman, The Ohio State University Moritz College of Law (June 28, 2017, at 13:50 EST) (on file with author).

2.　Speaking generally, *Jones* illuminates how procedural limitations on the right to marry can, at times, veer onto substantive terrain, limiting the right to marry and so violating the constitutional protections accorded to it. But the *Jones* court decision does not rule that the in-person marriage license requirement at issue in the case is always unconstitutional. Its judgment is highly contextualized. It declares this licensure requirement in this case to be a "direct and substantial" limitation on Jones's right to marry. What are the factors that lead the court to this conclusion? What do you make of the court's view that statistics on incarceration rates are relevant to the constitutional ruling it issues? What, precisely, is the court saying on this score, and do you agree or disagree, and why?

3.　*Jones* formally addresses how the in-person marriage license requirement challenged in the case violates Bradley Jones's constitutional right to marry. Along the way, the court's opinion suggests, without deciding, that Warden Janet Conover's decision not to transport Kathryn Brooke Sauer to the Shelby County Clerk's office in order to satisfy the Clerk's in-person licensure requirement might not have constituted a violation of Sauer's constitutional marriage rights, even though that decision practically blocked Sauer from satisfying the in-person licensure requirement, hence kept her, at least initially, from marrying Jones. Is the idea that thus emerges from the case that Jones's constitutional right to marry entitles him to marry Sauer but that Sauer's constitutional right to marry on its own may not entitle her to marry him? Is Sauer's right to marry Jones in this case, then, a function of his, and not her own, constitutional rights? Would that raise any legal concerns of its own?

4.   According to at least one newspaper report, the in-person marriage license requirement at issue in *Jones* traces to a desire "to ensure the bride and groom are 18 and of different sexes, as required by law, and to avoid other marriage fraud." Andrew Wolfson, *Kentucky Inmate Fights Marriage License's Revocation*, COURIER-J., Nov. 7, 2012, at A1, A6 (referring to comments by "Jerry Carlton, director of local government records," given in an interview). May States generally have in-person marriage license requirements in order to ensure that the parties to a marriage satisfy substantive marriage law rules?

CHAPTER 3

MARRIAGE

B. CHALLENGES TO THE TRADITIONAL MARRIAGE MODEL

2. CONSTITUTIONAL LIMITS ON SEX DISCRIMINATION

THE FOURTEENTH AMENDMENT

Page 214, Unabridged (Page 151, Concise). Replace *United States v. Flores-Villar* with the following case and notes.

Sessions v. Morales-Santana

Supreme Court of the United States, June 12, 2017.
582 U.S. ___, 137 S.Ct. 1678, 198 L.Ed.2d 150.

■ JUSTICE GINSBURG delivered the opinion of the Court.

This case concerns a gender-based differential in the law governing acquisition of U.S. citizenship by a child born abroad, when one parent is a U.S. citizen, the other, a citizen of another nation. The main rule appears in 8 U.S.C. § 1401(a)(7) (1958 ed.), now § 1401(g) (2012 ed.). Applicable to married couples, § 1401(a)(7) requires a period of physical presence in the United States for the U.S.-citizen parent. The requirement, as initially prescribed, was ten years' physical presence prior to the child's birth, § 601(g) (1940 ed.); currently, the requirement is five years prebirth, § 1401(g) (2012 ed.). That main rule is rendered applicable to unwed U.S.-citizen fathers by § 1409(a). Congress ordered an exception, however, for unwed U.S.-citizen mothers. Contained in § 1409(c), the exception allows an unwed mother to transmit her citizenship to a child born abroad if she has lived in the United States for just one year prior to the child's birth.

The respondent in this case, Luis Ramón Morales-Santana, was born in the Dominican Republic when his father was just 20 days short of meeting § 1401(a)(7)'s physical-presence requirement. Opposing removal to the Dominican Republic, Morales-Santana asserts that the equal protection principle implicit in the Fifth Amendment entitles him to citizenship stature. We hold that the gender line Congress drew is incompatible with the requirement that the Government accord to all persons "the equal protection of the laws." Nevertheless, we cannot convert § 1409(c)'s exception for unwed mothers into the main rule displacing § 1401(a)(7) (covering married couples) and § 1409(a) (covering unwed fathers). We must therefore leave it to Congress to select, going forward, a physical-presence requirement (ten years, one year, or some other period) uniformly applicable to all children born abroad with one U.S.-citizen and one alien parent, wed or unwed. In the interim, the Government must ensure that the laws in question are administered in a manner free from gender-based discrimination.

I

A

We first describe in greater detail the regime Congress constructed. The general rules for acquiring U.S. citizenship are found in 8 U.S.C. § 1401, the first section in Chapter 1 of Title III of the Immigration and Nationality Act (1952 Act or INA), § 301, 66 Stat. 235–236. Section 1401 sets forth the INA's rules for determining who "shall be nationals and citizens of the United States at birth" by establishing a range of residency and physical-presence requirements calibrated primarily to the parents' nationality and the child's place of birth. § 1401(a) (1958 ed.); § 1401 (2012 ed.). The primacy of § 1401 in the statutory scheme is evident. Comprehensive in coverage, § 1401 provides the general framework for the acquisition of citizenship at birth. In particular, at the time relevant here,[2] § 1401(a)(7) provided for the U.S. citizenship of

> "a person born outside the geographical limits of the United States and its outlying possessions of parents one of whom is an alien, and the other a citizen of the United States who, prior to the birth of such person, was physically present in the United States or its outlying possessions for a period or periods totaling not less than ten years, at least five of which were after attaining the age of fourteen years: *Provided*, That any periods of honorable service in the Armed Forces of the United States by such citizen parent may be included in computing the physical presence requirements of this paragraph."

Congress has since reduced the duration requirement to five years, two after age 14. § 1401(g) (2012 ed.).[3]

Section 1409 pertains specifically to children with unmarried parents. Its first subsection, § 1409(a), incorporates by reference the physical-presence requirements of § 1401, thereby allowing an acknowledged unwed citizen parent to transmit U.S. citizenship to a foreign-born child under the same terms as a married citizen parent. Section 1409(c)—a provision applicable only to unwed U.S.-citizen mothers—states an exception to the physical-presence requirements of §§ 1401 and 1409(a). Under § 1409(c)'s exception, only one year of continuous physical presence is required before unwed mothers may pass citizenship to their children born abroad.

---

[2]   Unless otherwise noted, references to 8 U.S.C. §§ 1401 and 1409 are to the 1958 edition of the U.S. Code, the version in effect when respondent Morales-Santana was born. Section 1409(a) and (c) have retained their numbering; § 1401(a)(7) has become § 1401(g).

[3]   The reduction affects only children born on or after November 14, 1986. § 8(r), 102 Stat. 2619; see §§ 12–13, 100 Stat. 3657. Because Morales-Santana was born in 1962, his challenge is to the ten-years, five-after-age-14 requirement applicable at the time of his birth.

B

Respondent Luis Ramón Morales-Santana moved to the United States at age 13, and has resided in this country most of his life. Now facing deportation, he asserts U.S. citizenship at birth based on the citizenship of his biological father, José Morales, who accepted parental responsibility and included Morales-Santana in his household.

José Morales was born in Guánica, Puerto Rico, on March 19, 1900. Puerto Rico was then, as it is now, part of the United States, and José became a U.S. citizen under the Organic Act of Puerto Rico, ch. 145, § 5, 39 Stat. 953 (a predecessor to 8 U.S.C. § 1402). After living in Puerto Rico for nearly two decades, José left his childhood home on February 27, 1919, 20 days short of his 19th birthday, therefore failing to satisfy § 1401(a)(7)'s requirement of five years' physical presence after age 14. He did so to take up employment as a builder-mechanic for a U.S. company in the then-U.S.-occupied Dominican Republic.

By 1959, José attested in a June 21, 1971 affidavit presented to the U.S. Embassy in the Dominican Republic, he was living with Yrma Santana Montilla, a Dominican woman he would eventually marry. In 1962, Yrma gave birth to their child, respondent Luis Morales-Santana. While the record before us reveals little about Morales-Santana's childhood, the Dominican archives disclose that Yrma and José married in 1970, and that José was then added to Morales-Santana's birth certificate as his father. José also related in the same affidavit that he was then saving money "for the susten[ance] of [his] family" in anticipation of undergoing surgery in Puerto Rico, where members of his family still resided. In 1975, when Morales-Santana was 13, he moved to Puerto Rico, and by 1976, the year his father died, he was attending public school in the Bronx, a New York City borough.[5]

C

In 2000, the Government placed Morales-Santana in removal proceedings based on several convictions for offenses under New York State Penal Law, all of them rendered on May 17, 1995. Morales-Santana ranked as an alien despite the many years he lived in the United States, because, at the time of his birth, his father did not satisfy the requirement of five years' physical presence after age 14. An immigration judge rejected Morales-Santana's claim to citizenship derived from the U.S. citizenship of his father, and ordered Morales-Santana's removal to the Dominican Republic. In 2010, Morales-Santana moved to reopen the proceedings, asserting that the Government's refusal to recognize that he derived citizenship from his U.S.-citizen father violated the Constitution's equal protection guarantee. The Board of Immigration Appeals (BIA) denied the motion.

---

[5] There is no question that Morales-Santana himself satisfied the five-year residence requirement that once conditioned a child's acquisition of citizenship under § 1401(a)(7). See § 1401(b).

The United States Court of Appeals for the Second Circuit reversed the BIA's decision. 804 F.3d 520, 524 (2015). Relying on this Court's post-1970 construction of the equal protection principle as it bears on gender-based classifications, the court held unconstitutional the differential treatment of unwed mothers and fathers. *Id.*, at 527–535. To cure the constitutional flaw, the court further held that Morales-Santana derived citizenship through his father, just as he would were his mother the U.S. citizen. *Id.*, at 535–538. In so ruling, the Second Circuit declined to follow the conflicting decision of the Ninth Circuit in *United States v. Flores-Villar*, 536 F.3d 990 (2008), see 804 F.3d, at 530, 535, n. 17. We granted certiorari in *Flores-Villar*, but ultimately affirmed by an equally divided Court. *Flores-Villar v. United States*, 564 U.S. 210 (2011) (*per curiam*). Taking up Morales-Santana's request for review, 579 U.S. ___ (2016), we consider the matter anew.

II

Because § 1409 treats sons and daughters alike, Morales-Santana does not suffer discrimination on the basis of *his* gender. He complains, instead, of gender-based discrimination against his father, who was unwed at the time of Morales-Santana's birth and was not accorded the right an unwed U.S.-citizen mother would have to transmit citizenship to her child. Although the Government does not contend otherwise, we briefly explain why Morales-Santana may seek to vindicate his father's right to the equal protection of the laws.

Ordinarily, a party "must assert his own legal rights" and "cannot rest his claim to relief on the legal rights . . . of third parties." *Warth v. Seldin*, 422 U.S. 490, 499 (1975). But we recognize an exception where, as here, "the party asserting the right has a close relationship with the person who possesses the right [and] there is a hindrance to the possessor's ability to protect his own interests." *Kowalski v. Tesmer*, 543 U.S. 125, 130 (2004) (quoting *Powers v. Ohio*, 499 U.S. 400, 411 (1991)). José Morales' ability to pass citizenship to his son, respondent Morales-Santana, easily satisfies the "close relationship" requirement. So, too, is the "hindrance" requirement well met. José Morales' failure to assert a claim in his own right "stems from disability," not "disinterest," *Miller v. Albright*, 523 U.S. 420, 450 (1998) (O'Connor, J., concurring in judgment), for José died in 1976, Record 140, many years before the current controversy arose. See *Hodel v. Irving*, 481 U.S. 704, 711–712, 723, n. 7 (1987) (children and their guardians may assert Fifth Amendment rights of deceased relatives). Morales-Santana is thus the "obvious claimant," see *Craig v. Boren*, 429 U.S. 190, 197 (1976), the "best available proponent," *Singleton v. Wulff*, 428 U.S. 106, 116 (1976), of his father's right to equal protection.

III

Sections 1401 and 1409, we note, date from an era when the lawbooks of our Nation were rife with overbroad generalizations about the way men and women are. See, *e.g., Hoyt v. Florida*, 368 U.S. 57, 62

(1961); *Goesaert v. Cleary*, 335 U.S. 464, 466 (1948). Today, laws of this kind are subject to review under the heightened scrutiny that now attends "all gender-based classifications." *J.E.B. v. Alabama ex rel. T. B.*, 511 U.S. 127, 136 (1994); see, *e.g.*, *United States v. Virginia*, 518 U.S. 515, 555–556 (1996).

Laws granting or denying benefits "on the basis of the sex of the qualifying parent," our post-1970 decisions affirm, differentiate on the basis of gender, and therefore attract heightened review under the Constitution's equal protection guarantee. *Califano v. Westcott*, 443 U.S. 76, 84 (1979); see *id.*, at 88–89.

Prescribing one rule for mothers, another for fathers, § 1409 is of the same genre as the classifications we declared unconstitutional in [a number of earlier cases]. . . . As in those cases, heightened scrutiny is in order. Successful defense of legislation that differentiates on the basis of gender, we have reiterated, requires an "exceedingly persuasive justification." *Virginia*, 518 U.S., at 531 (internal quotation marks omitted); *Kirchberg v. Feenstra*, 450 U.S. 455, 461 (1981) (internal quotation marks omitted).

A

The defender of legislation that differentiates on the basis of gender must show "at least that the [challenged] classification serves important governmental objectives and that the discriminatory means employed are substantially related to the achievement of those objectives." *Virginia*, 518 U.S., at 533 (quoting *Mississippi Univ. for Women v. Hogan*, 458 U.S. 718, 724 (1982); alteration in original); see *Tuan Anh Nguyen v. INS*, 533 U.S. 53, 60, 70 (2001). Moreover, the classification must substantially serve an important governmental interest *today*, for "in interpreting the [e]qual [p]rotection [guarantee], [we have] recognized that new insights and societal understandings can reveal unjustified inequality . . . that once passed unnoticed and unchallenged." *Obergefell v. Hodges*, 576 U.S. ___, ___ (2015) (slip op., at 20). Here, the Government has supplied no "exceedingly persuasive justification," *Virginia*, 518 U.S., at 531 (internal quotation marks omitted), for § 1409(a) and (c)'s "gender-based" and "gender-biased" disparity, *Westcott*, 443 U.S., at 84 (internal quotation marks omitted).

1

History reveals what lurks behind § 1409. Enacted in the Nationality Act of 1940 (1940 Act), see 54 Stat. 1139–1140, § 1409 ended a century and a half of congressional silence on the citizenship of children born abroad to unwed parents.[8] During this era, two once habitual, but now untenable, assumptions pervaded our Nation's citizenship laws and underpinned judicial and administrative rulings: In marriage, husband

---

[8]   The provision was first codified in 1940 at 8 U.S.C. § 605, see § 205, 54 Stat. 1139–1140, and recodified in 1952 at § 1409, see § 309, 66 Stat. 238–239. For simplicity, we here use the latter designation.

is dominant, wife subordinate; unwed mother is the natural and sole guardian of a nonmarital child.

Under the once entrenched principle of male dominance in marriage, the husband controlled both wife and child. "[D]ominance [of] the husband," this Court observed in 1915, "is an ancient principle of our jurisprudence." *Mackenzie v. Hare*, 239 U.S. 299, 311 (1915). Through the early 20th century, a male citizen automatically conferred U.S. citizenship on his alien wife. A female citizen, however, was incapable of conferring citizenship on her husband; indeed, she was subject to expatriation if she married an alien. The family of a citizen or a lawfully admitted permanent resident enjoyed statutory exemptions from entry requirements, but only if the citizen or resident was male. And from 1790 until 1934, the foreign-born child of a married couple gained U.S. citizenship only through the father.

For unwed parents, the father-controls tradition never held sway. Instead, the mother was regarded as the child's natural and sole guardian. At common law, the mother, and only the mother, was "bound to maintain [a nonmarital child] as its natural guardian." 2 J. KENT, COMMENTARIES ON AMERICAN LAW *215–*216 (8th ed. 1854). In line with that understanding, in the early 20th century, the State Department sometimes permitted unwed mothers to pass citizenship to their children, despite the absence of any statutory authority for the practice.

In the 1940 Act, Congress discarded the father-controls assumption concerning married parents, but codified the mother-as-sole-guardian perception regarding unmarried parents. The Roosevelt administration, which proposed § 1409, explained: "[T]he mother [of a nonmarital child] stands in the place of the father . . . [,] has a right to the custody and control of such a child as against the putative father, and is bound to maintain it as its natural guardian." 1940 Hearings 431 (internal quotation marks omitted).

This unwed-mother-as-natural-guardian notion renders § 1409's gender-based residency rules understandable. Fearing that a foreign-born child could turn out "more alien than American in character," the administration believed that a citizen parent with lengthy ties to the United States would counteract the influence of the alien parent. *Id.*, at 426–427. Concern about the attachment of foreign-born children to the United States explains the treatment of unwed citizen fathers, who, according to the familiar stereotype, would care little about, and have scant contact with, their nonmarital children. For unwed citizen mothers, however, there was no need for a prolonged residency prophylactic: The alien father, who might transmit foreign ways, was presumptively out of the picture. See *id.*, at 431.

2

For close to a half century, as earlier observed, see *supra*, at 7–8, this Court has viewed with suspicion laws that rely on "overbroad generalizations about the different talents, capacities, or preferences of males and females." *Virginia*, 518 U.S., at 533. In particular, we have recognized that if a "statutory objective is to exclude or 'protect' members of one gender" in reliance on "fixed notions concerning [that gender's] roles and abilities," the "objective itself is illegitimate." *Mississippi Univ. for Women*, 458 U.S., at 725.

In accord with this eventual understanding, the Court has held that no "important [governmental] interest" is served by laws grounded, as § 1409(a) and (c) are, in the obsolescing view that "unwed fathers [are] invariably less qualified and entitled than mothers" to take responsibility for nonmarital children. *Caban v. Mohammed*, 441 U.S. 380, 382, 394 (1979). Overbroad generalizations of that order, the Court has come to comprehend, have a constraining impact, descriptive though they may be of the way many people still order their lives. Laws according or denying benefits in reliance on "[s]tereotypes about women's domestic roles," the Court has observed, may "creat[e] a self-fulfilling cycle of discrimination that force[s] women to continue to assume the role of primary family caregiver." *Nevada Dept. of Human Resources v. Hibbs*, 538 U.S. 721, 736 (2003). Correspondingly, such laws may disserve men who exercise responsibility for raising their children. See *ibid.* In light of the equal protection jurisprudence this Court has developed since 1971, see *Virginia*, 518 U.S., at 531–534, § 1409(a) and (c)'s discrete duration-of-residence requirements for unwed mothers and fathers who have accepted parental responsibility is stunningly anachronistic.

B

In urging this Court nevertheless to reject Morales-Santana's equal protection plea, the Government cites three decisions of this Court: *Fiallo v. Bell*, 430 U.S. 787 (1977); *Miller v. Albright*, 523 U.S. 420 [(1998)]; and *Nguyen v. INS*, 533 U.S. 53. None controls this case.

The 1952 Act provision at issue in *Fiallo* gave special immigration preferences to alien children of citizen (or lawful-permanent-resident) mothers, and to alien unwed mothers of citizen (or lawful-permanent-resident) children. 430 U.S., at 788–789, and n. 1. Unwed fathers and their children, asserting their right to equal protection, sought the same preferences. *Id.*, at 791. Applying minimal scrutiny (rational-basis review), the Court upheld the provision, relying on Congress' "exceptionally broad power" to admit or exclude aliens. *Id.*, at 792, 794.[14] This case, however, involves no entry preference for aliens. Morales-Santana claims he is, and since birth has been, a U.S. citizen. Examining a claim of that order, the Court has not disclaimed, as it did in *Fiallo*, the

_____

[14] In 1986, nine years after the decision in *Fiallo*, Congress amended the governing law. The definition of "child" that included offspring of natural mothers but not fathers was altered to include children born out of wedlock who established a bona fide parent-child relationship with their natural fathers. See Immigration Reform and Control Act of 1986, § 315(a), 100 Stat. 3439, as amended, 8 U.S.C. § 1101(b)(1)(D) (1982 ed., Supp. IV).

application of an exacting standard of review. See *Nguyen*, 533 U.S., at 60–61, 70; *Miller*, 523 U.S., at 434–435, n. 11 (opinion of Stevens, J.).

The provision challenged in *Miller* and *Nguyen* as violative of equal protection requires unwed U.S.-citizen fathers, but not mothers, to formally acknowledge parenthood of their foreign-born children in order to transmit their U.S. citizenship to those children. See § 1409(a)(4) (2012 ed.).[15] After *Miller* produced no opinion for the Court, see 523 U.S., at 423, we took up the issue anew in *Nguyen*. There, the Court held that imposing a paternal-acknowledgment requirement on fathers was a justifiable, easily met means of ensuring the existence of a biological parent-child relationship, which the mother establishes by giving birth. See 533 U.S., at 62–63. Morales-Santana's challenge does not renew the contest over § 1409's paternal-acknowledgment requirement (whether the current version or that in effect in 1970), and the Government does not dispute that Morales-Santana's father, by marrying Morales-Santana's mother, satisfied that requirement.

Unlike the paternal-acknowledgment requirement at issue in *Nguyen* and *Miller*, the physical-presence requirements now before us relate solely to the duration of the parent's prebirth residency in the United States, not to the parent's filial tie to the child. As the Court of Appeals observed in this case, a man needs no more time in the United States than a woman "in order to have assimilated citizenship-related values to transmit to [his] child." 804 F.3d, at 531. And unlike *Nguyen*'s parental-acknowledgment requirement, § 1409(a)'s age-calibrated physical-presence requirements cannot fairly be described as "minimal." 533 U.S., at 70.

C

Notwithstanding § 1409(a) and (c)'s provenance in traditional notions of the way women and men are, the Government maintains that the statute serves two important objectives: (1) ensuring a connection between the child to become a citizen and the United States and (2)

---

[15] Section 1409(a), following amendments in 1986 and 1988, see § 13, 100 Stat. 3657; § 8(k), 102 Stat. 2618, now states:

"The provisions of paragraphs (c), (d), (e), and (g) of section 1401 of this title, . . . shall apply as of the date of birth to a person born out of wedlock if—

"(1) a blood relationship between the person and the father is established by clear and convincing evidence,

"(2) the father had the nationality of the United States at the time of the person's birth,

"(3) the father (unless deceased) has agreed in writing to provide financial support for the person until the person reaches the age of 18 years, and

"(4) while the person is under the age of 18 years—

"(A) the person is legitimated under the law of the person's residence or domicile,

"(B) the father acknowledges paternity of the person in writing under oath, or

"(C) the paternity of the person is established by adjudication of a competent court."

preventing "statelessness," *i.e.*, a child's possession of no citizenship at all. Even indulging the assumption that Congress intended § 1409 to serve these interests, neither rationale survives heightened scrutiny.

1

We take up first the Government's assertion that § 1409(a) and (c)'s gender-based differential ensures that a child born abroad has a connection to the United States of sufficient strength to warrant conferral of citizenship at birth. The Government does not contend, nor could it, that unmarried men take more time to absorb U.S. values than unmarried women do. See *supra*, at 16. Instead, it presents a novel argument, one it did not advance in *Flores-Villar*.

An unwed mother, the Government urges, is the child's only "legally recognized" parent at the time of childbirth. . . . An unwed citizen father enters the scene later, as a second parent. A longer physical connection to the United States is warranted for the unwed father, the Government maintains, because of the "competing national influence" of the alien mother. Congress, the Government suggests, designed the statute to bracket an unwed U.S.-citizen mother with a married couple in which both parents are U.S. citizens, and to align an unwed U.S.-citizen father with a married couple, one spouse a citizen, the other, an alien.

Underlying this apparent design is the assumption that the alien father of a nonmarital child born abroad to a U.S.-citizen mother will not accept parental responsibility. For an actual affiliation between alien father and nonmarital child would create the "competing national influence" that, according to the Government, justifies imposing on unwed U.S.-citizen fathers, but not unwed U.S.-citizen mothers, lengthy physical-presence requirements. Hardly gender neutral, that assumption conforms to the long-held view that unwed fathers care little about, indeed are strangers to, their children. Lump characterization of that kind, however, no longer passes equal protection inspection.

Accepting, *arguendo*, that Congress intended the diverse physical-presence prescriptions to serve an interest in ensuring a connection between the foreign-born nonmarital child and the United States, the gender-based means scarcely serve the posited end. The scheme permits the transmission of citizenship to children who have no tie to the United States so long as their mother was a U.S. citizen continuously present in the United States for one year at any point in her life *prior* to the child's birth. The transmission holds even if the mother marries the child's alien father immediately after the child's birth and never returns with the child to the United States. At the same time, the legislation precludes citizenship transmission by a U.S.-citizen father who falls a few days short of meeting § 1401(a)(7)'s longer physical-presence requirements, even if the father acknowledges paternity on the day of the child's birth and raises the child in the United States.[19] One cannot see in this driven-by-gender scheme the close means-end fit required to survive heightened scrutiny. See, *e.g.*, *Wengler v. Druggists Mut. Ins. Co.*, 446 U.S. 142, 151–152 (1980).

2

The Government maintains that Congress established the gender-based residency differential in § 1409(a) and (c) to reduce the risk that a foreign-born child of a U.S. citizen would be born stateless. This risk, according to the Government, was substantially greater for the foreign-born child of an unwed U.S.-citizen mother than it was for the foreign-born child of an unwed U.S.-citizen father. But there is little reason to believe that a statelessness concern prompted the diverse physical-presence requirements. Nor has the Government shown that the risk of statelessness disproportionately endangered the children of unwed mothers.

As the Court of Appeals pointed out, with one exception, nothing in the congressional hearings and reports on the 1940 and 1952 Acts "refer[s] to the problem of statelessness for children born abroad." 804 F.3d, at 532–533. Reducing the incidence of statelessness was the express goal of *other* sections of the 1940 Act. See 1940 Hearings 430 ("stateless[ness]" is "object" of section on foundlings). The justification for § 1409's gender-based dichotomy, however, was not the child's plight, it was the mother's role as the "natural guardian" of a nonmarital child. It will not do to "hypothesiz[e] or inven[t]" governmental purposes for gender classifications "*post hoc* in response to litigation." *Virginia*, 518 U.S., at 533, 535–536.

Infecting the Government's risk-of-statelessness argument is an assumption without foundation. "[F]oreign laws that would put the child of the U.S.-citizen mother at risk of statelessness (by not providing for the child to acquire the father's citizenship at birth)," the Government asserts, "would *protect* the child of the U.S.-citizen father against statelessness by providing that the child would take his mother's citizenship." The Government, however, neglected to expose this supposed "protection" to a reality check. Had it done so, it would have recognized the formidable impediments placed by foreign laws on an unwed mother's transmission of citizenship to her child.

Experts who have studied the issue report that, at the time relevant here, in "at least thirty countries," citizen mothers generally could not

---

[19] Brief for Respondent 26, n. 9, presents this example: "Child A is born in Germany and raised there by his U.S.-citizen mother who spent only a year of her life in the United States during infancy; Child B is born in Germany and is legitimated and raised in Germany by a U.S.-citizen father who spent his entire life in the United States before leaving for Germany one week before his nineteenth birthday. Notwithstanding the fact that Child A's 'legal relationship' with his U.S.-citizen mother may have been established 'at the moment of birth,' and Child B's 'legal relationship' with his U.S.-citizen father may have been established a few hours later, Child B is more likely than Child A to learn English and assimilate U.S. values. Nevertheless, under the discriminatory scheme, only Child A obtains U.S. citizenship at birth." . . .

transmit their citizenship to nonmarital children born within the mother's country. [See Brief for Scholars on Statelessness as *Amici Curiae*] 14. "[A]s many as forty-five countries," they further report, "did not permit their female citizens to assign nationality to a nonmarital child born outside the subject country with a foreign father." *Id.*, at 18; see *id.*, at 18–21. In still other countries, they also observed, there was no legislation in point, leaving the nationality of nonmarital children uncertain. *Id.*, at 21–22. Taking account of the foreign laws actually in force, these experts concluded, "the risk of parenting stateless children abroad was, as of [1940 and 1952], and remains today, substantial for unmarried U.S. fathers, a risk perhaps greater than that for unmarried U.S. mothers." [*Id.* at] 9–10. One can hardly characterize as gender neutral a scheme allegedly attending to the risk of statelessness for children of unwed U.S.-citizen mothers while ignoring the same risk for children of unwed U.S.-citizen fathers.

In 2014, the United Nations High Commissioner for Refugees (UNHCR) undertook a ten-year project to eliminate statelessness by 2024. See generally UNHCR, *Ending Statelessness Within 10 Years*, online at http://www.unhcr.org/en-us/protection/statelessness/54621 7229/special–report–ending–statelessness–10–years.html (all Internet materials as last visited June 9, 2017). Cognizant that discrimination against either mothers or fathers in citizenship and nationality laws is a major cause of statelessness, the Commissioner has made a key component of its project the elimination of gender discrimination in such laws. In this light, we cannot countenance risk of statelessness as a reason to uphold, rather than strike out, differential treatment of unmarried women and men with regard to transmission of citizenship to their children.

In sum, the Government has advanced no "exceedingly persuasive" justification for § 1409(a) and (c)'s gender-specific residency and age criteria. Those disparate criteria, we hold, cannot withstand inspection under a Constitution that requires the Government to respect the equal dignity and stature of its male and female citizens.

IV

While the equal protection infirmity in retaining a longer physical-presence requirement for unwed fathers than for unwed mothers is clear, this Court is not equipped to grant the relief Morales-Santana seeks, *i.e.*, extending to his father (and, derivatively, to him) the benefit of the one-year physical-presence term § 1409(c) reserves for unwed mothers.

There are "two remedial alternatives[ ]" . . . when a statute benefits one class (in this case, unwed mothers and their children), as § 1409(c) does, and excludes another from the benefit (here, unwed fathers and their children). "[A] court may either declare [the statute] a nullity and order that its benefits not extend to the class that the legislature intended to benefit, or it may extend the coverage of the statute to include those who are aggrieved by exclusion." *Westcott*, 443 U.S., at 89 (quoting

Welsh [v. United States], 398 U.S. [333], 361 [(1970)] (opinion of Harlan, J.)). . . .

The choice between these outcomes is governed by the legislature's intent, as revealed by the statute at hand.

Ordinarily, we have reiterated, "extension, rather than nullification, is the proper course." *Westcott*, 443 U.S., at 89. . . . Here, however, the discriminatory exception consists of *favorable* treatment for a discrete group (a shorter physical-presence requirement for unwed U.S.-citizen mothers giving birth abroad). Following the same approach as in [a series of other] . . . benefits cases—striking the discriminatory exception—leads here to extending the general rule of longer physical-presence requirements to cover the previously favored group.

The Court has looked to Justice Harlan's concurring opinion in *Welsh v. United States*, 398 U.S., at 361–367, in considering whether the legislature would have struck an exception and applied the general rule equally to all, or instead, would have broadened the exception to cure the equal protection violation. In making this assessment, a court should " 'measure the intensity of commitment to the residual policy' "—the main rule, not the exception—" 'and consider the degree of potential disruption of the statutory scheme that would occur by extension as opposed to abrogation.' " *Heckler [v. Mathews]*, 465 U.S. [728], 739, n. 5 [(1984)] (quoting *Welsh*, 398 U.S., at 365 (opinion of Harlan, J.)).

The residual policy here, the longer physical-presence requirement stated in §§ 1401(a)(7) and 1409, evidences Congress' recognition of "the importance of residence in this country as the talisman of dedicated attachment." *Rogers v. Bellei*, 401 U.S. 815, 834 (1971). And the potential for "disruption of the statutory scheme" is large. For if § 1409(c)'s one-year dispensation were extended to unwed citizen fathers, would it not be irrational to retain the longer term when the U.S.-citizen parent is married? Disadvantageous treatment of marital children in comparison to nonmarital children is scarcely a purpose one can sensibly attribute to Congress.

Although extension of benefits is customary in federal benefit cases, all indicators in this case point in the opposite direction. Put to the choice, Congress, we believe, would have abrogated § 1409(c)'s exception, preferring preservation of the general rule.

V

The gender-based distinction infecting §§ 1401(a)(7) and 1409(a) and (c), we hold, violates the equal protection principle, as the Court of Appeals correctly ruled. For the reasons stated, however, we must adopt the remedial course Congress likely would have chosen "had it been apprised of the constitutional infirmity." *Levin [v. Commerce Energy, Inc.]*, 560 U.S. [413], 427 [(2010)]. Although the preferred rule in the typical case is to extend favorable treatment, see *Westcott*, 443 U.S., at 89–90, this is hardly the typical case. Extension here would render the special treatment Congress prescribed in § 1409(c), the one-year physical-presence requirement for U.S.-citizen mothers, the general rule, no longer an exception. Section 1401(a)(7)'s longer physical-presence requirement, applicable to a substantial majority of children born abroad to one U.S.-citizen parent and one foreign-citizen parent, therefore, must hold sway. Going forward, Congress may address the issue and settle on a uniform prescription that neither favors nor disadvantages any person on the basis of gender. In the interim, as the Government suggests, § 1401(a)(7)'s now-five year requirement should apply, prospectively, to children born to unwed U.S.-citizen mothers.

* * *

The judgment of the Court of Appeals for the Second Circuit is affirmed in part and reversed in part, and the case is remanded for further proceedings consistent with this opinion.

It is so ordered.

■ JUSTICE GORSUCH took no part in the consideration or decision of this case.

■ JUSTICE THOMAS, with whom JUSTICE ALITO joins, concurring in the judgment in part.

The Court today holds that we are "not equipped to" remedy the equal protection injury that respondent claims his father suffered under the Immigration and Nationality Act (INA) of 1952. *Ante*, at 23. I agree with that holding. As the majority concludes, extending 8 U.S.C. § 1409(c)'s 1-year physical presence requirement to unwed citizen fathers (as respondent requests) is not, under this Court's precedent, an appropriate remedy for any equal protection violation. See *ante*, at 23. Indeed, I am skeptical that we even have the "power to provide relief of the sort requested in this suit—namely, conferral of citizenship on a basis other than that prescribed by Congress." *Tuan Anh Nguyen v. INS*, 533 U.S. 53, 73 (2001) (Scalia, J., joined by THOMAS, J., concurring) (citing *Miller v. Albright*, 523 U.S. 420, 452 (1998) (Scalia, J., joined by THOMAS, J., concurring in judgment)).

The Court's remedial holding resolves this case. Because respondent cannot obtain relief in any event, it is unnecessary for us to decide whether the 1952 version of the INA was constitutional, whether respondent has third-party standing to raise an equal protection claim on behalf of his father, or whether other immigration laws (such as the current versions of §§ 1401(g) and 1409) are constitutional. I therefore concur only in the judgment reversing the Second Circuit.

NOTES

1.   Justice Ginsburg's opinion for the Court in *Sessions v. Morales-Santana* indicates that "all gender-based classifications" are subject to "heightened scrutiny." Applying this standard of review, the majority opinion at different points speaks of the need for the government to explain sex-based

differential treatment by offering an "exceedingly persuasive justification" for it, an exacting standard that the government ultimately fails to satisfy in this case. What do the articulation of this standard and its application here suggest for the continuing validity of the "intermediate scrutiny" traditionally applied to sex-based legal classifications? What possibilities for facially sex-based differential treatment in law, including family law, remain after this ruling?

2.   Does the approving citation of *Obergefell v. Hodges* in *Morales-Santana* subtly indicate that Chief Justice Roberts may now be prepared to give *Obergefell* full respect as binding constitutional precedent despite the declaration in his *Obergefell* dissent that *Obergefell* has "nothing to do with" the U.S. Constitution? *Obergefell v. Hodges*, 135 S.Ct. 2584, 2626 (2015) (Roberts, C.J., dissenting) ("If you are among the many Americans—of whatever sexual orientation—who favor expanding same-sex marriage, by all means celebrate today's decision. . . . But do not celebrate the Constitution. It had nothing to do with it."); *see also id.* at 2612 ("The majority's decision is an act of will, not legal judgment. The right it announces has no basis in the Constitution or this Court's precedent."). *Cf.* Josh Blackmun, *In* Morales-Santana, *SCOTUS Reaffirms* Obergefell, *Hints that Ted Cruz is a Natural Born Citizen*, [http://joshblackman.com/blog/2017/06/18/in-morales-santana-scotus-reaffirms-obergefell-hints-that-ted-cruz-is-a-natural-born-citizen/] (Jun. 18, 2017) ("I am somewhat surprised that . . . Chief [Justice Roberts] did not balk at this citation [to *Obergefell*], as it expressly extends Justice Kennedy's scrutiny-less rubric to gender-based intermediate scrutiny."). As you read the tea leaves that *Morales-Santana* supplies, you might also wish to consider Chief Justice Roberts's decision to join the Court's opinion in *Pavan v. Smith*, 582 U.S. ___, 2017 WL 2722472 (June 26, 2017), on p. 153 of this Supplement.

3. STATUTORY LIMITS ON SEX DISCRIMINATION

a. TITLE VII

Page 229, Unabridged (Page 161, Concise). Insert the following case and note after *Hopkins v. Price Waterhouse*.

Hively v. Ivy Tech Community College of Indiana
U.S. Court of Appeals, Seventh Circuit, April 4, 2017.
853 F.3d 339.

■ WOOD, CHIEF JUDGE.

Title VII of the Civil Rights Act of 1964 makes it unlawful for employers subject to the Act to discriminate on the basis of a person's "race, color, religion, sex, or national origin. . . ." 42 U.S.C. § 2000e–2(a). For many years, the courts of appeals of this country understood the prohibition against sex discrimination to exclude discrimination on the basis of a person's sexual orientation. The Supreme Court, however, has never spoken to that question. In this case, we have been asked to take a fresh look at our position in light of developments at the Supreme Court extending over two decades. We have done so, and we conclude today that discrimination on the basis of sexual orientation is a form of sex discrimination. We therefore reverse the district court's judgment dismissing Kimberly Hively's suit against Ivy Tech Community College and remand for further proceedings.

I

Hively is openly lesbian. She began teaching as a part-time, adjunct professor at Ivy Tech Community College's South Bend campus in 2000. Hoping to improve her lot, she applied for at least six full-time positions between 2009 and 2014. These efforts were unsuccessful; worse yet, in July 2014 her part-time contract was not renewed. Believing that Ivy Tech was spurning her because of her sexual orientation, she filed a . . . charge with the Equal Employment Opportunity Commission on December 13, 2013. . . . After receiving a right-to-sue letter, she filed this action in the district court. . . . Ivy Tech responded with a motion to dismiss for failure to state a claim on which relief can be granted. It argued that sexual orientation is not a protected class under Title VII[.] . . . [T]he district court granted Ivy Tech's motion and dismissed Hively's case with prejudice.

. . . Hively . . . appealed to this court. . . .

. . .

II

A

The question before us is . . . what it means to discriminate on the basis of sex, and in particular, whether actions taken on the basis of sexual orientation are a subset of actions taken on the basis of sex. This is a pure question of statutory interpretation[.] . . .

. . .

Our interpretive task is guided by the Supreme Court's approach in the closely related case of *Oncale* [*v. Sundowner Offshore Services, Inc.*, 523 U.S. 75 (1998)], where [the Court] . . . had this to say as it addressed the question whether Title VII covers sexual harassment inflicted by a man on a male victim:

We see no justification in the statutory language or our precedents for a categorical rule excluding same-sex harassment claims from the coverage of Title VII. As some courts have observed, male-on-male sexual harassment in the workplace was assuredly not the principal evil Congress was concerned with when it enacted Title VII. But statutory prohibitions often go beyond the principal evil to cover reasonably comparable evils, and it is ultimately the provisions of our laws rather than the principal concerns of our legislators by which we are governed. Title VII prohibits "discriminat[ion]

... because of ... sex" in the "terms" or "conditions" of employment. Our holding that this includes sexual harassment must extend to sexual harassment of any kind that meets the statutory requirements.

523 U.S. at 79–80. The Court could not have been clearer: the fact that the enacting Congress may not have anticipated a particular application of the law cannot stand in the way of the provisions of the law that are on the books.

It is therefore neither here nor there that the Congress that enacted the Civil Rights Act in 1964 and chose to include sex as a prohibited basis for employment discrimination (no matter why it did so) may not have realized or understood the full scope of the words it chose. . . .

B

Hively offers two approaches in support of her contention that "sex discrimination" includes discrimination on the basis of sexual orientation. The first relies on the tried-and-true comparative method in which we attempt to isolate the significance of the plaintiff's sex to the employer's decision: has she described a situation in which, holding all other things constant and changing only her sex, she would have been treated the same way? The second relies on the *Loving v. Virginia*, 388 U.S. 1 (1967), line of cases, which she argues protect her right to associate intimately with a person of the same sex. . . .

1

. . .

Hively alleges that if she had been a man married to a woman (or living with a woman, or dating a woman) and everything else had stayed the same, Ivy Tech would not have refused to promote her and would not have fired her. (We take the facts in the light most favorable to her, because we are here on a Rule 12(b)(6) dismissal; naturally nothing we say will prevent Ivy Tech from contesting these points in later proceedings.) This describes paradigmatic sex discrimination. . . . Ivy Tech is disadvantaging her *because she is a woman.* . . .

. . . Hively represents the ultimate case of failure to conform to the female stereotype (at least as understood in a place such as modern America, which views heterosexuality as the norm and other forms of sexuality as exceptional): she is not heterosexual. . . . Hively's claim is no different from the claims brought by women who were rejected for jobs in traditionally male workplaces, such as fire departments, construction, and policing. The employers in those cases were policing the boundaries of what jobs or behaviors they found acceptable for a woman (or in some cases, for a man).

This was the critical point that the Supreme Court was making in [*Price Waterhouse v.*] *Hopkins*[, 490 U.S. 228 (1989)]. The four justices in the plurality and the two justices concurring in the judgment recognized that Hopkins had alleged that her employer was discriminating only against women who behaved in what the employer viewed as too "masculine" a way—no makeup, no jewelry, no fashion sense. . . . [A] policy that discriminates on the basis of sexual orientation does not affect every woman, or every man, but it is based on assumptions about the proper behavior for someone of a given sex. The discriminatory behavior does not exist without taking the victim's biological sex (either as observed at birth or as modified, in the case of transsexuals) into account. Any discomfort, disapproval, or job decision based on the fact that the complainant—woman or man—dresses differently, speaks differently, or dates or marries a same-sex partner, is a reaction purely and simply based on sex. That means that it falls within Title VII's prohibition against sex discrimination, if it affects employment in one of the specified ways.

    . . .

2

    . . . Hively also has argued that action based on sexual orientation is sex discrimination under the associational theory. It is now accepted that a person who is discriminated against because of the protected characteristic of one with whom she associates is actually being disadvantaged because of her own traits. This line of cases began with *Loving*, in which the Supreme Court held that "restricting the freedom to marry solely because of racial classifications violates the central meaning of the Equal Protection Clause." 388 U.S. at 12. The Court rejected the argument that miscegenation statutes do not violate equal protection because they "punish equally both the white and the Negro participants in an interracial marriage." *Id.* at 8. When dealing with a statute containing racial classifications, it wrote, "the fact of equal application does not immunize the statute from the very heavy burden of justification" required by the Fourteenth Amendment for lines drawn by race. *Id.* at 9.

    . . .

    The fact that *Loving* . . . deal[s] with racial associations, as opposed to those based on color, national origin, religion, or sex, is of no moment. The text of [Title VII] . . . draws no distinction, for this purpose, among the different varieties of discrimination it addresses[.] . . . This means that to the extent that the statute prohibits discrimination on the basis of the race of someone with whom the plaintiff associates, it also prohibits discrimination on the basis of the national origin, or the color, or the religion, or (as relevant here) the sex of the associate. No matter which category is involved, the essence of the claim is that the *plaintiff* would not be suffering the adverse action had his or her sex, race, color, national origin, or religion been different.

III

Today's decision must be understood against the backdrop of the Supreme Court's decisions, not only in the field of employment discrimination, but also in the area of broader discrimination on the basis of sexual orientation. We already have discussed the employment cases, especially *Hopkins* and *Oncale*. The latter line of cases began with *Romer v. Evans*, 517 U.S. 620 (1996), in which the Court held that a provision of the Colorado Constitution forbidding any organ of government in the state from taking action designed to protect "homosexual, lesbian, or bisexual" persons, *id.* at 624, violated the federal Equal Protection Clause. *Romer* was followed by *Lawrence v. Texas*, 539 U.S. 558 (2003), in which the Court found that a Texas statute criminalizing homosexual intimacy between consenting adults violated the liberty provision of the Due Process Clause. Next came *United States v. [Windsor]*, [570] U.S. ___, 133 S.Ct. 2675 (2013), which addressed the constitutionality of the part of the Defense of Marriage Act (DOMA) that excluded a same-sex partner from the definition of "spouse" in other federal statutes. The Court held that this part of DOMA "violate[d] basic due process and equal protection principles applicable to the Federal Government." *Id.* at 2693. Finally, the Court's decision in *Obergefell* [*v. Hodges*, 576 U.S. ___ (2015)], held that the right to marry is a fundamental liberty right, protected by the Due Process and Equal Protection Clauses of the Fourteenth Amendment. 135 S.Ct. at 2604. The Court wrote that "[i]t is now clear that the challenged laws burden the liberty of same-sex couples, and it must be further acknowledged that they abridge central precepts of equality." *Id.*

It would require considerable calisthenics to remove the "sex" from "sexual orientation." . . . The EEOC concluded[ ] in . . . *Baldwin* [*v. Foxx*, EEOC Appeal No. 0120133080, 2015 WL 4397641 (July 16, 2015)] . . . . that such an effort cannot be reconciled with the straightforward language of Title VII. Many district courts have come to the same conclusion. Many other courts have found that gender-identity claims are cognizable under Title VII.

This is not to say that authority to the contrary does not exist. . . . [I]t does. But this court sits en banc to consider what the correct rule of law is now in light of the Supreme Court's authoritative interpretations, not what someone thought it meant one, ten, or twenty years ago. The logic of the Supreme Court's decisions, as well as the common-sense reality that it is actually impossible to discriminate on the basis of sexual orientation without discriminating on the basis of sex, persuade us that the time has come to overrule our previous cases that have endeavored to find and observe that line.

. . .

We close by noting that we have decided only the issue put before us. Additional complications can be saved for another day, when they are actually involved in the case. Ivy Tech did not contend, for example, that it was a religious institution and the positions it denied to Hively related to a religious mission. See 42 U.S.C. § 2000e–1(a). Nor have we had any occasion to consider the meaning of discrimination in the context of the provision of social or public services. We hold only that a person who alleges that she experienced employment discrimination on the basis of her sexual orientation has put forth a case of sex discrimination for Title VII purposes. It was therefore wrong to dismiss Hively's complaint for failure to state a claim. The judgment of the district court is REVERSED and the case is REMANDED for further proceedings.

■ POSNER, CIRCUIT JUDGE, concurring.

I agree that we should reverse, and I join the majority opinion, but I wish to explore an alternative approach that may be more straightforward.

. . .

Title VII of the Civil Rights Act of 1964, now more than half a century old, invites an interpretation that will update it to the present, a present that differs markedly from the era in which the Act was enacted. But I need to emphasize that this . . . form of interpretation—call it judicial interpretive updating—presupposes a lengthy interval between enactment and (re)interpretation. A statute when passed has an understood meaning; it takes years, often many years, for a shift in the political and cultural environment to change the understanding of the statute.

Hively, the plaintiff, claims that because she's a lesbian her employer declined to either promote her to full-time employment or renew her part-time employment contract. She seeks redress on the basis of the provision of Title VII that forbids an employer "to fail or refuse to hire[,] or to discharge[,] any individual, or otherwise to discriminate against any individual with respect to his compensation, terms, conditions, or privileges of employment, because of such individual's . . . sex. . . ." 42 U.S.C. § 2000e–2(a)(1).

. . .

It is well-nigh certain that homosexuality, male or female, did not figure in the minds of the legislators who enacted Title VII. . . .

A diehard "originalist" would argue that what was believed in 1964 defines the scope of the statute for as long as the statutory text remains unchanged, and therefore until changed by Congress's amending or replacing the statute. But . . . statutory and constitutional provisions frequently are interpreted on the basis of present need and understanding rather than original meaning. Think for example of Justice Scalia's decisive fifth vote to hold that burning the American flag as a political protest is protected by the free-speech clause of the First Amendment, provided that it's your flag and is not burned in circumstances in which the fire might spread. *Texas v. Johnson*, 491 U.S. 397 (1989); *United States v. Eichman*, 496 U.S. 310 (1990). Burning a flag is not speech in the usual sense and there is no indication that the framers or ratifiers of the First Amendment thought that the word "speech" in the amendment embraced flag burning or other nonverbal methods of communicating.

. . . In effect the Supreme Court rewrote . . . the First Amendment in the flag-burning cases, . . . just as today we are rewriting Title VII. . . .

. . . Over and over again, old statutes, old constitutional provisions, are given new meaning, as explained so eloquently by Justice Holmes in *Missouri v. Holland*, 252 U.S. 416, 433–34 (1920):

> When we are dealing with words that also are a constituent act, like the Constitution of the United States, we must realize that they have called into life a being the development of which could not have been foreseen completely by the most gifted of its begetters. . . . The case before us must be considered in the light of our whole experience and not merely in that of what was said a hundred years ago. The treaty in question does not contravene any prohibitory words to be found in the Constitution. The only question is whether it is forbidden by some invisible radiation from the general terms of the Tenth Amendment. *We must consider what this country has become in deciding what that amendment has reserved* (emphasis added).

So by substituting Title VII for "that amendment" in Holmes's opinion, discrimination on grounds of "sex" in Title VII receives today a new, a broader, meaning. Nothing has changed more in the decades since the enactment of the statute than attitudes toward sex. 1964 was more than a decade before Richard Raskind underwent male-to-female sex reassignment surgery and took the name Renée Richards, becoming the first transgender celebrity; now of course transgender persons are common.

In 1964 (and indeed until the 2000s), and in some states until the Supreme Court's decision in *Obergefell v. Hodges*, [576] U.S. __, 135 S.Ct. 2584 (2015), men were not allowed to marry each other, nor women allowed to marry each other. If in those days an employer fired a lesbian because he didn't like lesbians, he would have said that he was not firing her because she was a woman—he would not have fired her had she been heterosexual—and so he was not discriminating on the basis of sex as understood by the authors and ratifiers of Title VII. But today "sex" has a broader meaning than the genitalia you're born with. In *Baskin v. Bogan*, 766 F.3d 648 (7th Cir. 2014), our court, anticipating *Obergefell* by invalidating laws in Indiana and Wisconsin that forbade same-sex marriage, discussed at length whether homosexual orientation is innate or chosen, and found that the scientific literature strongly supports the proposition that it is biological and innate, not a choice like deciding how to dress. The position of a woman discriminated against on account of being a lesbian is thus analogous to a woman's being discriminated against on account of being a woman. That woman didn't choose to be a woman; the lesbian didn't choose to be a lesbian. I don't see why firing a lesbian because she is in the subset of women who are lesbian should be thought any less a form of sex discrimination than firing a woman because she's a woman.

But it has taken our courts and our society a considerable while to realize that sexual harassment, which has been pervasive in many workplaces . . . , is a form of sex discrimination. It has taken a little longer for realization to dawn that discrimination based on a woman's failure to fulfill stereotypical gender roles is also a form of sex discrimination. And it has taken still longer, with a substantial volume of cases struggling and failing to maintain a plausible, defensible line between sex discrimination and sexual-orientation discrimination, to realize that homosexuality is nothing worse than failing to fulfill stereotypical gender roles.

It's true that even today if asked what is the sex of plaintiff Hively one would answer that she is female or that she is a woman, not that she is a lesbian. Lesbianism denotes a form of sexual or romantic attraction; it is not a physical sex identifier like masculinity or femininity. A broader understanding of the word "sex" in Title VII than the original understanding is thus required in order to be able to classify the discrimination of which Hively complains as a form of sex discrimination. That broader understanding is essential. Failure to adopt it would make the statute anachronistic[.] . . .

We now understand that homosexual men and women (and also bisexuals, defined as having both homosexual and heterosexual orientations) are normal in the ways that count, and beyond that have made many outstanding intellectual and cultural contributions to society (think for example of Tchaikovsky, Oscar Wilde, Jane Addams, André Gide, Thomas Mann, Marlene Dietrich, Bayard Rustin, Alan Turing, Alec Guinness, Leonard Bernstein, Van Cliburn, and James Baldwin—a very partial list). We now understand that homosexuals, male and female, play an essential role, in this country at any rate, as adopters of children from foster homes—a point emphasized in our *Baskin* decision. The compelling social interest in protecting homosexuals (male and female) from discrimination justifies an admittedly loose "interpretation" of the word "sex" in Title VII to embrace homosexuality: an interpretation that cannot be imputed to the framers of the statute but that we are entitled to adopt in light of (to quote Holmes) *"what this country has become*[.]*"* . . .

The majority opinion states that Congress in 1964 "may not have realized or understood the full scope of the words it chose." This could be understood to imply that the statute forbade discrimination against homosexuals but the framers and ratifiers of the statute were not smart enough to realize that. I would prefer to say that theirs was the then-current understanding of the key word—sex. "Sex" in 1964 meant gender, not sexual orientation. What the framers and ratifiers understandably didn't understand was how attitudes toward homosexuals would change in the following half century. They shouldn't be blamed for that failure of foresight. *We* understand the words of Title VII differently not because we're smarter than the statute's framers and ratifiers but because we live in a different era, a different culture. Congress in the 1960s did not foresee the sexual revolution of the 2000s. . . .

I would prefer to see us acknowledge openly that today we, who are judges rather than members of Congress, are imposing on a half-century-old statute a meaning of "sex discrimination" that the Congress that enacted it would not have accepted. This is something courts do fairly frequently to avoid statutory obsolescence and concomitantly to avoid placing the entire burden of updating old statutes on the legislative branch. We should not leave the impression that we are merely the obedient servants of the 88th Congress (1963–1965), carrying out their wishes. We are not. We are taking advantage of what the last half century has taught.

■ FLAUM, CIRCUIT JUDGE, joined by RIPPLE, CIRCUIT JUDGE, concurring.

I join Parts I and II of the majority opinion and agree that Title VII of the Civil Rights Act of 1964, 42 U.S.C. § 2000e–2(a), does not preclude Professor Hively's claim that Ivy Tech Community College engaged in unlawful employment discrimination. I find the issue before us is simply whether discriminating against an employee for being homosexual violates Title VII's prohibition against discriminating against that employee because of their sex. In my view, the answer is yes, and the statute's text commands as much.

. . .

Setting aside the treatment in the majority and dissenting opinions of sexual orientation as a freestanding concept, I conclude discrimination against an employee on the basis of their homosexuality is necessarily, in part, discrimination based on their sex. Fundamental to the definition of homosexuality is the sexual attraction to individuals of the "same sex." *Homosexual*, MERRIAM-WEBSTER DICTIONARY ONLINE, *available at* https://www.merriam-webster.com/dictionary/homosexual ("[O]f, relating to, or characterized by a tendency to direct sexual desire toward another of the *same sex*") (emphasis added) (last visited April 4, 2017); *see also Homosexual*, BLACK'S LAW DICTIONARY (10th ed. 2014) ("Of relating to, or characterized by sexual desire for a person of the *same sex*.") (emphasis added); *Homosexual*, OXFORD ENGLISH DICTIONARY (5th ed. 1964) ("Having a sexual propensity for persons of one's *own sex*.") (emphasis added). One cannot consider a person's homosexuality without also accounting for their sex: doing so would render "same" and "own" meaningless. As such, discriminating against that employee because they are homosexual constitutes discriminating against an employee because of (A) the employee's sex, *and* (B) their sexual attraction to individuals of the *same sex*. And "sex," under Title VII, is an enumerated trait.

. . . The [Supreme] Court [has] made clear that "[t]he critical inquiry . . . is whether gender was *a factor* in the employment decision" when it was made. [*Price Waterhouse v. Hopkins*, 490 U.S. 228,] 241 [(1989)] (emphasis added). So if discriminating against an employee because she is homosexual is equivalent to discriminating against her because she is (A) a woman who is (B) sexually attracted to women, then it is motivated, in part, by an enumerated trait: the employee's sex. That is all an employee must show to successfully allege a Title VII claim.

. . .

. . . Ivy Tech allegedly refused to promote Professor Hively because she was homosexual—or (A) a woman who is (B) sexually attracted to women. Thus, the College allegedly discriminated against Professor Hively, at least in part, because of her sex. I conclude that Title VII, as its text provides, does not allow this.

■ SYKES, CIRCUIT JUDGE, with whom BAUER and KANNE, CIRCUIT JUDGES, join, dissenting.

Any case heard by the full court is important. This one is momentous. . . . The question before the en banc court is one of statutory interpretation. The majority deploys a judge-empowering, common-law decision method that leaves a great deal of room for judicial discretion. So does Judge Posner in his concurrence. Neither is faithful to the statutory text, read fairly, as a reasonable person would have understood it when it was adopted. The result is a statutory amendment courtesy of unelected judges. Judge Posner admits this; he embraces and argues for this conception of judicial power. The majority does not, preferring instead to smuggle in the statutory amendment under cover of an aggressive reading of loosely related Supreme Court precedents. Either way, the result is the same: the circumvention of the legislative process by which the people govern themselves.

Respect for the constraints imposed on the judiciary by a system of written law must begin with fidelity to the traditional first principle of statutory interpretation: When a statute supplies the rule of decision, our role is to give effect to the enacted text, interpreting the statutory language as a reasonable person would have understood it at the time of enactment. We are not authorized to infuse the text with a new or unconventional meaning or to update it to respond to changed social, economic, or political conditions.

In a handful of statutory contexts, Congress has vested the federal courts with authority to consider and make new rules of law in the common-law way. The Sherman Act is the archetype of the so-called "common-law statutes," but there are very few of these and Title VII is not one of them. So our role is interpretive only; we lack the discretion to ascribe to Title VII a meaning it did not bear at its inception. Sitting en banc permits us to overturn our own precedents, but in a statutory case, we do not sit as a common-law court free to engage in "judicial interpretive updating," as Judge Posner calls it, or to do the same thing by pressing hard on tenuously related Supreme Court opinions, as the majority does.

Judicial statutory updating, whether overt or covert, cannot be reconciled with the constitutional design. The Constitution establishes a procedure for enacting and amending statutes: bicameralism and presentment. *See* U.S. CONST. art. I, § 7. Needless to say, statutory amendments brought to you by the judiciary do not pass through this process. That is why a textualist decision method matters: When we assume the power to alter the original public meaning of a statute through the process of interpretation, we assume a power that is not ours. The Constitution assigns the power to make and amend statutory law to the elected representatives of the people. However welcome today's decision might be as a policy matter, it comes at a great cost to representative self-government.

I

Title VII of the Civil Rights Act of 1964 makes it unlawful for an employer "to fail or refuse to hire or to discharge any individual, or otherwise to discriminate against any individual . . . because of such individual's race, color, religion, sex, or national origin." 42 U.S.C. § 2000e–2(a)(1). Sexual orientation is not on the list of forbidden categories of employment discrimination, and we have long and consistently held that employment decisions based on a person's sexual orientation do not classify people on the basis of sex and thus are not covered by Title VII's prohibition of discrimination "because of sex." *Hamm v. Weyauwega Milk Prods., Inc.*, 332 F.3d 1058, 1062 (7th Cir. 2003); *Spearman v. Ford Motor Co.*, 231 F.3d 1080, 1085 (7th Cir. 2000); *Hamner v. St. Vincent Hosp. & Health Care Ctr., Inc.*, 224 F.3d 701, 704 (7th Cir. 2000); *Ulane v. E. Airlines, Inc.*, 742 F.2d 1081, 1085 (7th Cir. 1984). This interpretation has been stable for many decades and is broadly accepted; all circuits agree that sexual-orientation discrimination is a distinct form of discrimination and is not synonymous with sex discrimination.

Today the court jettisons the prevailing interpretation and installs the polar opposite. Suddenly sexual-orientation discrimination *is* sex discrimination and thus is actionable under Title VII. . . .

. . . Attitudes about gay rights have dramatically shifted in the 53 years since the Civil Rights Act was adopted. . . .

This striking cultural change informs a case for legislative change and might eventually persuade the people's representatives to amend the statute to implement a new public policy. But it does not bear on the sole inquiry properly before the en banc court: Is the prevailing interpretation of Title VII—that discrimination on the basis of sexual orientation is different in kind and not a form of sex discrimination—*wrong as an original matter*?

A

On that question [Hively] . . . has not carried [her] . . . burden of legal persuasion. To be clear, I agree with my colleagues that the proposed new interpretation is not necessarily incorrect simply because no one in the 1964 Congress that adopted Title VII intended or anticipated its application to sexual-orientation discrimination. The subjective intentions of the legislators do not matter. Statutory interpretation is an objective inquiry that looks for the meaning the statutory language conveyed to a reasonable person at the time of enactment. The objective meaning of the text is not delimited by what individual lawmakers specifically had in mind when they voted for the statute. The Supreme Court made this point clear in *Oncale* when it said that "statutory prohibitions often go beyond the principal evil to cover reasonably comparable evils, and it is ultimately the provisions of our laws rather than the principal concerns of our legislators by which we are governed." *Oncale v. Sundowner Offshore Servs., Inc.*, 523 U.S. 75, 79 (1998). Broadly worded statutes are regularly applied to circumstances beyond the subjective contemplation of the lawmakers who adopted the text.

That much is uncontroversial. Indeed, it derives from a foundational rule-of-law principle:

> [I]t is simply incompatible with democratic government, or indeed, even with fair government, to have the meaning of a law determined by what the lawgiver meant, rather than by what the lawgiver promulgated. . . . [Ours is a] government of laws, not of men. Men may intend what they will; but it is only the laws that they enact which bind us.

ANTONIN SCALIA, A MATTER OF INTERPRETATION: FEDERAL COURTS AND THE LAW 17 (Amy Gutmann ed., 1997).

So as a matter of interpretive method, I agree with my colleagues that the scope of Title VII is not limited by the subjective intentions of the enacting legislators. . . .

B

That is where our agreement ends. The en banc majority rests its new interpretation of sex discrimination on a thought experiment drawn from the "tried-and-true" comparative method of proof often used by plaintiffs in discrimination cases. The majority also invokes *Loving v. Virginia*, 388 U.S. 1 (1967), the Supreme Court's historic decision striking down Virginia's miscegenation laws under the Fourteenth Amendment's Equal Protection Clause, as well as cases involving sex stereotyping, most prominently *Price Waterhouse v. Hopkins*, 490 U.S. 228 (1989).

But the analysis must begin with the statutory text; it largely ends there too. Is it even remotely plausible that in 1964, when Title VII was adopted, a reasonable person competent in the English language would have understood that a law banning employment discrimination "because of sex" also banned discrimination because of sexual orientation? The answer is no, of course not.

. . . The interpretive inquiry looks to the original public meaning of the statutory text.

Title VII does not define discrimination "because of sex." In common, ordinary usage in 1964—and now, for that matter—the word "sex" means biologically *male* or *female*; it does not also refer to sexual orientation. *See, e.g., Sex*, THE AMERICAN HERITAGE DICTIONARY OF THE ENGLISH LANGUAGE (1st ed. 1969) (defining "sex" as "[t]he property or quality by which organisms are classified according to their reproductive functions[;] [e]ither of two divisions, designated *male* and *female*, of this classification"); *Sex*, NEW OXFORD AMERICAN DICTIONARY (3d ed. 2010) (defining "sex" as "either of the two main categories (male and female) into which humans and many other living things are divided on the basis of their reproductive functions"); *Sex*, THE AMERICAN HERITAGE DESK DICTIONARY (5th ed. 2013) (defining "sex" as "[e]ither of the two divisions, female and male, by which most organisms are classified on the basis of their reproductive organs and functions[;] [t]he condition or character of being female or male").

To a fluent speaker of the English language—then and now—the ordinary meaning of the word "sex" does not fairly include the concept of "sexual orientation."[3] The two terms are never used interchangeably, and the latter is not subsumed within the former; there is no overlap in meaning. . . . More specifically to the point here, discrimination "because of sex" is not reasonably understood to include discrimination based on sexual orientation, a different immutable characteristic. Classifying people by sexual orientation is different than classifying them by sex. The two traits are categorically distinct and widely recognized as such. There is no ambiguity or vagueness here.

. . . Because sexual-orientation discrimination is not synonymous with sex discrimination in ordinary usage, Title VII does not prohibit sexual-orientation discrimination. Not expressly (obviously), and not by fair implication either.

C

This commonsense understanding is confirmed by the language Congress uses when it *does* legislate against sexual-orientation discrimination. For example, the Violence Against Women Act prohibits funded programs and activities from discriminating "on the basis of actual or perceived race, color, religion, national origin, *sex*, gender identity, . . . *sexual orientation*, or disability." 42 U.S.C. § 13925(b)(13)(A)

---

[3]   The term "sexual orientation" does not appear in dictionaries at or around the time of Title VII's enactment. According to the current definition, it is not synonymous with "sex." *Sexual Orientation*, OXFORD ENGLISH DICTIONARY (2009 ed.) ("Originally: (the process of) orientation with respect to a sexual goal, potential mate, partner, etc. Later chiefly: a person's sexual identity in relation to the gender to whom he or she is usually attracted; (broadly) the fact of being heterosexual, bisexual, or homosexual.").

(emphases added). If sex discrimination is commonly understood to encompass sexual-orientation discrimination, then listing the two categories separately, as this statute does, is needless surplusage. The federal Hate Crimes Act is another example. It imposes a heightened punishment for causing or attempting to cause bodily injury "to any person, because of the actual or perceived religion, national origin, *gender, sexual orientation*, gender identity, or disability of any person." 18 U.S.C. § 249(a)(2)(A) (emphases added).

Other examples can be found elsewhere in the U.S. Code.

State and local antidiscrimination laws likewise distinguish between sex discrimination and sexual-orientation discrimination by listing them separately as distinct forms of unlawful discrimination.

I could go on, but the point has been made. This uniformity of usage is powerful objective evidence that sexual-orientation discrimination is broadly recognized as an independent category of discrimination and is *not* synonymous with sex discrimination.

II

My colleagues in the majority superficially acknowledge *Ulane's* "truism" that sex discrimination is discrimination based on a person's biological sex. As they see it, however, even if sex discrimination is understood in the ordinary way, sexual-orientation discrimination *is* sex discrimination because "it is actually impossible to discriminate on the basis of sexual orientation without discriminating on the basis of sex."

Not true. An employer who refuses to hire homosexuals is not drawing a line based on the job applicant's sex. He is not excluding gay men because they are men and lesbians because they are women. His discriminatory motivation is independent of and unrelated to the applicant's sex. Sexism (misandry and misogyny) and homophobia are separate kinds of prejudice that classify people in distinct ways based on different immutable characteristics. Simply put, sexual-orientation discrimination doesn't classify people by sex; it doesn't draw male/female distinctions but instead targets homosexual men and women for harsher treatment than heterosexual men and women.

. . .

III

A

The majority also draws on *Loving*, the Supreme Court's iconic decision invalidating Virginia's miscegenation statutes on equal-protection grounds. This case is not a variant of *Loving*. Miscegenation laws plainly employ invidious racial classifications; they are inherently racially discriminatory. In contrast, sexual-orientation discrimination springs from a wholly different kind of bias than sex discrimination. The two forms of discrimination classify people based on different traits and thus are not the same.

. . .

. . . *Loving* rests on the inescapable truth that miscegenation laws are inherently racist. They are premised on invidious ideas about white superiority and use racial classifications toward the end of racial purity and white supremacy. Sexual-orientation discrimination, on the other hand, is not inherently *sexist*. No one argues that sexual-orientation discrimination aims to promote or perpetuate the supremacy of one sex. In short, *Loving* neither compels nor supports the majority's decision to upend the long-settled understanding that sex discrimination and sexual-orientation discrimination are distinct.

. . .

B

The majority also relies on cases involving sex stereotyping, most notably the Supreme Court's decision in *Price Waterhouse v. Hopkins*. More specifically, my colleagues conclude that a claim of sexual-orientation discrimination is indistinguishable from a claim involving sex stereotyping. I disagree. Nothing in *Hopkins* altered the traditional understanding that sexual-orientation discrimination is a distinct type of discrimination and is not synonymous with sex discrimination.

As a preliminary matter, neither *Hopkins* nor any other decision of the Supreme Court establishes an independent cause of action for, or "doctrine" or "theory" of, "sex stereotyping." *Hopkins* held only that the presence of sex stereotyping by an employer "can certainly be *evidence*" of sex discrimination; to prove her case, the plaintiff must always prove that "the employer *actually* relied on her gender in making its decision." 490 U.S. at 251 (second emphasis added).

. . .

. . . Regarding the *legal* significance of sex stereotyping as evidence of sex discrimination, the plurality had only this to say:

> In saying that gender played a motivating part in an employment decision, we mean that, if we asked the employer at the moment of the decision what its reasons were and if we received a truthful response, one of those reasons would be that the applicant or employee was a woman. In the specific context of sex stereotyping, an employer who acts on the basis of a belief that a woman cannot be aggressive, or that she must not be, has acted on the basis of gender.
>
> . . . As for the legal relevance of sex stereotyping, we are beyond the day when an employer could evaluate employees by assuming or insisting that they matched the stereotype associated with their group, for " '[i]n forbidding employers to discriminate against individuals because of their sex, Congress

> intended to strike at the entire spectrum of disparate treatment of men and women resulting from sex stereotypes.' " *Los Angeles Dept. of Water and Power v. Manhart*, 435 U.S. 702, 707, n.13 (1978), quoting *Sprogis v. United Air Lines, Inc.*, 444 F.2d 1194, 1198 (7th Cir. 1971). An employer who objects to aggressiveness in women but whose positions require this trait places women in an intolerable and impermissible catch 22; out of a job if they behave aggressively and out of a job if they do not. Title VII lifts women out of this bind.

Id. at 250–51 (footnote omitted). Nothing in this passage casts any doubt on the settled, long-understood distinction between sex discrimination and sexual-orientation discrimination.

. . .

So it's a serious mistake to think that *Hopkins* either supports or requires a new interpretation of Title VII that equates sexual-orientation discrimination with sex discrimination. To the contrary, *Hopkins* does not even gesture in that direction. . . .

C

Neither does *Oncale* compel or support today's decision. *Oncale* held only that same-sex sexual harassment may, in an appropriate case, support a claim under Title VII *provided* that it "meets the statutory requirements." 523 U.S. at 79–80. The Court reiterated that in *all* sex-discrimination cases, including sexual-harassment cases, "[t]he critical issue, Title VII's text indicates, is whether members of one sex are exposed to disadvantageous terms or conditions of employment to which members of the other sex are not exposed." *Id.* at 80 (quotation marks omitted).

. . .

. . . [I]n authorizing claims of same-sex harassment as a theoretical matter, the Court carefully tethered *all* sexual-harassment claims to the statutory requirement that the plaintiff prove discrimination "because of sex." Nothing in *Oncale* eroded the distinction between sex discrimination and sexual-orientation discrimination or opened the door to a new interpretation of Title VII.

. . .

D

The majority also finds support for its decision in "the backdrop of the Supreme Court's decisions . . . in the area of broader discrimination on the basis of sexual orientation," citing *Romer v. Evans*, 517 U.S. 620 (1996); *Lawrence v. Texas*, 539 U.S. 558 (2003); *United States v. Windsor*, [570] U.S. ___, 133 S.Ct. 2675 (2013); and *Obergefell v. Hodges*, [576] U.S. ___, 135 S.Ct. 2584 (2015).

But the majority's position is actually irreconcilable with these cases. First, *Lawrence* was decided solely under the Due Process Clause;

it was not an equal-protection case. 539 U.S. at 564. In the other cases, far from collapsing the well-understood distinction between sex discrimination and sexual-orientation discrimination, the Court actually preserved it. The Court assigned these two distinct forms of discrimination to different analytical categories for purposes of equal-protection scrutiny. If sex discrimination and sexual-orientation discrimination were really one and the same, then the Court would have applied the intermediate standard of scrutiny that governs judicial review of laws that classify people by sex. *See United States v. Virginia*, 518 U.S. 515, 531 (1996). It did not do so.

E

. . .

* * *

If Kimberly Hively was denied a job because of her sexual orientation, she was treated unjustly. But Title VII does not provide a remedy for this kind of discrimination. The argument that it *should* must be addressed to Congress.

IV

. . .

* * *

. . .

. . . Because Title VII does not by its terms prohibit sexual-orientation discrimination, Hively's case was properly dismissed. I respectfully dissent.

NOTE

1. The U.S. Supreme Court will be given the opportunity to engage the legal issue that *Hively v. Ivy Tech Community College of Indiana* addresses. Associated Press, *Court Declines to Rehear Gay Employee Discrimination Case*, N.Y. TIMES (July 6, 2017), https://www.nytimes.com/aponline/2017/07/06/us/ap-us-discrimination-lawsuit-lesbian.html. Were the Supreme Court to consider the issue, how do you expect that it would be resolved?

b. FAMILY AND MEDICAL LEAVE

Page 238, Unabridged. Replace Note 2 with the following note.

2. Although the protections of the FMLA did not extend to same-sex couples for some time in virtue of the federal Defense of Marriage Act, 1 U.S.C. § 7 (2006), they now do, on the same terms as for cross-sex couples. U.S. DEP'T OF LABOR, 29 CFR 825.102, 122(b), DEFINITION OF SPOUSE UNDER THE FAMILY AND MEDICAL LEAVE ACT (Mar. 27, 2015) ("Spouse, as defined in this statute, . . . includes an individual in a same-sex or common law marriage[.]")

C. ENCROACHMENTS ON THE DOCTRINE OF FAMILY PRIVACY

2. THE CONSTITUTIONAL RIGHT TO PRIVACY

Page 301, Unabridged (Page 215, Concise). Insert the following case and notes after *Gonzales v. Carhart*.

Whole Woman's Health v. Hellerstedt

Supreme Court of the United States, June 27, 2016.
579 U.S. ___, 136 S.Ct. 2292, 195 L.Ed.2d 665.

■ JUSTICE BREYER delivered the opinion of the Court.

In *Planned Parenthood of Southeastern Pa. v. Casey*, 505 U.S. 833, 878 (1992), a plurality of the Court concluded that there "exists" an "undue burden" on a woman's right to decide to have an abortion, and consequently a provision of law is constitutionally invalid, if the "*purpose or effect*" of the provision "*is to place a substantial obstacle* in the path of a woman seeking an abortion before the fetus attains viability." (Emphasis added.) The plurality added that "[u]nnecessary health regulations that have the purpose or effect of presenting a substantial obstacle to a woman seeking an abortion impose an undue burden on the right." *Ibid.*

We must here decide whether two provisions of Texas' House Bill 2 violate the Federal Constitution as interpreted in *Casey*. The first provision, which we shall call the "*admitting-privileges requirement*," says that

> "[a] physician performing or inducing an abortion . . . must, on the date the abortion is performed or induced, have active admitting privileges at a hospital that . . . is located not further than 30 miles from the location at which the abortion is performed or induced." Tex. Health & Safety Code Ann. § 171.0031(a) (West Cum.Supp.2015).

This provision amended Texas law that had previously required an abortion facility to maintain a written protocol "for managing medical emergencies and the transfer of patients requiring further emergency care to a hospital." 38 Tex. Reg. 6546 (2013).

The second provision, which we shall call the "*surgical-center requirement*," says that

> "the minimum standards for an abortion facility must be equivalent to the minimum standards adopted under [the Texas Health and Safety Code section] for ambulatory surgical centers." Tex. Health & Safety Code Ann. § 245.010(a).

We conclude that neither of these provisions confers medical benefits sufficient to justify the burdens upon access that each imposes. Each places a substantial obstacle in the path of women seeking a previability abortion, each constitutes an undue burden on abortion access, *Casey, supra,* at 878 (plurality opinion), and each violates the Federal Constitution. [U.S. CONST. amend. XIV, § 1].

. . .

III *Undue Burden—Legal Standard*

We begin with the standard, as described in *Casey*. We recognize that the "State has a legitimate interest in seeing to it that abortion, like any other medical procedure, is performed under circumstances that insure maximum safety for the patient." *Roe v. Wade,* 410 U.S. 113, 150 (1973). But, we added, "a statute which, while furthering [a] valid state interest, has the effect of placing a substantial obstacle in the path of a woman's choice cannot be considered a permissible means of serving its legitimate ends." *Casey,* 505 U.S., at 877 (plurality opinion). Moreover, "[u]nnecessary health regulations that have the purpose or effect of presenting a substantial obstacle to a woman seeking an abortion impose an undue burden on the right." *Id.,* at 878.

. . .

. . . The rule announced in *Casey* . . . requires that courts consider the burdens a law imposes on abortion access together with the benefits those laws confer. See 505 U.S., at 887–898 (opinion of the Court) (performing this balancing with respect to a spousal notification provision); *id.,* at 899–901 (joint opinion of O'Connor, KENNEDY, and Souter, JJ.) (same balancing with respect to a parental notification provision). . . .

. . . [T]he Court, when determining the constitutionality of laws regulating abortion procedures, has placed considerable weight upon evidence and argument presented in judicial proceedings. In *Casey,* for example, we relied heavily on the District Court's factual findings and the research-based submissions of *amici* in declaring a portion of the law at issue unconstitutional. 505 U.S., at 888–894 (opinion of the Court) (discussing evidence related to the prevalence of spousal abuse in determining that a spousal notification provision erected an undue burden to abortion access). And, in *Gonzales* [*v. Carhart*], the Court, while pointing out that we must review legislative "factfinding under a deferential standard," added that we must not "place dispositive weight" on those "findings." 550 U.S. [124,] 165 [(2007)]. *Gonzales* went on to point out that the "*Court retains an independent constitutional duty to review factual findings where constitutional rights are at stake.*" *Ibid.* (emphasis added). Although there we upheld a statute regulating abortion, we did not do so solely on the basis of legislative findings explicitly set forth in the statute, noting that "evidence presented in the District Courts contradicts" some of the legislative findings. *Id.,* at 166. In these circumstances, we said, "[u]ncritical deference to Congress' factual findings . . . is inappropriate." *Ibid.*

Unlike in *Gonzales*, the relevant statute here does not set forth any legislative findings. Rather, one is left to infer that the legislature sought to further a constitutionally acceptable objective (namely, protecting women's health). *Id.*, at 149–150. For a district court to give significant weight to evidence in the judicial record in these circumstances is consistent with this Court's case law. As we shall describe, the District Court did so here. It did not simply substitute its own judgment for that of the legislature. It considered the evidence in the record—including expert evidence, presented in stipulations, depositions, and testimony. It then weighed the asserted benefits against the burdens. We hold that, in so doing, the District Court applied the correct legal standard.

IV *Undue Burden—Admitting-Privileges Requirement*

. . . [W]e first consider the admitting-privileges requirement. Before the enactment of H.B. 2, doctors who provided abortions were required to "have admitting privileges *or* have a working arrangement with a physician(s) who has admitting privileges at a local hospital in order to ensure the necessary back up for medical complications." Tex. Admin. Code, tit. 25, § 139.56 (2009) (emphasis added). The new law changed this requirement by requiring that a "physician performing or inducing an abortion . . . must, on the date the abortion is performed or induced, have active admitting privileges at a hospital that . . . is located not further than 30 miles from the location at which the abortion is performed or induced." Tex. Health & Safety Code Ann. § 171.0031(a). The District Court held that the legislative change imposed an "undue burden" on a woman's right to have an abortion. We conclude that there is adequate legal and factual support for the District Court's conclusion.

The purpose of the admitting-privileges requirement is to help ensure that women have easy access to a hospital should complications arise during an abortion procedure. But the District Court found that it brought about no such health-related benefit. The court found that "[t]he great weight of evidence demonstrates that, before the act's passage, abortion in Texas was extremely safe with particularly low rates of serious complications and virtually no deaths occurring on account of the procedure." [*Whole Woman's Health v. Lakey*,] 46 F.Supp.3d [673,] 684 [(W.D. Tex. 2014)]. Thus, there was no significant health-related problem that the new law helped to cure.

The evidence upon which the court based this conclusion included, among other things:

- A collection of at least five peer-reviewed studies on abortion complications in the first trimester, showing that the highest rate of major complications—including those complications requiring hospital admission—was less than one-quarter of 1%. See App. 269–270.

- Figures in three peer-reviewed studies showing that the highest complication rate found for the much rarer second trimester abortion was less than one-half of 1% (0.45% or about 1 out of about 200). *Id.*, at 270.

- Expert testimony to the effect that complications rarely require hospital admission, much less immediate transfer to a hospital from an outpatient clinic. *Id.*, at 266–267 (citing a study of complications occurring within six weeks after 54,911 abortions that had been paid for by the fee-for-service California Medicaid Program finding that the incidence of complications was 2.1%, the incidence of complications requiring hospital admission was 0.23%, and that of the 54,911 abortion patients included in the study, only 15 required immediate transfer to the hospital on the day of the abortion).

- Expert testimony stating that "it is extremely unlikely that a patient will experience a serious complication at the clinic that requires emergent hospitalization" and "in the rare case in which [one does], the quality of care that the patient receives is not affected by whether the abortion provider has admitting privileges at the hospital." *Id.*, at 381.

- Expert testimony stating that in respect to surgical abortion patients who do suffer complications requiring hospitalization, most of these complications occur in the days after the abortion, not on the spot. See *id.*, at 382; see also *id.*, at 267.

- Expert testimony stating that a delay before the onset of complications is also expected for medical abortions, as "abortifacient drugs take time to exert their effects, and thus the abortion itself almost always occurs after the patient has left the abortion facility." *Id.*, at 278.

- Some experts added that, if a patient needs a hospital in the day or week following her abortion, she will likely seek medical attention at the hospital nearest her home. See, *e.g., id.*, at 153.

We have found nothing in Texas' record evidence that shows that, compared to prior law (which required a "working arrangement" with a doctor with admitting privileges), the new law advanced Texas' legitimate interest in protecting women's health.

We add that, when directly asked at oral argument whether Texas knew of a single instance in which the new requirement would have helped even one woman obtain better treatment, Texas admitted that there was no evidence in the record of such a case. See Tr. of Oral Arg. 47. This answer is consistent with the findings of the other Federal District Courts that have considered the health benefits of other States' similar admitting-privileges laws. See *Planned Parenthood of Wis., Inc. v. Van Hollen*, 94 F.Supp.3d 949, 953 (W.D. Wis. 2015), aff'd *sub nom.*

Planned Parenthood of Wis., Inc. v. Schimel, 806 F.3d 908 (C.A. 7 2015); *Planned Parenthood Southeast, Inc. v. Strange,* 33 F.Supp.3d 1330, 1378 (M.D. Ala. 2014).

At the same time, the record evidence indicates that the admitting-privileges requirement places a "substantial obstacle in the path of a woman's choice." *Casey,* 505 U.S., at 877 (plurality opinion). The District Court found, as of the time the admitting-privileges requirement began to be enforced, the number of facilities providing abortions dropped in half, from about 40 to about 20. 46 F.Supp.3d, at 681. Eight abortion clinics closed in the months leading up to the requirement's effective date. See App. 229–230; cf. Brief for Planned Parenthood Federation of America et al. as *Amici Curiae* 14 (noting that abortion facilities in Waco, San Angelo, and Midland no longer operate because Planned Parenthood is "unable to find local physicians in those communities with privileges who are willing to provide abortions due to the size of those communities and the hostility that abortion providers face"). Eleven more closed on the day the admitting-privileges requirement took effect. See App. 229–230; Tr. of Oral Arg. 58.

Other evidence helps to explain why the new requirement led to the closure of clinics. We read that other evidence in light of a brief filed in this Court by the Society of Hospital Medicine. That brief describes the undisputed general fact that "hospitals often condition admitting privileges on reaching a certain number of admissions per year." Brief for Society of Hospital Medicine et al. as *Amici Curiae* 11. Returning to the District Court record, we note that, in direct testimony, the president of Nova Health Systems, implicitly relying on this general fact, pointed out that it would be difficult for doctors regularly performing abortions at the El Paso clinic to obtain admitting privileges at nearby hospitals because "[d]uring the past 10 years, over 17,000 abortion procedures were performed at the El Paso clinic [and n]ot a single one of those patients had to be transferred to a hospital for emergency treatment, much less admitted to the hospital." App. 730. In a word, doctors would be unable to maintain admitting privileges or obtain those privileges for the future, because the fact that abortions are so safe meant that providers were unlikely to have any patients to admit.

Other *amicus* briefs filed here set forth without dispute other common prerequisites to obtaining admitting privileges that have nothing to do with ability to perform medical procedures. See Brief for Medical Staff Professionals as *Amici Curiae* 20–25 (listing, for example, requirements that an applicant has treated a high number of patients in the hospital setting in the past year, clinical data requirements, residency requirements, and other discretionary factors); see also Brief for American College of Obstetricians and Gynecologists et al. as *Amici Curiae* 16 (ACOG Brief) ("[S]ome academic hospitals will only allow medical staff membership for clinicians who also . . . accept faculty appointments"). . . . . [R]eturning to the District Court record, we note that

Dr. Lynn of the McAllen clinic, a veteran obstetrics and gynecology doctor who estimates that he has delivered over 15,000 babies in his 38 years in practice was unable to get admitting privileges at any of the seven hospitals within 30 miles of his clinic. App. 390–394. He was refused admitting privileges at a nearby hospital for reasons, as the hospital wrote, "not based on clinical competence considerations." *Id.*, at 393–394 (emphasis deleted). The admitting-privileges requirement does not serve any relevant credentialing function.

In our view, the record contains sufficient evidence that the admitting-privileges requirement led to the closure of half of Texas' clinics, or thereabouts. Those closures meant fewer doctors, longer waiting times, and increased crowding. Record evidence also supports the finding that after the admitting-privileges provision went into effect, the "number of women of reproductive age living in a county . . . more than 150 miles from a provider increased from approximately 86,000 to 400,000 . . . and the number of women living in a county more than 200 miles from a provider from approximately 10,000 to 290,000." 46 F.Supp.3d, at 681. We recognize that increased driving distances do not always constitute an "undue burden." See *Casey*, 505 U.S., at 885–887 (joint opinion of O'Connor, KENNEDY, and Souter, JJ.). But here, those increases are but one additional burden, which, when taken together with others that the closings brought about, and when viewed in light of the virtual absence of any health benefit, lead us to conclude that the record adequately supports the District Court's "undue burden" conclusion. Cf. *id.*, at 895 (opinion of the Court) (finding burden "undue" when requirement places "substantial obstacle to a woman's choice" in "a large fraction of the cases in which" it "is relevant").

The dissent's only argument why these clinic closures, as well as the ones discussed in Part V, *infra*, may not have imposed an undue burden is this: Although "H. B. 2 caused the closure of *some* clinics," other clinics may have closed for other reasons (so we should not "actually count" the burdens resulting from those closures against H.B. 2). But petitioners satisfied their burden to present evidence of causation by presenting direct testimony as well as plausible inferences to be drawn from the timing of the clinic closures. App. 182–183, 228–231. The District Court credited that evidence and concluded from it that H.B. 2 in fact led to the clinic closures. 46 F.Supp.3d, at 680–681. The dissent's speculation that perhaps other evidence, not presented at trial or credited by the District Court, might have shown that some clinics closed for unrelated reasons does not provide sufficient ground to disturb the District Court's factual finding on that issue.

In the same breath, the dissent suggests that one benefit of H.B. 2's requirements would be that they might "force unsafe facilities to shut down." . . . Determined wrongdoers, already ignoring existing statutes and safety measures, are unlikely to be convinced to adopt safe practices by a new overlay of regulations. . . . Pre-existing Texas law already contained numerous detailed regulations covering abortion facilities, including a requirement that facilities be inspected at least annually. The record contains nothing to suggest that H. B. 2 would be more effective than pre-existing Texas law at deterring wrongdoers . . . from criminal behavior.

V *Undue Burden—Surgical-Center Requirement*

The second challenged provision of Texas' new law sets forth the surgical-center requirement. Prior to enactment of the new requirement, Texas law required abortion facilities to meet a host of health and safety requirements. Under those pre-existing laws, facilities were subject to annual reporting and recordkeeping requirements, see Tex. Admin. Code, tit. 25, §§ 139.4, 139.5, 139.55, 139.58; a quality assurance program, see § 139.8; personnel policies and staffing requirements, see §§ 139.43, 139.46; physical and environmental requirements, see § 139.48; infection control standards, see § 139.49; disclosure requirements, see § 139.50; patient-rights standards, see § 139.51; and medical- and clinical-services standards, see § 139.53, including anesthesia standards, see § 139.59. These requirements are policed by random and announced inspections, at least annually, see §§ 139.23, 139.31; Tex. Health & Safety Code Ann. § 245.006(a) (West 2010), as well as administrative penalties, injunctions, civil penalties, and criminal penalties for certain violations, see Tex. Admin. Code, tit. 25, § 139.33; Tex. Health & Safety Code Ann. § 245.011 (criminal penalties for certain reporting violations).

H.B. 2 added the requirement that an "abortion facility" meet the "minimum standards . . . for ambulatory surgical centers" under Texas law. § 245.010(a) (West Cum.Supp.2015). The surgical-center regulations include, among other things, detailed specifications relating to the size of the nursing staff, building dimensions, and other building requirements. The nursing staff must comprise at least "an adequate number of [registered nurses] on duty to meet the following minimum staff requirements: director of the department (or designee), and supervisory and staff personnel for each service area to assure the immediate availability of [a registered nurse] for emergency care or for any patient when needed," Tex. Admin. Code, tit. 25, § 135.15(a)(3) (2016), as well as "a second individual on duty on the premises who is trained and currently certified in basic cardiac life support until all patients have been discharged from the facility" for facilities that provide moderate sedation, such as most abortion facilities, § 135.15(b)(2)(A). Facilities must include a full surgical suite with an operating room that has "a clear floor area of at least 240 square feet" in which "[t]he minimum clear dimension between built-in cabinets, counters, and shelves shall be 14 feet." § 135.52(d)(15)(A). There must be a preoperative patient holding room and a postoperative recovery suite. The former "shall be provided and arranged in a one-way traffic pattern so that patients entering from outside the surgical suite can change, gown, and move directly into the restricted corridor of the surgical suite," § 135.52(d)(10)(A), and the latter "shall be arranged to provide a one-way traffic pattern from the restricted surgical corridor to the postoperative recovery suite, and then to the extended observation rooms or discharge," § 135.52(d)(9)(A). Surgical centers must meet numerous other spatial requirements, see generally § 135.52, including specific corridor widths, § 135.52(e)(1)(B)(iii). Surgical centers must also have an advanced heating, ventilation, and air conditioning system, § 135.52(g)(5), and must satisfy particular piping system and plumbing requirements, § 135.52(h). Dozens of other sections list additional requirements that apply to surgical centers. See generally §§ 135.1–135.56.

There is considerable evidence in the record supporting the District Court's findings indicating that the statutory provision requiring all abortion facilities to meet all surgical-center standards does not benefit patients and is not necessary. The District Court found that "risks are not appreciably lowered for patients who undergo abortions at ambulatory surgical centers as compared to nonsurgical-center facilities." 46 F.Supp.3d, at 684. The court added that women "will not obtain better care or experience more frequent positive outcomes at an ambulatory surgical center as compared to a previously licensed facility." *Ibid.* And these findings are well supported.

The record makes clear that the surgical-center requirement provides no benefit when complications arise in the context of an abortion produced through medication. That is because, in such a case, complications would almost always arise only after the patient has left the facility. App. 278. The record also contains evidence indicating that abortions taking place in an abortion facility are safe—indeed, safer than numerous procedures that take place outside hospitals and to which Texas does not apply its surgical-center requirements. See, *e.g., id.*, at 223–224, 254, 275–279. The total number of deaths in Texas from abortions was five in the period from 2001 to 2012, or about one every two years (that is to say, one out of about 120,000 to 144,000 abortions). *Id.*, at 272. Nationwide, childbirth is 14 times more likely than abortion to result in death, *ibid.*, but Texas law allows a midwife to oversee childbirth in the patient's own home. Colonoscopy, a procedure that typically takes place outside a hospital (or surgical center) setting, has a mortality rate 10 times higher than an abortion. *Id.*, at 276–277; see ACOG Brief 15 (the mortality rate for liposuction, another outpatient procedure, is 28 times higher than the mortality rate for abortion). Medical treatment after an incomplete miscarriage often involves a procedure identical to that involved in a nonmedical abortion, but it often takes place outside a hospital or surgical center. App. 254; see ACOG Brief 14 (same). And Texas partly or wholly grandfathers (or waives in whole or in part the surgical-center requirement for) about two-thirds of the facilities to which the surgical-center standards apply. But it neither grandfathers nor provides waivers for any of the facilities that perform abortions. [*Lakey*,] 46 F.Supp.3d, at 680–681; see App. 184. These facts indicate that the surgical-center provision imposes "a requirement that simply is not based on differences" between abortion and other surgical procedures "that are reasonably related to" preserving women's health, the asserted "purpos[e] of the Act in which it is found." *Doe* [*v. Bolton*], 410 U.S. [179], 194 [(1973)] (quoting *Morey v. Doud*, 354 U.S. 457, 465 (1957); internal quotation marks omitted).

Moreover, many surgical-center requirements are inappropriate as applied to surgical abortions. Requiring scrub facilities; maintaining a one-way traffic pattern through the facility; having ceiling, wall, and floor finishes; separating soiled utility and sterilization rooms; and regulating air pressure, filtration, and humidity control can help reduce infection where doctors conduct procedures that penetrate the skin. App. 304. But abortions typically involve either the administration of medicines or procedures performed through the natural opening of the birth canal, which is itself not sterile. See *id.*, at 302–303. Nor do provisions designed to safeguard heavily sedated patients (unable to help themselves) during fire emergencies, see Tex. Admin. Code, tit. 25, § 135.41; App. 304, provide any help to abortion patients, as abortion facilities do not use general anesthesia or deep sedation, *id.*, at 304–305. Further, since the few instances in which serious complications do arise following an abortion almost always require hospitalization, not treatment at a surgical center, *id.*, at 255–256, surgical-center standards will not help in those instances either.

The upshot is that this record evidence, along with the absence of any evidence to the contrary, provides ample support for the District Court's conclusion that "[m]any of the building standards mandated by the act and its implementing rules have such a tangential relationship to patient safety in the context of abortion as to be nearly arbitrary." 46 F.Supp.3d, at 684. That conclusion, along with the supporting evidence, provides sufficient support for the more general conclusion that the surgical-center requirement "will not [provide] better care or . . . more frequent positive outcomes." *Ibid.* The record evidence thus supports the ultimate legal conclusion that the surgical-center requirement is not necessary.

At the same time, the record provides adequate evidentiary support for the District Court's conclusion that the surgical-center requirement places a substantial obstacle in the path of women seeking an abortion. The parties stipulated that the requirement would further reduce the number of abortion facilities available to seven or eight facilities, located in Houston, Austin, San Antonio, and Dallas/Fort Worth. See App. 182–183. In the District Court's view, the proposition that these "seven or eight providers could meet the demand of the entire State stretches credulity." 46 F.Supp.3d, at 682. We take this statement as a finding that these few facilities could not "meet" that "demand."

The Court of Appeals held that this finding was "clearly erroneous." [*Whole Woman's Health v. Cole*,] 790 F.3d [563,] 590 [(5th Cir. 2015)]. It wrote that the finding rested upon the " '*ipse dixit*' " of one expert, Dr. Grossman, and that there was no evidence that the current surgical centers (*i.e.*, the seven or eight) are operating at full capacity or could not increase capacity. *Ibid.* Unlike the Court of Appeals, however, we hold that the record provides adequate support for the District Court's finding.

For one thing, the record contains charts and oral testimony by Dr. Grossman, who said that, as a result of the surgical-center requirement, the number of abortions that the clinics would have to provide would rise from " '14,000 abortions annually' " to " '60,000 to 70,000' "—an increase by a factor of about five. *Id.*, at 589–590. The District Court credited Dr. Grossman as an expert witness. See 46 F.Supp.3d, at 678–679, n. 1; *id.*, at 681, n. 4 (finding "indicia of reliability" in Dr. Grossman's conclusions). The Federal Rules of Evidence state that an expert may testify in the "form of an opinion" as long as that opinion rests upon "sufficient facts or data" and "reliable principles and methods." [FED. R. EVID.] 702. In this case Dr. Grossman's opinion rested upon his participation, along with other university researchers, in research that tracked "the number of open facilities providing abortion care in the state by . . . requesting information from the Texas Department of State Health Services . . . [, t]hrough interviews with clinic staff[,] and review of publicly available information." App. 227. The District Court acted within its legal authority in determining that Dr. Grossman's testimony was admissible.

For another thing, common sense suggests that, more often than not, a physical facility that satisfies a certain physical demand will not be able to meet five times that demand without expanding or otherwise incurring significant costs. Suppose that we know only that a certain grocery store serves 200 customers per week, that a certain apartment building provides apartments for 200 families, that a certain train station welcomes 200 trains per day. While it is conceivable that the store, the apartment building, or the train station could just as easily provide for 1,000 customers, families, or trains at no significant additional cost, crowding, or delay, most of us would find this possibility highly improbable. The dissent takes issue with this general, intuitive point by arguing that many places operate below capacity and that in any event, facilities could simply hire additional providers. We disagree that, according to common sense, medical facilities, well known for their wait times, operate below capacity as a general matter. And the fact that so many facilities were forced to close by the admitting-privileges requirement means that hiring more physicians would not be quite as simple as the dissent suggests. Courts are free to base their findings on commonsense inferences drawn from the evidence. And that is what the District Court did here.

The dissent now seeks to discredit Dr. Grossman by pointing out that a preliminary prediction he made in his testimony in [*Planned*

Parenthood of Greater Tex. Surgical Heal Servs. v.] Abbott[, 951 F.Supp.2d 891 (W.D. Tex. 2013), aff'd in part and rev'd in part, 748 F.3d 583 (5th Cir. 2014)], about the effect of the admitting-privileges requirement on capacity was not borne out after that provision went into effect. If every expert who overestimated or underestimated any figure could not be credited, courts would struggle to find expert assistance. Moreover, making a hypothesis—and then attempting to verify that hypothesis with further studies, as Dr. Grossman did—is not irresponsible. It is an essential element of the scientific method. The District Court's decision to credit Dr. Grossman's testimony was sound, particularly given that Texas provided no credible experts to rebut it. See 46 F.Supp.3d, at 680, n. 3 (declining to credit Texas' expert witnesses, in part because Vincent Rue, a nonphysician consultant for Texas, had exercised "considerable editorial and discretionary control over the contents of the experts' reports").

Texas suggests that the seven or eight remaining clinics could expand sufficiently to provide abortions for the 60,000 to 72,000 Texas women who sought them each year. Because petitioners had satisfied their burden, the obligation was on Texas, if it could, to present evidence rebutting that issue to the District Court. Texas admitted that it presented no such evidence. Tr. of Oral Arg. 46. Instead, Texas argued before this Court that one new clinic now serves 9,000 women annually. *Ibid.* In addition to being outside the record, that example is not representative. The clinic to which Texas referred apparently cost $26 million to construct—a fact that even more clearly demonstrates that requiring seven or eight clinics to serve five times their usual number of patients does indeed represent an undue burden on abortion access. See *Planned Parenthood Debuts New Building: Its $26 Million Center in Houston is Largest of Its Kind in U. S.*, HOUSTON CHRONICLE, May 21, 2010, p. B1.

Attempting to provide the evidence that Texas did not, the dissent points to an exhibit submitted in *Abbott* showing that three Texas surgical centers, two in Dallas as well as the $26-million facility in Houston, are each capable of serving an average of 7,000 patients per year. That "average" is misleading. In addition to including the Houston clinic, which does not represent most facilities, it is underinclusive. It ignores the evidence as to the Whole Woman's Health surgical-center facility in San Antonio, the capacity of which is described as "severely limited." The exhibit does nothing to rebut the commonsense inference that the dramatic decline in the number of available facilities will cause a shortfall in capacity should H.B. 2 go into effect. And facilities that were still operating after the effective date of the admitting-privileges provision were not able to accommodate increased demand. See App. 238; Tr. of Oral Arg. 30–31; Brief for National Abortion Federation et al. as *Amici Curiae* 17–20 (citing clinics' experiences since the admitting-privileges requirement went into effect of 3-week wait times, staff burnout, and waiting rooms so full, patients had to sit on the floor or wait outside).

More fundamentally, in the face of no threat to women's health, Texas seeks to force women to travel long distances to get abortions in crammed-to-capacity superfacilities. Patients seeking these services are less likely to get the kind of individualized attention, serious conversation, and emotional support that doctors at less taxed facilities may have offered. Healthcare facilities and medical professionals are not fungible commodities. Surgical centers attempting to accommodate sudden, vastly increased demand, see 46 F.Supp.3d, at 682, may find that quality of care declines. Another commonsense inference that the District Court made is that these effects would be harmful to, not supportive of, women's health. See *id.*, at 682–683.

Finally, the District Court found that the costs that a currently licensed abortion facility would have to incur to meet the surgical-center requirements were considerable, ranging from $1 million per facility (for facilities with adequate space) to $3 million per facility (where additional land must be purchased). *Id.*, at 682. This evidence supports the conclusion that more surgical centers will not soon fill the gap when licensed facilities are forced to close.

We agree with the District Court that the surgical-center requirement, like the admitting-privileges requirement, provides few, if any, health benefits for women, poses a substantial obstacle to women seeking abortions, and constitutes an "undue burden" on their constitutional right to do so.

VI

We consider three additional arguments that Texas makes and deem none persuasive.

First, Texas argues that facial invalidation of both challenged provisions is precluded by H.B. 2's severability clause. See Brief for Respondents 50–52. The severability clause says that "every provision, section, subsection, sentence, clause, phrase, or word in this Act, and every application of the provision in this Act, are severable from each other." H.B. 2, § 10(b), App. to Pet. for Cert. 200a. It further provides that if "any application of any provision in this Act to any person, group of persons, or circumstances is found by a court to be invalid, the remaining applications of that provision to all other persons and circumstances shall be severed and may not be affected." *Ibid.* That language, Texas argues, means that facial invalidation of parts of the statute is not an option; instead, it says, the severability clause mandates a more narrowly tailored judicial remedy. But the challenged provisions of H.B. 2 close most of the abortion facilities in Texas and place added stress on those facilities able to remain open. They vastly increase the obstacles confronting women seeking abortions in Texas without providing any benefit to women's health capable of withstanding any meaningful scrutiny. The provisions are unconstitutional on their face: Including a severability provision in the law does not change that conclusion.

Severability clauses, it is true, do express the enacting legislature's preference for a narrow judicial remedy. As a general matter, we attempt to honor that preference. But our cases have never required us to proceed application by conceivable application when confronted with a facially unconstitutional statutory provision. . . . [I]f a severability clause could impose such a requirement on courts, legislatures would easily be able to insulate unconstitutional statutes from most facial review. . . . We reject Texas' invitation to pave the way for legislatures to immunize their statutes from facial review.

Texas similarly argues that instead of finding the entire surgical-center provision unconstitutional, we should invalidate (as applied to abortion clinics) only those specific surgical-center regulations that unduly burden the provision of abortions, while leaving in place other surgical-center regulations (for example, the reader could pick any of the various examples provided by the dissent). See Brief for Respondents 52–53. As we have explained, Texas' attempt to broadly draft a requirement to sever "applications" does not require us to proceed in piecemeal fashion when we have found the statutory provisions at issue facially unconstitutional.

. . .

Second, Texas claims that the provisions at issue here do not impose a substantial obstacle because the women affected by those laws are not a "large fraction" of Texan women "of reproductive age," which Texas reads *Casey* to have required. See Brief for Respondents 45, 48. But *Casey* used the language "large fraction" to refer to "a large fraction of cases in which [the provision at issue] is *relevant*," a class narrower than "all women," "pregnant women," or even "the class of *women seeking abortions* identified by the State." 505 U.S., at 894–895 (opinion of the Court) (emphasis added). Here, as in *Casey*, the relevant denominator is "those [women] for whom [the provision] is an actual rather than an irrelevant restriction." *Id.*, at 895.

Third, Texas looks for support to *Simopoulos v. Virginia*, 462 U.S. 506 (1983), a case in which this Court upheld a surgical-center requirement as applied to second-trimester abortions. This case, however, unlike *Simopoulos*, involves restrictions applicable to all abortions, not simply to those that take place during the second trimester. Most abortions in Texas occur in the first trimester, not the second. App. 236. More importantly, in *Casey* we discarded the trimester framework, and we now use "viability" as the relevant point at which a State may begin limiting women's access to abortion for reasons unrelated to maternal health. 505 U.S., at 878 (plurality opinion). Because the second trimester includes time that is both previability and postviability, *Simopoulos* cannot provide clear guidance. Further, the Court in *Simopoulos* found that the petitioner in that case, unlike petitioners here, had waived any argument that the regulation did not significantly help protect women's health. 462 U.S., at 517.

* * *

For these reasons the judgment of the Court of Appeals is reversed, and the case is remanded for further proceedings consistent with this opinion.

It is so ordered.

■ JUSTICE GINSBURG, concurring.

The Texas law called H.B. 2 inevitably will reduce the number of clinics and doctors allowed to provide abortion services. Texas argues that H.B. 2's restrictions are constitutional because they protect the health of women who experience complications from abortions. In truth, "complications from an abortion are both rare and rarely dangerous." *Planned Parenthood of Wis., Inc. v. Schimel*, 806 F.3d 908, 912 (C.A. 7 2015). See Brief for American College of Obstetricians and Gynecologists et al. as *Amici Curiae* 6–10 (collecting studies and concluding "[a]bortion is one of the safest medical procedures performed in the United States"); Brief for Social Science Researchers as *Amici Curiae* 5–9 (compiling studies that show "[c]omplication rates from abortion are very low"). Many medical procedures, including childbirth, are far more dangerous to patients, yet are not subject to ambulatory-surgical-center or hospital admitting-privileges requirements. See *Planned Parenthood of Wis.*, 806 F.3d, at 921–922. See also Brief for Social Science Researchers 9–11 (comparing statistics on risks for abortion with tonsillectomy, colonoscopy, and in-office dental surgery); Brief for American Civil Liberties Union et al. as *Amici Curiae* 7 (all District Courts to consider admitting-privileges requirements found abortion "is at least as safe as other medical procedures routinely performed in outpatient settings"). Given those realities, it is beyond rational belief that H.B. 2 could genuinely protect the health of women, and certain that the law "would simply make it more difficult for them to obtain abortions." *Planned Parenthood of Wis.*, 806 F.3d, at 910. When a State severely limits access to safe and legal procedures, women in desperate circumstances may resort to unlicensed rogue practitioners, *faute de mieux*, at great risk to their health and safety. See Brief for Ten Pennsylvania Abortion Care Providers as *Amici Curiae* 17–22. So long as this Court adheres to *Roe v. Wade*, 410 U.S. 113 (1973), and *Planned Parenthood of Southeastern Pa. v. Casey*, 505 U.S. 833 (1992), Targeted Regulation of Abortion Providers laws like H.B. 2 that "do little or nothing for health, but rather strew impediments to abortion," *Planned Parenthood of Wis.*, 806 F.3d, at 921, cannot survive judicial inspection.

■ JUSTICE THOMAS, dissenting.

Today the Court strikes down two state statutory provisions in all of their applications, at the behest of abortion clinics and doctors. That decision exemplifies the Court's troubling tendency "to bend the rules when any effort to limit abortion, or even to speak in opposition to abortion, is at issue." *Stenberg v. Carhart*, 530 U.S. 914, 954 (2000) (Scalia, J., dissenting). . . . I write separately to emphasize how today's decision perpetuates the Court's habit of applying different rules to different constitutional rights—especially the putative right to abortion.

. . .

. . .

II

Today's opinion . . . reimagines the undue-burden standard used to assess the constitutionality of abortion restrictions. Nearly 25 years ago, in *Planned Parenthood of Southeastern Pa. v. Casey*, 505 U.S. 833 [(1992)], a plurality of this Court invented the "undue burden" standard as a special test for gauging the permissibility of abortion restrictions. *Casey* held that a law is unconstitutional if it imposes an "undue burden" on a woman's ability to choose to have an abortion, meaning that it "has the purpose or effect of placing a substantial obstacle in the path of a woman seeking an abortion of a nonviable fetus." *Id.*, at 877. *Casey* thus instructed courts to look to whether a law substantially impedes women's access to abortion, and whether it is reasonably related to legitimate state interests. As the Court explained, "[w]here it has a rational basis to act, and it does not impose an undue burden, the State may use its regulatory power" to regulate aspects of abortion procedures, "all in furtherance of its legitimate interests in regulating the medical profession in order to promote respect for life, including life of the unborn." *Gonzales v. Carhart*, 550 U.S. 124, 158 (2007).

I remain fundamentally opposed to the Court's abortion jurisprudence. *E.g., id.*, at 168–169 (THOMAS, J., concurring); *Stenberg*, 530 U.S., at 980, 982 (THOMAS, J., dissenting). Even taking *Casey* as the baseline, however, the majority radically rewrites the undue-burden test in three ways. First, today's decision requires courts to "consider the burdens a law imposes on abortion access together with the benefits those laws confer." Second, today's opinion tells the courts that, when the law's justifications are medically uncertain, they need not defer to the legislature, and must instead assess medical justifications for abortion restrictions by scrutinizing the record themselves. Finally, even if a law imposes no "substantial obstacle" to women's access to abortions, the law now must have more than a "reasonabl[e] relat[ion] to . . . a legitimate state interest." These precepts are nowhere to be found in *Casey* or its successors, and transform the undue-burden test to something much more akin to strict scrutiny.

First, the majority's free-form balancing test is contrary to *Casey*. When assessing Pennsylvania's recordkeeping requirements for abortion providers, for instance, *Casey* did not weigh its benefits and burdens. Rather, *Casey* held that the law had a legitimate purpose because data collection advances medical research, "so it cannot be said that the requirements serve no purpose other than to make abortions more difficult." 505 U.S., at 901 (joint opinion of O'Connor, KENNEDY, and Souter, JJ.). The opinion then asked whether the recordkeeping requirements imposed a "substantial obstacle," and found none. *Ibid.* Contrary to the majority's statements, *Casey* did not balance the benefits and burdens of Pennsylvania's spousal and parental notification provisions, either. Pennsylvania's spousal notification requirement, the plurality said, imposed an undue burden because findings established that the requirement would "likely . . . prevent a significant number of women from obtaining an abortion"—not because these burdens outweighed its benefits. 505 U.S., at 893 (majority opinion); see *id.*, at 887–894. And *Casey* summarily upheld parental notification provisions because even pre-*Casey* decisions had done so. *Id.*, at 899–900 (joint opinion).

Decisions in *Casey*'s wake further refute the majority's benefits-and-burdens balancing test. The Court in *Mazurek v. Armstrong*, 520 U.S. 968 (1997) (*per curiam*), had no difficulty upholding a Montana law authorizing only physicians to perform abortions—even though no legislative findings supported the law, and the challengers claimed that "all health evidence contradict[ed] the claim that there is any health basis for the law." *Id.*, at 973 (internal quotation marks omitted). *Mazurek* also deemed objections to the law's lack of benefits "squarely foreclosed by *Casey* itself." *Ibid.* Instead, the Court explained, " 'the Constitution gives the States broad latitude to decide that particular functions may be performed only by licensed professionals, *even if an objective assessment might suggest that those same tasks could be performed by others.*' " *Ibid.* (quoting *Casey*, *supra*, at 885; emphasis in original); see *Gonzales*, *supra*, at 164 (relying on *Mazurek*).

Second, by rejecting the notion that "legislatures, and not courts, must resolve questions of medical uncertainty," the majority discards another core element of the *Casey* framework. Before today, this Court had "given state and federal legislatures wide discretion to pass legislation in areas where there is medical and scientific uncertainty." *Gonzales*, 550 U.S., at 163. This Court emphasized that this "traditional rule" of deference "is consistent with *Casey*." *Ibid.* This Court underscored that legislatures should not be hamstrung "if some part of the medical community were disinclined to follow the proscription." *Id.*, at 166. And this Court concluded that "[c]onsiderations of marginal safety, including the balance of risks, are within the legislative competence when the regulation is rational and in pursuit of legitimate ends." *Ibid.*; see *Stenberg*, *supra*, at 971 (KENNEDY, J., dissenting) ("the right of the legislature to resolve matters on which physicians disagreed" is "establish[ed] beyond doubt"). This Court could not have been clearer: Whenever medical justifications for an abortion restriction are debatable, that "provides a sufficient basis to conclude in [a] facial attack that the

[law] does not impose an undue burden." *Gonzales*, 550 U.S., at 164. Otherwise, legislatures would face "too exacting" a standard. *Id.*, at 166.

Today, however, the majority refuses to leave disputed medical science to the legislature because past cases "placed considerable weight upon the evidence and argument presented in judicial proceedings." But while *Casey* relied on record evidence to uphold Pennsylvania's spousal-notification requirement, that requirement had nothing to do with debated medical science. 505 U.S., at 888–894 (majority opinion). And while *Gonzales* observed that courts need not blindly accept all legislative findings, that does not help the majority. *Gonzales* refused to accept Congress' finding of "a medical consensus that the prohibited procedure is never medically necessary" because the procedure's necessity was debated within the medical community. 550 U.S., at 165–166. Having identified medical uncertainty, *Gonzales* explained how courts should resolve conflicting positions: by respecting the legislature's judgment. See *id.*, at 164.

Finally, the majority overrules another central aspect of *Casey* by requiring laws to have more than a rational basis even if they do not substantially impede access to abortion. "Where [the State] *has a rational basis to act* and it does not impose an undue burden," this Court previously held, "the State may use its regulatory power" to impose regulations "in furtherance of its legitimate interests in regulating the medical profession in order to promote respect for life, including life of the unborn." *Gonzales*, *supra*, at 158 (emphasis added); see *Casey*, *supra*, at 878 (plurality opinion) (similar). No longer. Though the majority declines to say how substantial a State's interest must be, one thing is clear: The State's burden has been ratcheted to a level that has not applied for a quarter century.

Today's opinion does resemble *Casey* in one respect: After disregarding significant aspects of the Court's prior jurisprudence, the majority applies the undue-burden standard in a way that will surely mystify lower courts for years to come. As in *Casey*, today's opinion "simply . . . highlight[s] certain facts in the record that apparently strike the . . . Justices as particularly significant in establishing (or refuting) the existence of an undue burden." 505 U.S., at 991 (Scalia, J., concurring in judgment in part and dissenting in part). As in *Casey*, "the opinion then simply announces that the provision either does or does not impose a 'substantial obstacle' or an 'undue burden.'" 505 U.S., at 991 (opinion of Scalia, J). And still "[w]e do not know whether the same conclusions could have been reached on a different record, or in what respects the record would have had to differ before an opposite conclusion would have been appropriate." 505 U.S., at 991 (opinion of Scalia, J.). All we know is that an undue burden now has little to do with whether the law, in a "real sense, deprive[s] women of the ultimate decision," *Casey*, *supra*, at 875, and more to do with the loss of "individualized attention, serious conversation, and emotional support[.]"

The majority's undue-burden test looks far less like our post-*Casey* precedents and far more like the strict-scrutiny standard that *Casey* rejected, under which only the most compelling rationales justified restrictions on abortion. See *Casey, supra,* at 871, 874–875 (plurality opinion). One searches the majority opinion in vain for any acknowledgment of the "premise central" to *Casey*'s rejection of strict scrutiny: "that the government has a legitimate and substantial interest in preserving and promoting fetal life" from conception, not just in regulating medical procedures. *Gonzales, supra,* at 145 (internal quotation marks omitted); see *Casey, supra,* at 846 (majority opinion), 871 (plurality opinion). Meanwhile, the majority's undue-burden balancing approach risks ruling out even minor, previously valid infringements on access to abortion. Moreover, by second-guessing medical evidence and making its own assessments of "quality of care" issues, the majority reappoints this Court as "the country's *ex officio* medical board with powers to disapprove medical and operative practices and standards throughout the United States." *Gonzales, supra,* at 164 (internal quotation marks omitted). And the majority seriously burdens States, which must guess at how much more compelling their interests must be to pass muster and what "commonsense inferences" of an undue burden this Court will identify next.

III

The majority's furtive reconfiguration of the standard of scrutiny applicable to abortion restrictions also points to a deeper problem. The undue-burden standard is just one variant of the Court's tiers-of-scrutiny approach to constitutional adjudication. And the label the Court affixes to its level of scrutiny in assessing whether the government can restrict a given right—be it "rational basis," intermediate, strict, or something else—is increasingly a meaningless formalism. As the Court applies whatever standard it likes to any given case, nothing but empty words separates our constitutional decisions from judicial fiat.

Though the tiers of scrutiny have become a ubiquitous feature of constitutional law, they are of recent vintage. Only in the 1960's did the Court begin in earnest to speak of "strict scrutiny" versus reviewing legislation for mere rationality, and to develop the contours of these tests. See Fallon, *Strict Judicial Scrutiny,* 54 UCLA L.REV. 1267, 1274, 1284– 1285 (2007). In short order, the Court adopted strict scrutiny as the standard for reviewing everything from race-based classifications under the Equal Protection Clause to restrictions on constitutionally protected speech. *Id.,* at 1275–1283. *Roe v. Wade,* 410 U.S. 113 [(1973)], then applied strict scrutiny to a purportedly "fundamental" substantive due process right for the first time. *Id.,* at 162–164; see Fallon, *supra,* at 1283; accord, *Casey, supra,* at 871 (plurality opinion) (noting that post-*Roe* cases interpreted *Roe* to demand "strict scrutiny"). Then the tiers of scrutiny proliferated into ever more gradations. See, *e.g., Craig* [*v. Boren*], 429 U.S. [190,] 197–198 [(1976)] (intermediate scrutiny for sex-based classifications); *Lawrence v. Texas*, 539 U.S. 558, 580 (2003) (O'Connor, J., concurring in judgment) ("a more searching form of rational basis review" applies to laws reflecting "a desire to harm a politically unpopular group"); *Buckley v. Valeo*, 424 U.S. 1, 25 (1976) (*per curiam*) (applying " 'closest scrutiny' " to campaign-finance contribution limits). *Casey*'s undue-burden test added yet another right-specific test on the spectrum between rational-basis and strict-scrutiny review.

The illegitimacy of using "made-up tests" to "displace longstanding national traditions as the primary determinant of what the Constitution means" has long been apparent. *United States v. Virginia*, 518 U.S. 515, 570 (1996) (Scalia, J., dissenting). The Constitution does not prescribe tiers of scrutiny. The three basic tiers—"rational basis," intermediate, and strict scrutiny—"are no more scientific than their names suggest, and a further element of randomness is added by the fact that it is largely up to us which test will be applied in each case." *Id.*, at 567.

But the problem now goes beyond that. If our recent cases illustrate anything, it is how easily the Court tinkers with levels of scrutiny to achieve its desired result. This Term, it is easier for a State to survive strict scrutiny despite discriminating on the basis of race in college admissions than it is for the same State to regulate how abortion doctors and clinics operate under the putatively less stringent undue-burden test. All the State apparently needs to show to survive strict scrutiny is a list of aspirational educational goals (such as the "cultivat[ion of] a set of leaders with legitimacy in the eyes of the citizenry") and a "reasoned, principled explanation" for why it is pursuing them—then this Court defers. *Fisher v. University of Tex. at Austin*, [579 U.S. ___ (2016)] [(slip op.] at 7, 12[ )] (internal quotation marks omitted). Yet the same State gets no deference under the undue-burden test, despite producing evidence that abortion safety, one rationale for Texas' law, is medically debated. See *Whole Woman's Health v. Lakey*, 46 F.Supp.3d 673, 684 (W.D. Tex. 2014) (noting conflict in expert testimony about abortion safety). Likewise, it is now easier for the government to restrict judicial candidates' campaign speech than for the Government to define marriage—even though the former is subject to strict scrutiny and the latter was supposedly subject to some form of rational-basis review. Compare *Williams-Yulee v. Florida Bar*, 575 U.S. ___, [135 S.Ct. 1656] (2015) (slip op., at 8–9), with *United States v. Windsor*, 570 U.S. ___, [133 S.Ct. 2675] (2013) (slip op., at 20).

These more recent decisions reflect the Court's tendency to relax purportedly higher standards of review for less-preferred rights. *E.g., Nixon v. Shrink Missouri Government PAC*, 528 U.S. 377, 421 (2000) (THOMAS, J., dissenting) ("The Court makes no effort to justify its deviation from the tests we traditionally employ in free speech cases" to review caps on political contributions). Meanwhile, the Court selectively applies rational-basis review—under which the question is supposed to be whether "any state of facts reasonably may be conceived to justify" the law, *McGowan v. Maryland*, 366 U.S. 420, 426 (1961)—with formidable toughness. *E.g., Lawrence*, 539 U.S., at 580 (O'Connor, J., concurring in judgment) (at least in equal protection cases, the Court is "most likely" to find no rational basis for a law if "the challenged legislation inhibits personal relationships"); see *id.*, at 586 (Scalia, J., dissenting) (faulting the Court for applying "an unheard-of form of rational-basis review").

These labels now mean little. Whatever the Court claims to be doing, in practice it is treating its "doctrine referring to tiers of scrutiny as guidelines informing our approach to the case at hand, not tests to be mechanically applied." *Williams-Yulee, supra*, at ___ (slip op., at 1) (BREYER, J., concurring). The Court should abandon the pretense that anything other than policy preferences underlies its balancing of constitutional rights and interests in any given case.

IV

It is tempting to identify the Court's invention of a constitutional right to abortion in *Roe v. Wade*, 410 U.S. 113, as the tipping point that transformed ... the tiers of scrutiny into an unworkable morass of special exceptions and arbitrary applications. But those roots run deeper, to the very notion that some constitutional rights demand preferential treatment. During the *Lochner* era, the Court considered the right to contract and other economic liberties to be fundamental requirements of due process of law. See *Lochner v. New York*, 198 U.S. 45 (1905). The Court in 1937 repudiated *Lochner*'s foundations. See *West Coast Hotel Co. v. Parrish*, 300 U.S. 379, 386–387, 400 (1937). But the Court then created a new taxonomy of preferred rights.

In 1938, seven Justices heard a constitutional challenge to a federal ban on shipping adulterated milk in interstate commerce. Without economic substantive due process, the ban clearly invaded no constitutional right. See *United States v. Carolene Products Co.*, 304 U.S. 144, 152–153 (1938). Within Justice Stone's opinion for the Court, however, was a footnote that just three other Justices joined—the famous *Carolene Products* Footnote 4. See *ibid.*, n. 4; Lusky, *Footnote Redux: A Carolene Products Reminiscence*, 82 COLUM. L.REV. 1093, 1097 (1982). The footnote's first paragraph suggested that the presumption of constitutionality that ordinarily attaches to legislation might be "narrower ... when legislation appears on its face to be within a specific prohibition of the Constitution." 304 U.S., at 152–153, n. 4. Its second paragraph appeared to question "whether legislation which restricts those political processes, which can ordinarily be expected to bring about repeal of undesirable legislation, is to be subjected to more exacting judicial scrutiny under the general prohibitions of the [14th] Amendment than are most other types of legislation." *Ibid.* And its third and most familiar paragraph raised the question "whether prejudice against discrete and insular minorities may be a special condition, which tends seriously to curtail the operation of those political processes ordinarily to be relied upon to protect minorities, and which may call for a correspondingly more searching judicial inquiry." *Ibid.*

Though the footnote was pure dicta, the Court seized upon it to justify its special treatment of certain personal liberties like the First Amendment and the right against discrimination on the basis of race— but also rights not enumerated in the Constitution. As the Court identified which rights deserved special protection, it developed the tiers of scrutiny as part of its equal protection (and, later, due process) jurisprudence as a way to demand extra justifications for encroachments on these rights. See Fallon, 54 UCLA L.REV., at 1270–1273, 1281–1285. And, having created a new category of fundamental rights, the Court loosened the reins to recognize even putative rights like abortion, see *Roe,* 410 U.S., at 162–164, which hardly implicate "discrete and insular minorities."

. . .

Eighty years on, the Court has come full circle. The Court has simultaneously transformed judicially created rights like the right to abortion into preferred constitutional rights, while disfavoring many of the rights actually enumerated in the Constitution. But our Constitution renounces the notion that some constitutional rights are more equal than others. A plaintiff either possesses the constitutional right he is asserting, or not—and if not, the judiciary has no business creating ad hoc exceptions so that others can assert rights that seem especially important to vindicate. A law either infringes a constitutional right, or not; there is no room for the judiciary to invent tolerable degrees of encroachment. Unless the Court abides by one set of rules to adjudicate constitutional rights, it will continue reducing constitutional law to policy-driven value judgments until the last shreds of its legitimacy disappear.

* * *

Today's decision will prompt some to claim victory, just as it will stiffen opponents' will to object. But the entire Nation has lost something essential. The majority's embrace of a jurisprudence of rights-specific exceptions and balancing tests is "a regrettable concession of defeat—an acknowledgement that we have passed the point where 'law,' properly speaking, has any further application." Scalia, *The Rule of Law as a Law of Rules,* 56 U. CHI. L.REV. 1175, 1182 (1989). I respectfully dissent.

■ JUSTICE ALITO, with whom THE CHIEF JUSTICE and JUSTICE THOMAS join, dissenting.

. . .

III

. . . Petitioners in this case are abortion clinics and physicians who perform abortions. If they were simply asserting a constitutional right to conduct a business or to practice a profession without unnecessary state regulation, they would have little chance of success. See, *e.g., Williamson v. Lee Optical of Okla., Inc.*, 348 U.S. 483 (1955). Under our abortion cases, however, they are permitted to rely on the right of the abortion patients they serve. See *Doe v. Bolton*, 410 U.S. 179, 188 (1973).

Thus, what matters for present purposes is not the effect of the H.B. 2 provisions on petitioners but the effect on their patients. Under our cases, petitioners must show that the admitting privileges and [ambulatory surgical centers ("ACSs")] requirements impose an "undue burden" on women seeking abortions. *Gonzales v. Carhart*, 550 U.S. 124, 146 (2007). And in order to obtain the sweeping relief they seek—facial invalidation of those provisions—they must show, at a minimum, that these provisions have an unconstitutional impact on at least a "large fraction" of Texas women of reproductive age.[11] *Id.*, at 167–168. Such a situation could result if the clinics able to comply with the new requirements either lacked the requisite overall capacity or were located too far away to serve a "large fraction" of the women in question.

Petitioners did not make that showing. Instead of offering direct evidence, they relied on two crude inferences. First, they pointed to the number of abortion clinics that closed after the enactment of H.B. 2, and asked that it be inferred that all these closures resulted from the two challenged provisions. See Brief for Petitioners 23–24. They made little effort to show why particular clinics closed. Second, they pointed to the number of abortions performed annually at ASCs before H.B. 2 took effect and, because this figure is well below the total number of abortions performed each year in the State, they asked that it be inferred that ASC-compliant clinics could not meet the demands of women in the State. See App. 237–238. Petitioners failed to provide any evidence of the actual capacity of the facilities that would be available to perform abortions in compliance with the new law[.] . . .

A

I do not dispute the fact that H.B. 2 caused the closure of some clinics. Indeed, it seems clear that H.B. 2 was intended to force unsafe facilities to shut down. . . .

While there can be no doubt that H.B. 2 caused some clinics to cease operation, the absence of proof regarding the reasons for particular closures is a problem because some clinics have or may have closed for at

---

[11] The proper standard for facial challenges is unsettled in the abortion context. See *Gonzales,* 550 U.S., at 167–168. Like the Court in *Gonzales, supra,* at 167–168, I do not decide the question, and use the more plaintiff-friendly "large fraction" formulation only because petitioners cannot meet even that test.

The Court, by contrast, applies the "large fraction" standard without even acknowledging the open question. In a similar vein, it holds that the fraction's "relevant denominator is 'those [women] for whom [the provision] is an actual rather than an irrelevant restriction.'" *Ibid.* (quoting *Casey,* 505 U.S., at 895). I must confess that I do not understand this holding. The purpose of the large-fraction analysis, presumably, is to compare the number of women *actually* burdened with the number *potentially* burdened. Under the Court's holding, we are supposed to use the same figure (women actually burdened) as both the numerator and the denominator. By my math, that fraction is always "1," which is pretty large as fractions go.

least four reasons other than the two H.B. 2 requirements at issue here. These are:

1. *H. B. 2's restriction on medication abortion.* . . . The record in this case indicates that in the first six months after [a "provision of H.B. 2 that regulates medication abortion"] took effect, the number of medication abortions dropped by 6,957 (compared to the same period the previous year). App. 236.

2. *Withdrawal of Texas family planning funds.* In 2011, Texas passed a law preventing family planning grants to providers that perform abortions and their affiliates. . . . [S]ome clinics closed "as a result of the defunding," and . . . this withdrawal appears specifically to have caused multiple clinic closures in West Texas.

3. *The nationwide decline in abortion demand.* Petitioners' expert testimony relies on a study from the Guttmacher Institute which concludes that " '[t]he national abortion rate has resumed its decline, and *no evidence was found that the overall drop in abortion incidence was related to the decrease in providers or to restrictions implemented between 2008 and 2011.*' " App. 1117 (direct testimony of Dr. Peter Uhlenberg) (quoting R. Jones & J. Jerman, Abortion Incidence and Service Availability In the United States, 2011, 46 Perspectives on Sexual and Reproductive Health 3 (2014); emphasis in testimony). Consistent with that trend, "[t]he number of abortions to residents of Texas declined by 4,956 between 2010 and 2011 and by 3,905 between 2011 and 2012." App. 1118.

4. *Physician retirement (or other localized factors).* Like everyone else, most physicians eventually retire, and the retirement of a physician who performs abortions can cause the closing of a clinic or a reduction in the number of abortions that a clinic can perform. When this happens, the closure of the clinic or the reduction in capacity cannot be attributed to H.B. 2 unless it is shown that the retirement was caused by the admitting privileges or surgical center requirements as opposed to age or some other factor.

At least nine Texas clinics may have ceased performing abortions (or reduced capacity) for one or more of the reasons having nothing to do with the provisions challenged here. . . .

Neither petitioners nor the District Court properly addressed these complexities in assessing causation—and for no good reason. The total number of abortion clinics in the State was not large. Petitioners could have put on evidence . . . about the challenged provisions' role in causing the closure of each clinic, and the court could have made a factual finding as to the cause of each closure.

Precise findings are important because the key issue here is not the number or percentage of clinics affected, but the effect of the closures on women seeking abortions, *i.e.*, on the capacity and geographic distribution of clinics used by those women. To the extent that clinics closed (or experienced a reduction in capacity) for any reason unrelated to the challenged provisions of H.B. 2, the corresponding burden on abortion access may not be factored into the access analysis. Because there was ample reason to believe that some closures were caused by these other factors, the District Court's failure to ascertain the reasons for clinic closures means that, on the record before us, there is no way to tell which closures actually count. Petitioners—who, as plaintiffs, bore the burden of proof—cannot simply point to temporal correlation and call it causation.

B

Even if the District Court had properly filtered out immaterial closures, its analysis would have been incomplete for a second reason. Petitioners offered scant evidence on the capacity of the clinics that are able to comply with the admitting privileges and ASC requirements, or on those clinics' geographic distribution. Reviewing the evidence in the record, it is far from clear that there has been a material impact on access to abortion.

On clinic capacity, the Court relies on petitioners' expert Dr. Grossman, who compared the number of abortions performed at Texas ASCs before the enactment of H.B. 2 (about 14,000 per year) with the total number of abortions per year in the State (between 60,000–70,000 per year).[21] Applying what the Court terms "common sense," the Court infers that the ASCs that performed abortions at the time of H.B. 2's enactment lacked the capacity to perform all the abortions sought by women in Texas.

The Court's inference has obvious limitations. First, it is not unassailable "common sense" to hold that current utilization equals capacity[.] . . . Faced with increased demand, ASCs could potentially

---

[21] . . . [I]n this case, in fact, Dr. Grossman admitted that [a] . . . prediction [that he and a co-author made] turned out to be wildly inaccurate. Specifically, he provided a new figure (approximately 9,200) that was less than half of his earlier prediction. And he then admitted that he had not proven any causal link between the admitting privileges requirement and that smaller decline.

Dr. Grossman's testimony in this case, furthermore, suggested that H.B. 2's restriction on medication abortion (whose impact on clinics cannot be attributed to the provisions challenged in this case) was a major cause in the decline in the abortion rate. After the medication abortion restriction and admitting privileges requirement took effect, over the next six months the number of medication abortions dropped by 6,957 compared to the same period in the previous year. See App. 236. The corresponding number of surgical abortions rose by 2,343. See *ibid.* If that net decline of 4,614 in six months is doubled to approximate the annual trend (which is apparently the methodology Dr. Grossman used to arrive at his 9,200 figure, see 90 Contraception, *supra*, at 500), then the year's drop of 9,228 abortions seems to be *entirely* the product of the medication abortion restriction. Taken together, these figures make it difficult to conclude that the admitting privileges requirement actually depressed the abortion rate *at all*.

In light of all this, it is unclear why the Court takes Dr. Grossman's testimony at face value.

increase the number of abortions performed without prohibitively expensive changes. Among other things, they might hire more physicians who perform abortions,[22] utilize their facilities more intensively or efficiently, or shift the mix of services provided. Second, what matters for present purposes is not the capacity of just those ASCs that performed abortions prior to the enactment of H.B. 2 but the capacity of those that would be available to perform abortions after the statute took effect. And since the enactment of H.B. 2, the number of ASCs performing abortions has increased by 50%—from six in 2012 to nine today.[23]

The most serious problem with the Court's reasoning is that its conclusion is belied by petitioners' own submissions to this Court. . . . Three of the facilities listed on [a] chart [submitted by petitioners in an earlier case] were ASCs, and their capacity was shown as follows:

- Southwestern Women's Surgery Center in Dallas was said to have the capacity for 5,720 abortions a year (110 per week);

- Planned Parenthood Surgical Health Services Center in Dallas was said to have the capacity for 6,240 abortions a year (120 per week); and

- Planned Parenthood Center for Choice in Houston was said to have the capacity for 9,100 abortions a year (175 per week). See Appendix, *infra*.

The average capacity of these three ASCs was 7,020 abortions per year. If the nine ASCs now performing abortions in Texas have the same average capacity, they have a total capacity of 63,180. Add in the assumed capacity for two other clinics that are operating pursuant to the judgment of the Fifth Circuit (over 3,100 abortions per year), and the total for the State is 66,280 abortions per year. That is comparable to the 68,298 total abortions performed in Texas in 2012, the year before H.B. 2 was enacted, App. 236, and well in excess of the abortion rate one would expect—59,070—if subtracting the apparent impact of the medication abortion restriction, see n. 21, *supra*.

To be clear, I do not vouch for the accuracy of this calculation. It might be too high or too low. The important point is that petitioners put on evidence of actual clinic capacity in their earlier case, and there is no apparent reason why they could not have done the same here. Indeed, the Court asserts that, after the admitting privileges requirement took effect, clinics "were not able to accommodate increased demand," but

---

[22] The Court asserts that the admitting privileges requirement is a bottleneck on capacity, but it musters no evidence and does not even dispute petitioners' own evidence that the admitting privileges requirement may have had *zero* impact on the Texas abortion rate, n. 21, *supra*.

[23] Two of the three new surgical centers opened since this case was filed are operated by Planned Parenthood (which now owns five of the nine surgical centers in the State). See App. 182–183, 1436. Planned Parenthood is obviously able to comply with the challenged H.B. 2 requirements. . . .

petitioners' own evidence suggested that the requirement had *no* effect on capacity. On this point, like the question of the reason for clinic closures, petitioners did not discharge their burden, and the District Court did not engage in the type of analysis that should have been conducted before enjoining an important state law.

So much for capacity. The other[30] potential obstacle to abortion access is the distribution of facilities throughout the State. This might occur if the two challenged H.B. 2 requirements, by causing the closure of clinics in some rural areas, led to a situation in which a "large fraction" of women of reproductive age live too far away from any open clinic. Based on the Court's holding in *Planned Parenthood of Southeastern Pa. v. Casey*, 505 U.S. 833, it appears that the need to travel up to 150 miles is not an undue burden,[32] and the evidence in this case shows that if the only clinics in the State were those that would have remained open if the judgment of the Fifth Circuit had not been enjoined, roughly 95% of the women of reproductive age in the State would live within 150 miles of an open facility (or lived outside that range before H.B. 2). Because the record does not show why particular facilities closed, the real figure may be even higher than 95%.

We should decline to hold that these statistics justify the facial invalidation of the H.B. 2 requirements. The possibility that the admitting privileges requirement *might* have caused a closure in Lubbock is no reason to issue a facial injunction exempting Houston clinics from that requirement. I do not dismiss the situation of those women who would no longer live within 150 miles of a clinic as a result of H.B. 2. But under current doctrine such localized problems can be addressed by narrow as-applied challenges.

IV

Even if the Court were right to hold . . . that H.B. 2 imposes an undue burden on abortion access—it is, in fact, wrong [to do so] . . .—it is still wrong to conclude that the admitting privileges and surgical center provisions must be enjoined in their entirety. H.B. 2 has an extraordinarily broad severability clause that must be considered before enjoining any portion or application of the law. Both challenged provisions should survive in substantial part if the Court faithfully applies that clause. Regrettably, it enjoins both in full, heedless of the (controlling) intent of the state legislature. Cf. *Leavitt v. Jane L.*, 518 U.S.

---

30   The Court also gives weight to supposed reductions in "individualized attention, serious conversation, and emotional support" in its undue-burden analysis. But those "facts" are not in the record, so I have no way of addressing them.

32   The District Court in *Casey* found that 42% of Pennsylvania women "must travel for at least one hour, and sometimes longer than three hours, to obtain an abortion from the *nearest* provider." 744 F.Supp. 1323, 1352 (E.D. Pa. 1990), aff'd in part, rev'd in part, 947 F.2d 682 (C.A. 3 1991), aff'd in part, rev'd in part, 505 U.S. 833 (1992). In that case, this Court recognized that the challenged 24-hour waiting period would require some women to make that trip twice, and yet upheld the law regardless. See *id.*, at 886–887.

137, 139 (1996) (*per curiam*) ("Severability is of course a matter of state law").

A

Applying H.B. 2's severability clause to the admitting privileges requirement is easy. Simply put, the requirement must be upheld in every city in which its application does not pose an undue burden. It surely does not pose that burden anywhere in the eastern half of the State, where most Texans live and where virtually no woman of reproductive age lives more than 150 miles from an open clinic. See App. 242, 244 (petitioners' expert testimony that 82.5% of Texas women of reproductive age live within 150 miles of open clinics in Austin, Dallas, Fort Worth, Houston, and San Antonio). (Unfortunately, the Court does not address the State's argument to this effect. See Brief for Respondents 51.) And petitioners would need to show that the requirement caused specific West Texas clinics to close before they could be entitled to an injunction tailored to address those closures.

B

Applying severability to the surgical center requirement calls for the identification of the particular provisions of the ASC regulations that result in the imposition of an undue burden. These regulations are lengthy and detailed, and while compliance with some might be expensive, compliance with many others would not. And many serve important health and safety purposes. Thus, the surgical center requirements cannot be judged as a package. But the District Court nevertheless held that all the surgical center requirements are unconstitutional in all cases, and the Court sustains this holding on grounds that are hard to take seriously.

When the Texas Legislature passed H.B. 2, it left no doubt about its intent on the question of severability. It included a provision mandating the greatest degree of severability possible. . . . [I]t is enough to note that under this provision "every provision, section, subsection, sentence, clause, phrase, or word in this Act, and every application of the provisions in this Act, are severable from each other." H.B. 2, § 10(b), App. to Pet. for Cert. 200a. And to drive home the point about the severability of applications of the law, the provision adds:

> "If any application of any provision in this Act to any person, group of persons, or circumstances is found by a court to be invalid, the remaining applications of that provision to all other persons and circumstances shall be severed and may not be affected. All constitutionally valid applications of this Act shall be severed from any applications that a court finds to be invalid, leaving the valid applications in force, because it is the legislature's intent and priority that the valid applications be allowed to stand alone." *Ibid.*

This provision indisputably requires that all surgical center regulations that are not themselves unconstitutional be left standing. Requiring an abortion facility to comply with any provision of the regulations applicable to surgical centers is an "application of the provision" of H.B. 2 that requires abortion clinics to meet surgical center standards. Therefore, if some such applications are unconstitutional, the severability clause plainly requires that those applications be severed and that the rest be left intact.

How can the Court possibly escape this painfully obvious conclusion? Its main argument is that it need not honor the severability provision because doing so would be too burdensome. This is a remarkable argument.

Under the Supremacy Clause, federal courts may strike down state laws that violate the Constitution or conflict with federal statutes, Art. VI, cl. 2, but in exercising this power, federal courts must take great care. The power to invalidate a state law implicates sensitive federal-state relations. Federal courts have no authority to carpet-bomb state laws, knocking out provisions that are perfectly consistent with federal law, just because it would be too much bother to separate them from unconstitutional provisions.

In any event, it should not have been hard in this case for the District Court to separate any bad provisions from the good. Petitioners should have identified the particular provisions that would entail what they regard as an undue expense, and the District Court could have then concentrated its analysis on those provisions. In fact, petitioners *did* do this in their trial brief, Doc. 185, p. 8 in [*Whole Woman's Health v.*] *Lakey*, [46 F.Supp.3d 673] ([W.D. Tex.] 2014) ("It is the construction and nursing requirements that form the basis of Plaintiffs' challenge"), but they changed their position once the District Court awarded blanket relief, see 790 F.3d, at 582 (petitioners told the Fifth Circuit that they "challenge H.B. 2 broadly, with no effort whatsoever to parse out specific aspects of the ASC requirement that they find onerous or otherwise infirm"). In its own review of the ASC requirement, in fact, the Court follows petitioners' original playbook and focuses on the construction and nursing requirements as well. I do not see how it "would inflict enormous costs on both courts and litigants[ ]" to single out the ASC regulations that this Court and petitioners have both targeted as the core of the challenge.

By forgoing severability, the Court strikes down numerous provisions that could not plausibly impose an undue burden. For example, surgical center patients must "be treated with respect, consideration, and dignity." Tex. Admin. Code, tit. 25, § 135.5(a). That's now enjoined. Patients may not be given misleading "advertising regarding the competence and/or capabilities of the organization." § 135.5(g). Enjoined. Centers must maintain fire alarm and emergency communications systems, §§ 135.41(d), 135.42(e), and eliminate "[h]azards that might lead to slipping, falling, electrical shock, burns, poisoning, or other trauma," § 135.10(b). Enjoined and enjoined. When a center is being remodeled while still in use, "[t]emporary sound barriers shall be provided where intense, prolonged construction noises will disturb patients or staff in the occupied portions of the building." § 135.51(b)(3)(B)(vi). Enjoined. Centers must develop and enforce policies concerning teaching and publishing by staff. §§ 135.16(a), (c). Enjoined. They must obtain informed consent before doing research on patients. § 135.17(e). Enjoined. And each center "shall develop, implement[,] and maintain an effective, ongoing, organization-wide, data driven patient safety program." § 135.27(b). Also enjoined. These are but a few of the innocuous requirements that the Court invalidates with nary a wave of the hand.

Any responsible application of the H.B. 2 severability provision would leave much of the law intact. At a minimum, both of the requirements challenged here should be held constitutional as applied to clinics in any Texas city that will have a surgical center providing abortions (*i.e.*, those areas in which there cannot possibly have been an undue burden on abortion access). Moreover, as even the District Court found, the surgical center requirement is clearly constitutional as to new abortion facilities and facilities already licensed as surgical centers. *Lakey*, 46 F.Supp.3d, at 676. And we should uphold every application of every surgical center regulation that does not pose an undue burden—at the very least, all of the regulations as to which petitioners have never made a specific complaint supported by specific evidence. The Court's wholesale refusal to engage in the required severability analysis here revives the "antagonistic 'canon of construction under which in cases involving abortion, a permissible reading of a statute is to be avoided at all costs.'" *Gonzales*, 550 U.S., at 153–154 (quoting *Stenberg v. Carhart*, 530 U.S. 914, 977 (2000) (KENNEDY, J., dissenting); some internal quotation marks omitted).

If the Court is unwilling to undertake the careful severability analysis required, that is no reason to strike down all applications of the challenged provisions. The proper course would be to remand to the lower courts for a remedy tailored to the specific facts shown in this case, to "try to limit the solution to the problem." *Ayotte v. Planned Parenthood of Northern New Eng.*, 546 U.S. 320, 328 (2006).

V

. . .

I . . . respectfully dissent.

NOTES

1. Justice Breyer's opinion for the Court in *Whole Woman's Health v. Hellerstedt* formally operates within the doctrinal rubric constructed by the plurality opinion in *Planned Parenthood v. Casey*, just as the Supreme Court's earlier decision in *Gonzales v. Carhart* did. Do you see *Whole*

Woman's Health and *Gonzales* reflecting the same judicial attitude toward abortion and abortion regulations? Do the two cases actually adopt the same approach to reviewing legislative limitations on abortion that are advanced in the name of protecting women's health? Consider Erika Bachiochi, Symposium: *Is* Hellerstedt *this Generation's* Roe?, SCOTUSBLOG (June 28, 2016 11:46 A.M.), http://www.scotusblog.com/2016/06/symposium-is-hellerstedt-this-generations-roe/ ("Balancing may seem the more fair and modest approach, but it is not an act for which courts are designed. It's the proper role of the legislature, as recognized in *Gonzales v. Carhart*, the 2007 decision [that *Whole Woman's Health*] mostly ignored in its desire to impose super-legislative tasks on the judiciary.").

2. Justice Thomas's dissent in *Whole Women's Health* observes that the Court's opinion in the case "transform[s] the undue-burden test [of *Casey*] to something more akin to strict scrutiny." Do you agree? If so, does *Whole Woman's Health* contain within it the seeds for a return to the Court's decision in *Roe v. Wade*? More modestly, does *Whole Woman's Health* amount to a step, while portending additional steps, in that direction?

3. How much guidance does *Whole Woman's Health* practically offer to lower courts about how they should apply the balancing approach to abortion regulation that it itself takes? Does the Court's fact-centered and skeptical approach to Texas's abortion laws provide a template for lower courts to follow? Or is the balancing approach of *Whole Woman's Health* more open-ended than that? Consider Kevin C. Walsh, Symposium: *The constitutional law of abortion after* Whole Woman's Health—What Comes next?, SCOTUSBLOG (June 28, 2016 10:56 A.M.), http://www.scotusblog.com/2016/06/symposium-the-constitutional-law-of-abortion-after-whole-womans-health-what-comes-next/ ("Take, for example, a law that bans abortions after twenty weeks gestational age. Hard to deny that this twenty-plus-week-old human fetus is a human baby. . . . What does, or will, our law say about the costs and benefits of a law that protects these babies, or of a constitutional regime that disables meaningful legal protection for them? I'll bet that depends on which judge you ask.").

CHAPTER 4

PARENTING

D. ADOPTION

STANDARDS

RACE AND ETHNICITY

Page 453, Unabridged (Page 318, Concise). Insert the following case and notes at the end of the section.

Adoptive Couple v. Baby Girl

Supreme Court of the United States, 2013.
570 U.S. ___, 133 S.Ct. 2552, 186 L.Ed.2d 729.

■ JUSTICE ALITO delivered the opinion of the Court.

This case is about a little girl (Baby Girl) who is classified as an Indian because she is 1.2% (3/256) Cherokee. Because Baby Girl is classified in this way, the South Carolina Supreme Court held that certain provisions of the federal Indian Child Welfare Act of 1978 required her to be taken, at the age of 27 months, from the only parents she had ever known and handed over to her biological father, who had attempted to relinquish his parental rights and who had no prior contact with the child. The provisions of the federal statute at issue here do not demand this result.

. . .

I

"The Indian Child Welfare Act of 1978 (ICWA), 92 Stat. 3069, 25 U.S.C. §§ 1901–1963, was the product of rising concern in the mid-1970's over the consequences to Indian children, Indian families, and Indian tribes of abusive child welfare practices that resulted in the separation of large numbers of Indian children from their families and tribes through adoption or foster care placement, usually in non-Indian homes." *Mississippi Band of Choctaw Indians v. Holyfield*, 490 U.S. 30, 32 (1989). Congress found that "an alarmingly high percentage of Indian families [were being] broken up by the removal, often unwarranted, of their children from them by nontribal public and private agencies." § 1901(4). This "wholesale removal of Indian children from their homes" prompted Congress to enact the ICWA, which establishes federal standards that govern state-court child custody proceedings involving Indian children. *Id.*, at 32, 36 (internal quotation marks omitted).[1]

---

[1] It is undisputed that Baby Girl is an "Indian child" as defined by the ICWA because she is an unmarried minor who "is eligible for membership in an Indian tribe and is the biological

Three provisions of the ICWA are especially relevant to this case. First, "[a]ny party seeking" an involuntary termination of parental rights to an Indian child under state law must demonstrate that "active efforts have been made to provide remedial services and rehabilitative programs designed to prevent the breakup of the Indian family and that these efforts have proved unsuccessful." § 1912(d). Second, a state court may not involuntarily terminate parental rights to an Indian child "in the absence of a determination, supported by evidence beyond a reasonable doubt, including testimony of qualified expert witnesses, that the continued custody of the child by the parent or Indian custodian is likely to result in serious emotional or physical damage to the child." § 1912(f). Third, with respect to adoptive placements for an Indian child under state law, "a preference shall be given, in the absence of good cause to the contrary, to a placement with (1) a member of the child's extended family; (2) other members of the Indian child's tribe; or (3) other Indian families." § 1915(a).

II

In this case, Birth Mother (who is predominantly Hispanic) and Biological Father (who is a member of the Cherokee Nation) became engaged in December 2008. One month later, Birth Mother informed Biological Father, who lived about four hours away, that she was pregnant. After learning of the pregnancy, Biological Father asked Birth Mother to move up the date of the wedding. He also refused to provide any financial support until after the two had married. The couple's relationship deteriorated, and Birth Mother broke off the engagement in May 2009. In June, Birth Mother sent Biological Father a text message asking if he would rather pay child support or relinquish his parental rights. Biological Father responded via text message that he relinquished his rights.

Birth Mother then decided to put Baby Girl up for adoption. Because Birth Mother believed that Biological Father had Cherokee Indian heritage, her attorney contacted the Cherokee Nation to determine whether Biological Father was formally enrolled. The inquiry letter misspelled Biological Father's first name and incorrectly stated his birthday, and the Cherokee Nation responded that, based on the information provided, it could not verify Biological Father's membership in the tribal records.

Working through a private adoption agency, Birth Mother selected Adoptive Couple, non-Indians living in South Carolina, to adopt Baby Girl. Adoptive Couple supported Birth Mother both emotionally and financially throughout her pregnancy. Adoptive Couple was present at Baby Girl's birth in Oklahoma on September 15, 2009, and Adoptive Father even cut the umbilical cord. The next morning, Birth Mother

---

child of a member of an Indian tribe," § 1903(4)(b). It is also undisputed that the present case concerns a "child custody proceeding," which the ICWA defines to include proceedings that involve "termination of parental rights" and "adoptive placement," § 1903(1).

signed forms relinquishing her parental rights and consenting to the adoption. Adoptive Couple initiated adoption proceedings in South Carolina a few days later, and returned there with Baby Girl. After returning to South Carolina, Adoptive Couple allowed Birth Mother to visit and communicate with Baby Girl.

It is undisputed that, for the duration of the pregnancy and the first four months after Baby Girl's birth, Biological Father provided no financial assistance to Birth Mother or Baby Girl, even though he had the ability to do so. Indeed, Biological Father "made no meaningful attempts to assume his responsibility of parenthood" during this period.

Approximately four months after Baby Girl's birth, Adoptive Couple served Biological Father with notice of the pending adoption. (This was the first notification that they had provided to Biological Father regarding the adoption proceeding.) Biological Father signed papers stating that he accepted service and that he was "not contesting the adoption." But Biological Father later testified that, at the time he signed the papers, he thought that he was relinquishing his rights to Birth Mother, not to Adoptive Couple.

Biological Father contacted a lawyer the day after signing the papers, and subsequently requested a stay of the adoption proceedings.[2] In the adoption proceedings, Biological Father sought custody and stated that he did not consent to Baby Girl's adoption. Moreover, Biological Father took a paternity test, which verified that he was Baby Girl's biological father.

A trial took place in the South Carolina Family Court in September 2011, by which time Baby Girl was two years old. The Family Court concluded that Adoptive Couple had not carried the heightened burden under § 1912(f) of proving that Baby Girl would suffer serious emotional or physical damage if Biological Father had custody. The Family Court therefore denied Adoptive Couple's petition for adoption and awarded custody to Biological Father. On December 31, 2011, at the age of 27 months, Baby Girl was handed over to Biological Father, whom she had never met.

The South Carolina Supreme Court affirmed the Family Court's denial of the adoption and the award of custody to Biological Father. . . .

III

It is undisputed that, had Baby Girl not been 3/256 Cherokee, Biological Father would have had no right to object to her adoption under South Carolina law. The South Carolina Supreme Court held, however, that Biological Father is a "parent" under the ICWA and that two statutory provisions—namely, § 1912(f) and § 1912(d)—bar the termination of his parental rights. . . . We need not—and therefore do

---

[2]   Around the same time, the Cherokee Nation identified Biological Father as a registered member and concluded that Baby Girl was an "Indian child" as defined in the ICWA. The Cherokee Nation intervened in the litigation approximately three months later.

not—decide whether Biological Father is a "parent." See § 1903(9). Rather, assuming for the sake of argument that he is a "parent," we hold that neither § 1912(f) nor § 1912(d) bars the termination of his parental rights.

A

Section 1912(f) addresses the involuntary termination of parental rights with respect to an Indian child. Specifically, § 1912(f) provides that "[n]o termination of parental rights may be ordered in such proceeding in the absence of a determination, supported by evidence beyond a reasonable doubt, . . . that the *continued custody* of the child by the parent or Indian custodian is likely to result in serious emotional or physical damage to the child." (Emphasis added.) The South Carolina Supreme Court held that Adoptive Couple failed to satisfy § 1912(f) because they did not make a heightened showing that Biological Father's "prospective legal and physical custody" would likely result in serious damage to the child. That holding was error.

Section 1912(f) conditions the involuntary termination of parental rights on a showing regarding the merits of "*continued* custody of the child by the parent." (Emphasis added.) The adjective "continued" plainly refers to a pre-existing state. . . . The term "continued" also can mean "resumed after interruption." The phrase "continued custody" therefore refers to custody that a parent already has (or at least had at some point in the past). As a result, § 1912(f) does not apply in cases where the Indian parent never had custody of the Indian child.

. . .

Our reading of § 1912(f) comports with the statutory text demonstrating that the primary mischief the ICWA was designed to counteract was the unwarranted removal of Indian children from Indian families due to the cultural insensitivity and biases of social workers and state courts. . . . And if the legislative history of the ICWA is thought to be relevant, it further underscores that the Act was primarily intended to stem the unwarranted removal of Indian children from intact Indian families. In sum, when, as here, the adoption of an Indian child is voluntarily and lawfully initiated by a non-Indian parent with sole custodial rights, the ICWA's primary goal of preventing the unwarranted removal of Indian children and the dissolution of Indian families is not implicated.

. . .

Under our reading of § 1912(f), Biological Father should not have been able to invoke § 1912(f) in this case, because he had never had legal or physical custody of Baby Girl as of the time of the adoption proceedings. . . .

In sum, the South Carolina Supreme Court erred in finding that § 1912(f) barred termination of Biological Father's parental rights.

B

Section 1912(d) provides that "[a]ny party" seeking to terminate parental rights to an Indian child under state law "shall satisfy the court that active efforts have been made to provide remedial services and rehabilitative programs designed to *prevent the breakup of the Indian family* and that these efforts have proved unsuccessful." (Emphasis added.) The South Carolina Supreme Court found that Biological Father's parental rights could not be terminated because Adoptive Couple had not demonstrated that Biological Father had been provided remedial services in accordance with § 1912(d). We disagree.

Consistent with the statutory text, we hold that § 1912(d) applies only in cases where an Indian family's "breakup" would be precipitated by the termination of the parent's rights. The term "breakup" refers in this context to "[t]he discontinuance of a relationship," American Heritage Dictionary 235 (3d ed. 1992), or "an ending as an effective entity," Webster's [Third New International Dictionary] 273 [(1961)]. But when an Indian parent abandons an Indian child prior to birth and that child has never been in the Indian parent's legal or physical custody, there is no "relationship" that would be "discontinu[ed]"—and no "effective entity" that would be "end[ed]"—by the termination of the Indian parent's rights. In such a situation, the "breakup of the Indian family" has long since occurred, and § 1912(d) is inapplicable.

Our interpretation of § 1912(d) is, like our interpretation of § 1912(f), consistent with the explicit congressional purpose of providing certain "standards for the *removal* of Indian children from their families." § 1902 (emphasis added). . . .

. . .

In sum, the South Carolina Supreme Court erred in finding that § 1912(d) barred termination of Biological Father's parental rights.

IV

In the decision below, the South Carolina Supreme Court suggested that if it had terminated Biological Father's rights, then § 1915(a)'s preferences for the adoptive placement of an Indian child would have been applicable. In so doing, however, the court failed to recognize a critical limitation on the scope of § 1915(a).

Section 1915(a) provides that "[i]n any adoptive placement of an Indian child under State law, a preference shall be given, in the absence of good cause to the contrary, to a placement with (1) a member of the child's extended family; (2) other members of the Indian child's tribe; or (3) other Indian families." Contrary to the South Carolina Supreme Court's suggestion, § 1915(a)'s preferences are inapplicable in cases where no alternative party has formally sought to adopt the child. This is because there simply is no "preference" to apply if no alternative party that is eligible to be preferred under § 1915(a) has come forward.

In this case, Adoptive Couple was the only party that sought to adopt Baby Girl in the Family Court or the South Carolina Supreme Court. Biological Father is not covered by § 1915(a) because he did not seek to *adopt* Baby Girl; instead, he argued that his parental rights should not be terminated in the first place. Moreover, Baby Girl's paternal grandparents never sought custody of Baby Girl. Nor did other members of the Cherokee Nation or "other Indian families" seek to adopt Baby Girl, even though the Cherokee Nation had notice of—and intervened in—the adoption proceedings.

3

The Indian Child Welfare Act was enacted to help preserve the cultural identity and heritage of Indian tribes, but under the State Supreme Court's reading, the Act would put certain vulnerable children at a great disadvantage solely because an ancestor—even a remote one— was an Indian. As the State Supreme Court read §§ 1912(d) and (f), a biological Indian father could abandon his child in utero and refuse any support for the birth mother—perhaps contributing to the mother's decision to put the child up for adoption—and then could play his ICWA trump card at the eleventh hour to override the mother's decision and the child's best interests. If this were possible, many prospective adoptive parents would surely pause before adopting any child who might possibly qualify as an Indian under the ICWA. Such an interpretation would raise equal protection concerns, but the plain text of §§ 1912(f) and (d) makes clear that neither provision applies in the present context. Nor do § 1915(a)'s rebuttable adoption preferences apply when no alternative party has formally sought to adopt the child. We therefore reverse the judgment of the South Carolina Supreme Court and remand the case for further proceedings not inconsistent with this opinion.

It is so ordered.

■ JUSTICE THOMAS, concurring.

. . . Each party in this case has put forward a plausible interpretation of the relevant sections of the Indian Child Welfare Act (ICWA). However, the interpretations offered by respondent Birth Father and the United States raise significant constitutional problems as applied to this case. Because the Court's decision avoids those problems, I concur in its interpretation.

I

. . .

The ICWA recognizes States' inherent "jurisdiction over Indian child custody proceedings," § 1901(5), but asserts that federal regulation is necessary because States "have often failed to recognize the essential tribal relations of Indian people and the cultural and social standards prevailing in Indian communities and families[.]" *Id.* However, Congress may regulate areas of traditional state concern only if the Constitution grants it such power. Admt. 10. The threshold question, then, is whether the Constitution grants Congress power to override state custody law whenever an Indian is involved.

II

The ICWA asserts that the Indian Commerce Clause, Art. I, § 8, cl. 3, and "other constitutional authority" provides Congress with "plenary power over Indian affairs." § 1901(1). The reference to "other constitutional authority" is not illuminating, and I am aware of no other enumerated power that could even arguably support Congress' intrusion into this area of traditional state authority. The assertion of plenary authority must, therefore, stand or fall on Congress' power under the Indian Commerce Clause. Although this Court has said that the "central function of the Indian Commerce Clause is to provide Congress with plenary power to legislate in the field of Indian affairs," *Cotton Petroleum Corp. v. New Mexico*, 490 U.S. 163, 192 (1989), neither the text nor the original understanding of the Clause supports Congress' claim to such "plenary" power.

A

The Indian Commerce Clause gives Congress authority "[t]o regulate Commerce . . . with the Indian tribes." Art. I, § 8, cl. 3 (emphasis added). "At the time the original Constitution was ratified, 'commerce' consisted of selling, buying, and bartering, as well as transporting for these purposes." *United States v. Lopez*, 514 U.S. 549, 585 (1995) (Thomas, J., concurring). . . . The term "commerce" did not include economic activity such as "manufacturing and agriculture," *id.*, let alone noneconomic activity such as adoption of children.

Furthermore, the term "commerce with Indian tribes" was invariably used during the time of the founding to mean "'trade with Indians.'" And regulation of Indian commerce generally referred to legal structures governing "the conduct of the merchants engaged in the Indian trade, the nature of the goods they sold, the prices charged, and similar matters."

The Indian Commerce Clause contains an additional textual limitation relevant to this case: Congress is given the power to regulate Commerce "with the Indian tribes." The Clause does not give Congress the power to regulate commerce with all Indian persons any more than the Foreign Commerce Clause gives Congress the power to regulate commerce with all foreign nationals traveling within the United States. A straightforward reading of the text, thus, confirms that Congress may only regulate commercial interactions—"commerce"—taking place with established Indian communities—"tribes." That power is far from "plenary."

B

Congress' assertion of "plenary power" over Indian affairs is also inconsistent with the history of the Indian Commerce Clause. At the time of the founding, the Clause was understood to reserve to the States general police powers with respect to Indians who were citizens of the several States. The Clause instead conferred on Congress the much narrower power to regulate trade with Indian tribes—that is, Indians who had not been incorporated into the body-politic of any State.

. . .

2

. . .

. . . [T]he Framers of the Constitution were alert to the difference between the power to regulate trade with the Indians and the power to regulate all Indian affairs. By limiting Congress' power to the former, the Framers declined to grant Congress the same broad powers over Indian affairs conferred by the Articles of Confederation.

. . .

III

In light of the original understanding of the Indian Commerce Clause, the constitutional problems that would be created by application of the ICWA here are evident. First, the statute deals with "child custody proceedings," § 1903(1), not "commerce." . . .

Second, the portions of the ICWA at issue here do not regulate Indian tribes as tribes. . . . Sections 1912(d) and (f), and § 1915(a) apply to all child custody proceedings involving an Indian child, regardless of whether an Indian tribe is involved. This case thus does not directly implicate Congress' power to "legislate in respect to Indian tribes." *United States v. Lara*, 541 U.S. 193, 200 (2004) (emphasis added). Baby Girl was never domiciled on an Indian Reservation, and the Cherokee Nation had no jurisdiction over her. Cf. *Mississippi Band of Choctaw Indians v. Holyfield*, 490 U.S. 30, 53–54 (1989). Although Birth Father is a registered member of The Cherokee Nation, he did not live on a reservation either. He was, thus, subject to the laws of the State in which he resided (Oklahoma) and of the State where his daughter resided during the custody proceedings (South Carolina). Nothing in the Indian Commerce Clause permits Congress to enact special laws applicable to Birth Father merely because of his status as an Indian.[3]

Because adoption proceedings like this one involve neither "commerce" nor "Indian tribes," there is simply no constitutional basis for Congress' assertion of authority over such proceedings. . . . Accordingly, application of the ICWA to these child custody proceedings would be unconstitutional.

---

[3] Petitioners and the guardian ad litem contend that applying the ICWA to child custody proceedings on the basis of race implicates equal protection concerns. I need not address this argument because I am satisfied that Congress lacks authority to regulate the child custody proceedings in this case.

3

Because the Court's plausible interpretation of the relevant sections of the ICWA avoids these constitutional problems, I concur.

■ JUSTICE BREYER, concurring.

. . .

. . . [W]e should decide here no more than is necessary. Thus, this case does not involve a father with visitation rights or a father who has paid "all of his child support obligations." Neither does it involve special circumstances such as a father who was deceived about the existence of the child or a father who was prevented from supporting his child. . . .

. . .

■ JUSTICE SCALIA, dissenting.

I join Justice Sotomayor's dissent except as to one detail. I reject the conclusion that the Court draws from the words "continued custody" in 25 U.S.C. § 1912(f) not because "literalness may strangle meaning," but because there is no reason that "continued" must refer to custody in the past rather than custody in the future. . . . For the reasons set forth in Justice Sotomayor's dissent, that connotation is much more in accord with the rest of the statute.

While I am at it, I will add one thought. The Court's opinion, it seems to me, needlessly demeans the rights of parenthood. It has been the constant practice of the common law to respect the entitlement of those who bring a child into the world to raise that child. We do not inquire whether leaving a child with his parents is "in the best interest of the child." It sometimes is not; he would be better off raised by someone else. But parents have their rights, no less than children do. This father wants to raise his daughter, and the statute amply protects his right to do so. There is no reason in law or policy to dilute that protection.

■ JUSTICE SOTOMAYOR, with whom JUSTICE GINSBURG and JUSTICE KAGAN join, and with whom JUSTICE SCALIA joins in part, dissenting.

. . . [T]he path from the text of the Indian Child Welfare Act of 1978 (ICWA) to the result the Court reaches is anything but clear, and its result anything but right.

. . .

II

. . .

B

. . . [T]he majority intimates that ICWA grants Birth Father an undeserved windfall: in the majority's words, an "ICWA trump card" he can "play . . . at the eleventh hour to override the mother's decision and the child's best interests." The implicit argument is that Congress could not possibly have intended to recognize a parent-child relationship between Birth Father and Baby Girl that would have to be legally terminated (either by valid consent or involuntary termination) before the adoption could proceed.

But this supposed anomaly is illusory. In fact, the law of at least 15 States did precisely that at the time ICWA was passed. And the law of a number of States still does so. The State of Arizona, for example, requires that notice of an adoption petition be given to all "potential father[s]" and that they be informed of their "right to seek custody." Ariz. Rev. Stat. §§ 8–106(G)–(J) (West Supp.2012). In Washington, an "alleged father['s]" consent to adoption is required absent the termination of his parental rights, Wash. Rev. Code §§ 26.33.020(1), 26.33.160(1)(b) (2012); and those rights may be terminated only "upon a showing by clear, cogent, and convincing evidence" not only that termination is in the best interest of the child and that the father is withholding his consent to adoption contrary to child's best interests, but also that the father "has failed to perform parental duties under circumstances showing a substantial lack of regard for his parental obligations," § 26.33.120(2).

Without doubt, laws protecting biological fathers' parental rights can lead—even outside the context of ICWA—to outcomes that are painful and distressing for both would-be adoptive families, who lose a much wanted child, and children who must make a difficult transition. On the other hand, these rules recognize that biological fathers have a valid interest in a relationship with their child. And children have a reciprocal interest in knowing their biological parents. These rules also reflect the understanding that the biological bond between a parent and a child is a strong foundation on which a stable and caring relationship may be built. Many jurisdictions apply a custodial preference for a fit natural parent over a party lacking this biological link. This preference is founded in the "presumption that fit parents act in the best interests of their children." *Troxel v. Granville*, 530 U.S. 57, 68 (2000) (plurality opinion). . . .

Balancing the legitimate interests of unwed biological fathers against the need for stability in a child's family situation is difficult, to be sure, and States have, over the years, taken different approaches to the problem. Some States, like South Carolina, have opted to hew to the constitutional baseline established by this Court's precedents and do not require a biological father's consent to adoption unless he has provided financial support during pregnancy. See *Quilloin v. Walcott*, 434 U.S. 246, 254–256 (1978); *Lehr* [*v. Robertson*], 463 U.S. 248, 261 [(1983)]. Other States, however, have decided to give the rights of biological fathers more robust protection and to afford them consent rights on the basis of their biological link to the child. At the time that ICWA was passed, as noted, over one-fourth of States did so.

ICWA, on a straightforward reading of the statute, is consistent with the law of those States that protected, and protect, birth fathers' rights more vigorously. This reading can hardly be said to generate an anomaly.

ICWA, as all acknowledge, was "the product of rising concern . . . [about] abusive child welfare practices that resulted in the separation of large numbers of Indian children from their families." [*Miss. Band of Choctaw Indians v.*] *Holyfield*, 490 U.S. [30,] 32 [(1989)]. It stands to reason that the Act would not render the legal status of an Indian father's relationship with his biological child fragile, but would instead grant it a degree of protection commensurate with the more robust state-law standards.

C

The majority also protests that a contrary result to the one it reaches would interfere with the adoption of Indian children. This claim is the most perplexing of all. A central purpose of ICWA is to "promote the stability and security of Indian . . . families," 25 U.S.C. § 1902, in part by countering the trend of placing "an alarmingly high percentage of [Indian] children . . . in non-Indian foster and adoptive homes and institutions." § 1901(4). The Act accomplishes this goal by, first, protecting the familial bonds of Indian parents and children; and, second, establishing placement preferences should an adoption take place, see § 1915(a). ICWA does not interfere with the adoption of Indian children except to the extent that it attempts to avert the necessity of adoptive placement and makes adoptions of Indian children by non-Indian families less likely.

The majority may consider this scheme unwise. But no principle of construction licenses a court to interpret a statute with a view to averting the very consequences Congress expressly stated it was trying to bring about. . . .

The majority further claims that its reading is consistent with the "primary" purpose of the Act, which in the majority's view was to prevent the dissolution of "intact" Indian families. We may not, however, give effect only to congressional goals we designate "primary" while casting aside others classed as "secondary"; we must apply the entire statute Congress has written. While there are indications that central among Congress' concerns in enacting ICWA was the removal of Indian children from homes in which Indian parents or other guardians had custody of them, see, *e.g.*, §§ 1901(4), 1902, Congress also recognized that "there is no resource that is more vital to the continued existence and integrity of Indian tribes than their children," § 1901(3). As we observed in *Holyfield*, ICWA protects not only Indian parents' interests but also those of Indian tribes. See 490 U.S., at 34, 52. A tribe's interest in its next generation of citizens is adversely affected by the placement of Indian children in homes with no connection to the tribe, whether or not those children were initially in the custody of an Indian parent.

Moreover, the majority's focus on "intact" families, begs the question of what Congress set out to accomplish with ICWA. In an ideal world, perhaps all parents would be perfect. They would live up to their parental responsibilities by providing the fullest possible financial and emotional support to their children. They would never suffer mental health problems, lose their jobs, struggle with substance dependency, or encounter any of the other multitudinous personal crises that can make it difficult to meet these responsibilities. In an ideal world parents would never become estranged and leave their children caught in the middle. But we do not live in such a world. Even happy families do not always fit the custodial-parent mold for which the majority would reserve ICWA's substantive protections; unhappy families all too often do not. They are families nonetheless. Congress understood as much. ICWA's definitions of "parent" and "termination of parental rights" provided in § 1903 sweep broadly. They should be honored.

D

The majority does not rely on the theory pressed by petitioners and the guardian ad litem that the canon of constitutional avoidance compels the conclusion that ICWA is inapplicable here. It states instead that it finds the statute clear. But the majority nevertheless offers the suggestion that a contrary result would create an equal protection problem.

It is difficult to make sense of this suggestion in light of our precedents, which squarely hold that classifications based on Indian tribal membership are not impermissible racial classifications. See *United States v. Antelope*, 430 U.S. 641, 645–647 (1977); *Morton v. Mancari*, 417 U.S. 535, 553–554 (1974). The majority's repeated, analytically unnecessary references to the fact that Baby Girl is 3/256 Cherokee by ancestry do nothing to elucidate its intimation that the statute may violate the Equal Protection Clause as applied here. I see no ground for this Court to second-guess the membership requirements of federally recognized Indian tribes, which are independent political entities. See *Santa Clara Pueblo v. Martinez*, 436 U.S. 49, 72, n. 32 (1978). I am particularly averse to doing so when the Federal Government requires Indian tribes, as a prerequisite for official recognition, to make "descen[t] from a historical Indian tribe" a condition of membership. 25 CFR § 83.7(e) (2012).

The majority's treatment of this issue, in the end, does no more than create a lingering mood of disapprobation of the criteria for membership adopted by the Cherokee Nation that, in turn, make Baby Girl an "Indian child" under the statute. Its hints at lurking constitutional problems are, by its own account, irrelevant to its statutory analysis, and accordingly need not detain us any longer.

III

Because I would affirm the South Carolina Supreme Court on the ground that § 1912 bars the termination of Birth Father's parental rights, I would not reach the question of the applicability of the adoptive placement preferences of § 1915. I note, however, that the majority does not and cannot foreclose the possibility that on remand, Baby Girl's paternal grandparents or other members of the Cherokee Nation may formally petition for adoption of Baby Girl. If these parties do so, and if on remand Birth Father's parental rights are terminated so that an adoption becomes possible, they will then be entitled to consideration under the order of preference established in § 1915. The majority cannot rule prospectively that § 1915 would not apply to an adoption petition that has not yet been filed. Indeed, the statute applies "[i]n *any* adoptive placement of an Indian child under State law," 25 U.S.C. § 1915(a) (emphasis added), and contains no temporal qualifications. It would indeed be an odd result for this Court, in the name of the child's best interests, to purport to exclude from the proceedings possible custodians for Baby Girl, such as her paternal grandparents, who may have well-established relationships with her.

* * *

. . .

The majority casts Birth Father as responsible for the painful circumstances in this case, suggesting that he intervened "at the eleventh hour to override the mother's decision and the child's best interests[.]" I have no wish to minimize the trauma of removing a 27-month-old child from her adoptive family. It bears remembering, however, that Birth Father took action to assert his parental rights when Baby Girl was four months old, as soon as he learned of the impending adoption. As the South Carolina Supreme Court recognized, " '[h]ad the mandate of . . . ICWA been followed [in 2010], . . . much potential anguish might have been avoided[;] and in any case the law cannot be applied so as automatically to "reward those who obtain custody, whether lawfully or otherwise, and maintain it during any ensuing (and protracted) litigation." ' "

The majority's hollow literalism distorts the statute and ignores Congress' purpose in order to rectify a perceived wrong that, while heartbreaking at the time, was a correct application of federal law and that in any case cannot be undone. Baby Girl has now resided with her father for 18 months. However difficult it must have been for her to leave Adoptive Couple's home when she was just over 2 years old, it will be equally devastating now if, at the age of 3 1/2, she is again removed from her home and sent to live halfway across the country. Such a fate is not foreordained, of course. But it can be said with certainty that the anguish this case has caused will only be compounded by today's decision.

I believe that the South Carolina Supreme Court's judgment was correct, and I would affirm it. I respectfully dissent.

NOTES

1. After the U.S. Supreme Court's decision in the case, on July 17, 2013, the South Carolina Supreme Court, in a 3–2 ruling, decided that Baby Girl, whose name is Veronica, should be returned to Adoptive Couple, whose

names are Melanie and Matt Capobianco. According to a news story that appeared in the Cherokee Phoenix, the Capobiancos commented:

> We are thrilled that after 18 long months, our daughter finally will be coming home[.] . . . We look forward to seeing Veronica's smiling face in the coming days and will do everything in our power to make her homecoming as smooth as possible. We also want to thank everyone who has supported us throughout this ordeal. Our prayers have been answered.

Associated Press, *Court Orders 'Baby Girl' Returned to South Carolina Couple*, CHEROKEE PHOENIX (July 18, 2013), http://www.cherokeephoenix .org/Article/Index/7430. Dusten Brown, Veronica's biological father, and his family also released a statement to the press about the South Carolina Supreme Court's decision:

> We are outraged that the South Carolina Supreme Court would order the adoption of our child finalized without a proper hearing to determine what is in Veronica's best interests. This child has been back with her family for 19 months and to tear her away from us, the family she loves and the only family she knows or remembers, would be devastating to her. This is an Oklahoma child and her placement should not be considered by a court in South Carolina. We have contacted our U.S. Senator and encourage each of you to do the same, in order to help us keep Veronica in her home, which is a safe, loving and nurturing environment. We will never give up the fight to raise our daughter.

Press Release, Dusten Brown, Brown Family Reaction to South Carolina Supreme Court Order (July 18, 2013), http://www.cherokee.org/News/Stories/ BrownfamilyreactiontoSouthCarolinaSupremeCourtorder.aspx. The Cherokee Nation itself reacted to the South Carolina Supreme Court's ruling this way:

> We are outraged and saddened that the South Carolina Supreme Court would order the transfer of this child without a hearing to determine what is in her best interests, particularly in light of the fact that this very same court previously found "we cannot say that Baby Girl's best interests are not served by the grant of custody to Father, as Appellants have not presented evidence that Baby Girl would not be safe, loved, and cared for if raised by Father and his family."

Press Release, Cherokee Nation, Cherokee Nation Statement re: Baby Veronica (July 17, 2013), http://www.cherokee.org/News/Stories/CherokeeNation statementreBabyVeronica.aspx. For other developments in and related to the case, see Associated Press, *Court Orders 'Baby Girl' Returned to South Carolina Couple*, CHEROKEE PHOENIX (July 18, 2013), http://www.cherokee phoenix.org/Article/Index/7430; *see also* Josh Voorhees, *The Long, Complicated "Baby Veronica" Saga Comes to an Unsatisfying End*, SLATE MAGAZINE (July 17, 2013), http://www.slate.com/blogs/the_slatest/2013/ 07/17/adoptive_couple_vs_baby_girl_south_carolina_court_sends_baby_ veronica_back.html; Lyle Denniston, *"Baby Veronica" Adoption Allowed*, SCOTUSBLOG (July 17, 2013, 5:34 PM), http://www.scotusblog.com/?p=167

497; Lyle Denniston, *"Baby Veronica" Adoption Finalized*, SCOTUSBLOG (July 24, 2013, 4:22 PM), http://www.scotusblog.com/2013/07/baby-veronica-adoption-finalized; Michael Overall, *Dusten Brown Makes First Public Comments Since 'Baby Veronica' Custody Battle*, TULSA WORLD (May 15, 2015), http://www.tulsaworld.com/news/local/dusten-brown-issues-first-public-comments-since-baby-veronica-custody/article_b9da8f5f-7aa1-55d4-a960-39 b2fc2add05.html; *cf.* 25 C.F.R § 23 (2016); Suzette Brewer, *BIA Releases New ICWA Guidelines to Protect Native Families and Children*, INDIAN COUNTRY TODAY MEDIA NETWORK (Feb. 26, 2016), http://indiancountrytodaymedia network.com/2015/02/26/bia-releases-new-icwa-guidelines-protect-native-families-and-children-159392.

2. Does the majority opinion in *Adoptive Couple v. Baby Girl* afford adequate respect to the biological tie between Baby Girl and her father—or not enough? *See* Marcia Zug, *The Court Got Baby Veronica Wrong*, SLATE MAGAZINE (June 26, 2013), http://www.slate.com/articles/double_x/doublex/ 2013/06/baby_veronica_indian_adoption_case_the_supreme_court_got_it _wrong.html; *see also* Marcia A. Yablon-Zug, *Adoptive Couple v. Baby Girl: Two-and-a-Half Ways to Destroy Indian Law*, 111 MICH. L. REV. FIRST IMPRESSIONS 46 (2014), http://repository.law.umich.edu/mlr_fi/vol111/iss1/5. Also consider:

> You don't have to dig too deeply to uncover clues that explain the majority's holding. The opinion noted that, had the father not been Indian, the whole case wouldn't have arisen, because ordinary "best interests of the child" analysis the hallmark of family law would have given the child to her adoptive parents. Conservatives have never liked ICWA, with its special granting of rights to Indians on the basis of their tribal sovereignty and the associated whiff of racial discrimination. But equal protection wasn't the majority five's motivating factor. Rather, it was their embrace of the norms of parental adoption and a distaste for a law that prefers biological parents to adopted ones.

Noah Feldman, *The Momentous Supreme Court Ruling You Totally Missed*, BLOOMBERG.COM (June 27, 2013), https://www.bloomberg.com/view/articles/ 2013-06-27/the-momentous-supreme-court-ruling-you-totally-missed.

3. How much is the majority's holding driven by equal protection concerns along the lines of race? Earlier decisions by the Supreme Court "squarely" held "that classifications based on Indian tribal membership are not impermissible racial classifications." *Adoptive Couple v. Baby Girl*, 133 S.Ct. 2552, 2584 (2013) (Sotomayor, J., dissenting). Do the majority's "references to the fact that Baby Girl is 3/256 Cherokee by ancestry," *id.*, raise the specter that the Indian Child Welfare Act of 1978—if not interpreted as the majority opinion interprets it in *Adoptive Couple v. Baby Girl*—may be tantamount to a constitutionally illegitimate "one drop" or, more exactly, a "3/256's drop" rule?

SEXUAL ORIENTATION

Page 453, Unabridged (Page 318, Concise). Substitute the following case for the materials in the section.

Campaign for Southern Equality v. Miss. Dep't of Human Services

United States District Court, S.D. Mississippi, March 31, 2016.
175 F.Supp.3d 691.

■ DANIEL P. JORDAN, III, DISTRICT JUDGE.

ORDER

Plaintiffs seek a declaration that Mississippi Code section 93–17–3(5)—which prohibits adoption by married gay couples—violates the Due Process and Equal Protection Clauses of the United States Constitution. They named as defendants the Mississippi Department of Human Services ("DHS"), DHS's Executive Director, three chancery courts, nine chancellors from those three courts, and Mississippi's Governor and Attorney General.

Defendants have offered a tepid defense of the statute itself, focusing instead on Plaintiffs' right to sue them. They argue that even assuming section 93–17–3(5) is unconstitutional, Plaintiffs lack Article III standing and cannot overcome Eleventh Amendment immunity. The Governor, Attorney General, and Executive Director further contend that there is no injury because those Defendants either lack authority to enforce the ban or would not enforce it to impede an otherwise valid gay adoption. . . . [T]he Court finds that Plaintiffs have standing as to DHS's Executive Director but no other defendant.* And finding a justiciable claim, Plaintiffs' motion for preliminary injunction is granted.

I. Background and Procedural History

Mississippi Code section 93–17–3(5) states simply: "Adoption by couples of the same gender is prohibited." Four lesbian couples residing in Mississippi and two advocacy groups now challenge that statute under the Due Process and Equal Protection Clauses of the United States Constitution. Two of the couples seek a private adoption involving the biological child of one of the partners. The others desire adoption through Mississippi's foster-care system.

. . .

[I]II. Plaintiffs' Motion for Preliminary Injunction

"A preliminary injunction is an extraordinary remedy never awarded as of right." *Winter v. Nat. Res. Def. Council, Inc.*, 555 U.S. 7, 24

---

*   Eds.: The court's analysis of the jurisdictional questions is omitted.

(2008). To obtain this relief, Plaintiffs must demonstrate four familiar requirements:

> (1) [a] substantial likelihood of success on the merits; (2) [a] substantial threat that plaintiff[s] will suffer irreparable injury; (3) [that the] injury outweighs any harm the injunction might cause the defendant[s]; and (4) [that the] injunction is in the public interest.

Women's Med. Ctr. of Nw. Hous. v. Bell, 248 F.3d 411, 419 n. 15 (5th Cir. 2001).

A. Likelihood of Success on the Merits

Obergefell [*v. Hodges*, 570 U.S. ___, 135 S.Ct. 2584 (2015),] held that bans on gay marriage violate the due-process and equal-protection clauses. It is the equal-protection component of the opinion that is relevant in the present dispute over Mississippi's ban on gay adoptions. Under traditional equal-protection analysis, a law that does not "target[ ] a suspect class" or involve a fundamental right will be upheld, "so long as it bears a rational relation to some legitimate end." *Romer v. Evans*, 517 U.S. 620, 631 (1996). Conversely, "if a classification does target a suspect class or impact a fundamental right, it will be strictly scrutinized and upheld only if it is precisely tailored to further a compelling government interest." *Sonnier v. Quarterman*, 476 F.3d 349, 368 (5th Cir. 2007) (citation omitted).

In this case, Defendants argue that rational-basis review applies. But *Obergefell* made no reference to that or any other test in its equal-protection analysis. That omission must have been consciously made given the Chief Justice's full-throated dissent. 135 S.Ct. 2623 (Roberts, C.J., dissenting) ("Absent from this portion of the opinion, however, is anything resembling our usual framework for deciding equal protection cases. . . .").

While the majority's approach could cause confusion if applied in lower courts to future cases involving marriage-related benefits, it evidences the majority's intent for sweeping change. For example, the majority clearly holds that marriage itself is a fundamental right when addressing the due-process issue. *Id.* at 2602. In the equal-protection context, that would require strict scrutiny. But the opinion also addresses the benefits of marriage, noting that marriage and those varied rights associated with it are recognized as a "unified whole." *Id.* at 2600. And it further states that "the marriage laws enforced by the respondents are in essence unequal: same-sex couples are denied all the *benefits* afforded to opposite-sex couples *and* are barred from exercising a fundamental right." *Id.* at 2604 (emphasis added).

Of course the Court did not state whether these other benefits are fundamental rights or whether gays are a suspect class. Had the classification not been suspect and the benefits not fundamental, then rational-basis review would have followed. It did not. Instead, it seems clear the Court applied something greater than rational-basis review. Indeed, the majority never discusses the states' reasons for adopting their bans on gay marriage and never mentions the word "rational."

While it may be hard to discern a precise test, the Court extended its holding to marriage-related benefits—which includes the right to adopt. And it did so despite those who urged restraint while marriage-related-benefits cases worked their way through the lower courts. According to the majority, "Were the Court to stay its hand to allow slower, case-by-case determination of the required *availability of specific public benefits to same-sex couples, it still would deny gays and lesbians many rights and responsibilities intertwined with marriage.*" *Id.* at 2606 (emphasis added).

The full impact of that statement was not lost on the minority. Chief Justice Roberts first took issue with the majority's failure to "note with precision which laws petitioners have challenged." *Id.* at 2623 (Roberts, C.J., dissenting). He then criticized the majority for jumping the gun on marriage-related cases that might otherwise develop:

> Although [the majority] discuss[es] some of the ancillary legal benefits that accompany marriage, such as hospital visitation rights and recognition of spousal status on official documents, petitioners' lawsuits target the laws defining marriage generally rather than those allocating benefits specifically. . . .
> Of course, *those more selective claims will not arise now* that the Court has taken the drastic step of requiring every State to license and recognize marriages between same-sex couples.

Id. at 2623–24 (Roberts, C.J., dissenting) (emphasis added).

In sum, the majority opinion foreclosed litigation over laws interfering with the right to marry and "rights and responsibilities intertwined with marriage." *Id.* at 2606. It also seems highly unlikely that the same court that held a state cannot ban gay marriage because it would deny benefits—expressly including the right to adopt—would then conclude that married gay couples can be denied that very same benefit.

Obergefell obviously reflects conflicting judicial philosophies. While an understanding of those positions is necessary for this ruling, it is not this Court's place nor intent to criticize either approach. The majority of the United States Supreme Court dictates the law of the land, and lower courts are bound to follow it. In this case, that means that section 93–17–3(5) violates the Equal Protection Clause of the United States Constitution.

2. Irreparable Injury

"An injury is 'irreparable' only if it cannot be undone through monetary remedies." *Deerfield Med. Ctr. v. City of Deerfield Beach*, 661 F.2d 328, 338 (5th Cir. 1981); *see also Spiegel v. City of Hous.*, 636 F.2d 997 (5th Cir. 1981). Defendants contend that Plaintiffs' injury is not irreparable, in part because only an adoption decree will remedy

Plaintiffs' damages. Defs.' Mem. [21] at 19. But "[d]iscriminatory treatment at the hands of the government is an injury 'long recognized as judicially cognizable.'" *Tex. Cable & Telecomm. Ass'n v. Hudson*, 265 Fed.Appx. 210, 218 (5th Cir. 2008) (quoting *Heckler v. Mathews*, 465 U.S. 728, 738 (1984)). And while Plaintiffs must undergo the adoption process to fully remedy their injuries, the current law imposes an unconstitutional impediment that has caused stigmatic and more practical injuries. Plaintiffs addressed these concerns in their testimony and Amended Complaint, and Defendants have not demonstrated that they could be undone with a monetary award. The Court finds irreparable harm.

3. Balance of Harms

Plaintiffs have also met their burden regarding the balance of harms. DHS has taken the position, through its Director of the Division of Family and Children's Services, that it will not impede an otherwise valid gay adoption, so this ruling merely memorializes what DHS has promised.

4. Public Interest

"[I]t is always in the public interest to prevent the violation of a party's constitutional rights." *Awad v. Ziriax*, 670 F.3d 1111, 1132 (10th Cir. 2012) (cited with approval in *Jackson Women's Health Org. v. Currier*, 760 F.3d 448, 470 n. 9 (5th Cir. 2014)).

[IV]. Conclusion

. . .

The Executive Director of DHS is hereby preliminarily enjoined from enforcing Mississippi Code section 93–17–3(5).

POST-ADOPTION ISSUES

Page 464, Unabridged (Page 324, Concise). Add new subsection a. with the following case and note. Reletter the remaining sections under "Post-Adoption Issues."

a. CONSTITUTIONAL BACKGROUND: FULL FAITH AND CREDIT CLAUSE

V.L. v. E.L., et al.

Supreme Court of the United States, 2016.
577 U.S. ___, 136 S.Ct. 1017, 194 L.Ed.2d 92.

■ PER CURIAM.

A Georgia court entered a final judgment of adoption making petitioner V.L. a legal parent of the children that she and respondent E.L. had raised together from birth. V.L. and E.L. later separated while living in Alabama. V.L. asked the Alabama courts to enforce the Georgia judgment and grant her custody or visitation rights. The Alabama Supreme Court ruled against her, holding that the Full Faith and Credit Clause of the United States Constitution does not require the Alabama courts to respect the Georgia judgment. That judgment of the Alabama Supreme Court is now reversed by this summary disposition.

I

V.L. and E.L. are two women who were in a relationship from approximately 1995 until 2011. Through assisted reproductive technology, E.L. gave birth to a child named S.L. in 2002 and to twins named N.L. and H.L. in 2004. After the children were born, V.L. and E.L. raised them together as joint parents.

V.L. and E.L. eventually decided to give legal status to the relationship between V.L. and the children by having V.L. formally adopt them. To facilitate the adoption, the couple rented a house in Alpharetta, Georgia. V.L. then filed an adoption petition in the Superior Court of Fulton County, Georgia. E.L. also appeared in that proceeding. While not relinquishing her own parental rights, she gave her express consent to V.L.'s adoption of the children as a second parent. The Georgia court determined that V.L. had complied with the applicable requirements of Georgia law, and entered a final decree of adoption allowing V.L. to adopt the children and recognizing both V.L. and E.L. as their legal parents.

V.L. and E.L. ended their relationship in 2011, while living in Alabama, and V.L. moved out of the house that the couple had shared. V.L. later filed a petition in the Circuit Court of Jefferson County, Alabama, alleging that E.L. had denied her access to the children and interfered with her ability to exercise her parental rights. She asked the Alabama court to register the Georgia adoption judgment and award her some measure of custody or visitation rights. The matter was transferred to the Family Court of Jefferson County. That court entered an order awarding V.L. scheduled visitation with the children.

E.L. appealed the visitation order to the Alabama Court of Civil Appeals. She argued, among other points, that the Alabama courts should not recognize the Georgia judgment because the Georgia court lacked subject-matter jurisdiction to enter it. The Court of Civil Appeals rejected that argument. It held, however, that the Alabama family court had erred by failing to conduct an evidentiary hearing before awarding V.L. visitation rights, and so it remanded for the family court to conduct that hearing.

The Alabama Supreme Court reversed. It held that the Georgia court had no subject-matter jurisdiction under Georgia law to enter a judgment allowing V.L. to adopt the children while still recognizing E.L.'s parental rights. As a consequence, the Alabama Supreme Court held Alabama courts were not required to accord full faith and credit to the Georgia judgment.

II

The Constitution provides that "Full Faith and Credit shall be given in each State to the public Acts, Records, and judicial Proceedings of every other State." U.S. Const., Art. IV, § 1. That Clause requires each State to recognize and give effect to valid judgments rendered by the courts of its sister States. . . .

With respect to judgments, "the full faith and credit obligation is exacting." *Baker v. General Motors Corp.*, 522 U.S. 222, 233 (1998). "A final judgment in one State, if rendered by a court with adjudicatory authority over the subject matter and persons governed by the judgment, qualifies for recognition throughout the land." *Ibid.* A State may not disregard the judgment of a sister State because it disagrees with the reasoning underlying the judgment or deems it to be wrong on the merits. On the contrary, "the full faith and credit clause of the Constitution precludes any inquiry into the merits of the cause of action, the logic or consistency of the decision, or the validity of the legal principles on which the judgment is based." *Milliken v. Meyer*, 311 U.S. 457, 462 (1940).

A State is not required, however, to afford full faith and credit to a judgment rendered by a court that "did not have jurisdiction over the subject matter or the relevant parties." *Underwriters Nat. Assurance Co. v. North Carolina Life & Accident & Health Ins. Guaranty Assn.*, 455 U.S. 691, 705 (1982). "Consequently, before a court is bound by [a] judgment rendered in another State, it may inquire into the jurisdictional basis of the foreign court's decree." *Ibid.* That jurisdictional inquiry, however, is a limited one. "[I]f the judgment on its face appears to be a 'record of a court of general jurisdiction, such jurisdiction over the cause and the parties is to be presumed unless disproved by extrinsic evidence, or by the record itself.' " *Milliken, supra*, at 462 (quoting *Adam v. Saenger*, 303 U.S. 59, 62 (1938)).

Those principles resolve this case. Under Georgia law, as relevant here, "[t]he superior courts of the several counties shall have exclusive jurisdiction in all matters of adoption." Ga.Code Ann. § 19–8–2(a) (2015). That provision on its face gave the Georgia Superior Court subject-matter jurisdiction to hear and decide the adoption petition at issue here. The Superior Court resolved that matter by entering a final judgment that made V.L. the legal adoptive parent of the children. Whatever the merits of that judgment, it was within the statutory grant of jurisdiction over "all matters of adoption." *Ibid.* The Georgia court thus had the "adjudicatory authority over the subject matter" required to entitle its judgment to full faith and credit. *Baker, supra*, at 233.

The Alabama Supreme Court reached a different result by relying on Ga.Code Ann. § 19–8–5(a). That statute states (as relevant here) that "a child who has any living parent or guardian may be adopted by a third party . . . only if each such living parent and each such guardian has voluntarily and in writing surrendered all of his or her rights to such child." The Alabama Supreme Court concluded that this provision prohibited the Georgia Superior Court from allowing V.L. to adopt the children while also allowing E.L. to keep her existing parental rights. It further concluded that this provision went not to the merits but to the Georgia court's subject-matter jurisdiction. In reaching that crucial second conclusion, the Alabama Supreme Court seems to have relied solely on the fact that the right to adoption under Georgia law is purely statutory, and " '[t]he requirements of Georgia's adoptions statutes are mandatory and must be strictly construed in favor of the natural parents.' " App. to Pet. for Cert. 23a–24a (quoting *In re Marks*, 684 S.E.2d 364, 367 ([Ga. App.] 2009)).

That analysis is not consistent with this Court's controlling precedent. Where a judgment indicates on its face that it was rendered by a court of competent jurisdiction, such jurisdiction " 'is to be presumed unless disproved.' " *Milliken, supra*, at 462 (quoting *Adam, supra*, at 62). There is nothing here to rebut that presumption. The Georgia statute on which the Alabama Supreme Court relied, Ga.Code Ann. § 19–8–5(a), does not speak in jurisdictional terms; for instance, it does not say that a Georgia court "shall have jurisdiction to enter an adoption decree" only if each existing parent or guardian has surrendered his or her parental rights. Neither the Georgia Supreme Court nor any Georgia appellate court, moreover, has construed § 19–8–5(a) as jurisdictional. That construction would also be difficult to reconcile with Georgia law. Georgia recognizes that in general, subject-matter jurisdiction addresses "whether a court has jurisdiction to decide a particular class of cases," *Goodrum v. Goodrum*, 657 S.E.2d 192 ([Ga.] 2008), not whether a court should grant relief in any given case. Unlike § 19–8–2(a), which expressly gives Georgia superior courts "exclusive jurisdiction in all matters of adoption," § 19–8–5(a) does not speak to whether a court has the power to decide a general class of cases. It only provides a rule of decision to apply in determining if a particular adoption should be allowed.

Section 19–8–5(a) does not become jurisdictional just because it is " 'mandatory' " and " 'must be strictly construed.' " App. to Pet. for Cert. 23a–24a (quoting *Marks*, 684 S.E.2d, at 367). This Court "has long rejected the notion that all mandatory prescriptions, however emphatic, are properly typed jurisdictional." *Gonzalez v. Thaler*, 565 U.S. 134 (2012) (internal quotation marks and ellipsis omitted). Indeed, the Alabama Supreme Court's reasoning would give jurisdictional status to *every* requirement of the Georgia adoption statutes, since Georgia law indicates those requirements are all mandatory and must be strictly construed. *Marks*, 684 S.E.2d, at 367. That result would comport neither with Georgia law nor with common sense.

As Justice Holmes observed more than a century ago, "it sometimes may be difficult to decide whether certain words in a statute are directed to jurisdiction or to merits." *Fauntleroy v. Lum*, 210 U.S. 230, 234–235 (1908). In such cases, especially where the Full Faith and Credit Clause is concerned, a court must be "slow to read ambiguous words, as meaning to leave the judgment open to dispute, or as intended to do more than fix the rule by which the court should decide." *Id.*, at 235. That time-honored rule controls here. The Georgia judgment appears on its face to have been issued by a court with jurisdiction, and there is no established Georgia law to the contrary. It follows that the Alabama Supreme Court erred in refusing to grant that judgment full faith and credit.

The petition for writ of certiorari is granted. The judgment of the Alabama Supreme Court is reversed, and the case is remanded for further proceedings not inconsistent with this opinion.

It is so ordered.

NOTE

1.   Does it strike you as curious that the Supreme Court's *per curiam* opinion in this case, which follows in the wake of *Obergefell v. Hodges* (*supra*, p. 18), avoids any engagement with it? Is *Obergefell* wholly doctrinally irrelevant to the disposition of this case?

CHAPTER 5

THE NONTRADITIONAL FAMILY

A. UNMARRIED ADULTS

3. LEGAL DEVELOPMENTS

Page 512, Unabridged (Page 357, Concise). Insert the following case and notes at the end of the note following the ALI Principles of the Law of Family Dissolution.

Blumenthal v. Brewer

Supreme Court of Illinois, August 18, 2016.
69 N.E.3d 834.

■ JUSTICE KARMEIER delivered the judgment of the court, with opinion.

In this case we are called on to consider the continued viability and applicability of our decision in *Hewitt v. Hewitt*, 394 N.E.2d 1204 ([Ill.] 1979), which held that Illinois public policy, as set forth in this State's statutory prohibition against common-law marriage, precludes unmarried cohabitants from bringing claims against one another to enforce mutual property rights where the rights asserted are rooted in a marriage-like relationship between the parties.

The issue has arisen here in the context of an action brought by Dr. Jane E. Blumenthal for partition of the family home she shared and jointly owned with Judge Eileen M. Brewer. The couple had maintained a long-term, domestic relationship and raised a family together but had never married. Blumenthal sought partition of the residence when the relationship ended and she moved out.

. . .

ANALYSIS

. . .

Common-law marriages are invalid in Illinois and have been since the early part of the last century. The prohibition is statutory and unequivocal. Section 214 of the Marriage and Dissolution Act (750 ILCS 5/214 (West 2010)) expressly provides that "[c]ommon law marriages contracted in this State after June 30, 1905 are invalid."

. . .

At issue in *Hewitt* was whether public policy barred the granting of common-law relief to plaintiff Victoria Hewitt, who was in a cohabiting, marriage-like relationship with the defendant, Robert Hewitt. Victoria and Robert commenced their relationship in 1960, while they were attending college in Iowa. After Victoria became pregnant, Robert proclaimed to Victoria "that they were husband and wife and would live as such, no formal ceremony being necessary, and that he would 'share his life, his future, his earnings and his property' with her." The parties immediately began holding themselves out as a married couple. Relying on Robert's promises, Victoria began to assist in paying for Robert's education and establishing a dental practice, helping him earn more than $80,000 annually and accumulate large amounts of property, owned either jointly with Victoria or separately.

After several years together, the relationship became sour, and Victoria filed for divorce, which the circuit court dismissed because the parties were never married. Victoria filed an amended complaint that sought an equitable one-half share of the parties' assets, based upon theories of implied contract, constructive trust, and unjust enrichment, which resulted from their "family relationship." The circuit court dismissed the amended complaint, "finding that Illinois law and public policy require such claims to be based on a valid marriage."

The appellate court reversed[.] . . . The appellate court noted that the "single flaw" of Robert's and Victoria's relationship was the lack of a valid marriage. . . . Adopting the reasoning of the "widely publicized" case of *Marvin v. Marvin*, 557 P.2d 106 ([Ca.] 1976), the appellate court held that the amended complaint stated a cause of action on an express oral contract. . . .

On appeal to this court, we unanimously reversed the appellate court's decision. . . .

In our view, the legislature intended marriage to be the only legally protected family relationship under Illinois law, and permitting unmarried partners to enforce mutual property rights might "encourage formation of such relationships and weaken marriage as the foundation of our family-based society." [*Hewitt*, 394 N.E.2d 1204 at 1207.] . . . We reasoned that an opposite outcome of judicially recognizing mutual property rights between knowingly unmarried cohabitants—where the claim is based upon or intimately related to the cohabitation of the parties—would effectively reinstate common-law marriage and violate the public policy of this state since 1905, when the legislature abolished common-law marriage. [*Id.* at] 1204.

Notably, . . . we emphatically rejected the holding in *Marvin* on which the appellate court relied. In doing so, we found that provisions of the Marriage and Dissolution Act—retaining fault as grounds for dissolution of marriage and allowing an unmarried person to acquire the rights of a legal spouse only if he or she goes through a marriage ceremony and cohabits with another in the good-faith belief that he is validly married—indicated the public policy and the judgment of the legislature disfavoring private contractual alternatives to marriage or the grant of property rights to unmarried cohabitants. In rejecting Victoria's public policy arguments, this court recognized that cohabitation by the unmarried parties may not prevent them from forming valid contracts about independent matters, for which sexual relations do not form part of the consideration and do not closely resemble those arising from conventional marriages. However, that was not the type of claim Victoria brought; thus, her claim failed.

The facts of the present case are almost indistinguishable from *Hewitt*, except, in this case, the parties were in a same-sex relationship. . . .

. . .

When considering the property rights of unmarried cohabitants, our view of *Hewitt*'s holding has not changed. . . .

Because rejection of *Hewitt* is essential to her counterclaim, Brewer requests that we revisit the decision and overrule it. . . .

. . .

Since this court's decision in *Hewitt*, the General Assembly has enacted, repealed, and amended numerous family-related statutes. . . .

These post-*Hewitt* amendments demonstrate that the legislature knows how to alter family-related statutes and does not hesitate to do so when and if it believes public policy so requires. Nothing in these post-*Hewitt* changes, however, can be interpreted as evincing an intention by the legislature to change the public policy concerning the situation presently before this court. To the contrary, the claim that our legislature is moving toward granting additional property rights to unmarried cohabitants in derogation of the prohibition against common-law marriage is flatly contradicted by the undeniable fact that for almost four decades since *Hewitt*, and despite all of these numerous changes to other family-related statutes, the statutory prohibition against common-law marriage set forth in section 214 of the Marriage and Dissolution Act has remained completely untouched and unqualified. That is so even though this court in *Hewitt* explicitly deferred any policy change to the legislature.

. . . If this court were to recognize the legal status desired by Brewer, we would infringe on the duty of the legislature to set policy in the area of domestic relations. . . .

. . .

We also reject Brewer's argument that changes in law since *Hewitt* demonstrate that the "legislature no longer considers withholding protection from nonmarital families to be a legitimate means of advancing the state's interest in marriage." To the contrary, this court finds that the current legislative and judicial trend is to uphold the institution of marriage. Most notably, within the past year, the United States Supreme Court in *Obergefell v. Hodges*, 576 U.S. ___, ___, 135 S.Ct. 2584 (2015), held that same-sex couples cannot be denied the right to marry. In doing so, the Court found that "new insights [from the developments in the institution of marriage over the past centuries] have strengthened, not weakened, the institution of marriage." 135 S.Ct. at 2596. For the institution of marriage has been a keystone of our social order and "remains a building block of our national community." *Id.* at 2601. Accordingly, the Court invalidated any state legislation prohibiting same-sex marriage because excluding same-sex couples from marriage would be excluding them "from one of civilization's oldest institutions." *Id.* at 2608.

. . . [N]ow that the centrality of the marriage has been recognized as a fundamental right for all, it is perhaps more imperative than before that we leave it to the legislative branch to determine whether and under what circumstances a change in the public policy governing the rights of parties in nonmarital relationships is necessary.

. . .

. . . Brewer, the supporting *amici*, and the partial dissent cite to numerous cases from our sister state courts and other secondary sources that support Brewer's public policy arguments. . . . [I]t should be noted that these cases and secondary sources were written prior to, and therefore did not consider, the fundamental change the United States Supreme Court decision in *Obergefell* had on legal rights of same-sex partners.

Due Process and Equal Protection Claims

. . .

We disagree with Brewer's claim that *Hewitt*'s holding denies unmarried domestic partners the ability to bring common-law claims solely because they are in an intimate relationship with another. . . . *Hewitt*'s holding does not prevent or penalize unmarried partners from entering into intimate relationships. Rather, it acknowledges the legislative intent to provide certain rights and benefits to those who participate in the institution of marriage.

The State's interest in the creation, regulation, and dissolution of the marriage relationship is beyond question. . . . In enacting the Marriage and Dissolution Act (Pub. Act 80–923 (eff. Oct. 1, 1977) (codified at 750 ILCS 5/101 *et seq.* (West 2014))), the Illinois legislature has shown its rightful interest in defining and regulating domestic relationships.

Since marriage is a legal relationship that all individuals may or may not enter into, Illinois does not act irrationally or discriminatorily in refusing to grant benefits and protections under the Marriage and Dissolution Act to those who do not participate in the institution of marriage. As noted in *Hewitt* and the line of cases that follow its holding, unmarried individuals may make express or implied contracts with one another, and such contracts will be enforceable if they are not based on a relationship indistinguishable from marriage. . . . We, therefore, reject Brewer's claims.

. . .

■ CHIEF JUSTICE GARMAN and JUSTICES FREEMAN, THOMAS, and KILBRIDE concurred in the judgment and opinion.

. . .

■ JUSTICE THEIS, concurring in part and dissenting in part:

. . .

. . . In my view, there is good cause to overrule *Hewitt* [*v. Hewitt*, 394 N.E.2d 1204 ([Ill.] 1979)]. The court's decision in that case was clouded by an inappropriate and moralistic view of domestic partners who cohabit and founded upon legal principles that have changed significantly.

According to the majority, *Hewitt* "did no more than follow the statutory provision abolishing common-law marriage, which embodied the public policy of Illinois that individuals acting privately by themselves, without the involvement of the State, cannot create marriage-like benefits." In fact, *Hewitt* did much more. It etched into the Illinois Reports the arcane view that domestic partners who choose to cohabit, but not marry, are engaged in "illicit" or "meretricious" behavior at odds with foundational values of "our family-based society." *Hewitt*, 394 N.E.2d [at 1207]. "Meretricious" means "of or relating to a prostitute" (WEBSTER'S THIRD NEW INTERNATIONAL DICTIONARY 1413 (1986)), so this court labeled such people as prostitutes.

The majority's attempt to distance itself from *Hewitt*'s sweeping and near-defamatory statement is unconvincing. Though the majority assures that "this court does not share the same concern or characterization of domestic partners who cohabit, nor do we condone such comparisons[,]" its disavowal of *Hewitt* is literally subtextual, occurring only in a footnote.* Elsewhere, the majority borrows troubling language from that case. In *Hewitt*, the court stated that "the situation" between the parties was "not the kind of arm's length bargain envisioned by traditional contract principles, but an intimate arrangement of a fundamentally different kind." *Hewitt*, 394 N.E.2d [at 1209] . . . The majority cleverly tries to cloak the real meaning of *Hewitt*, but what makes these "arrangements" fundamentally different is the same for the *Hewitt* court and the majority.

To state uncategorically that "our view of *Hewitt*'s holding has not changed" and insist that "it remains good law" is to reaffirm an oddly myopic and moralistic view of cohabitation. . . . Insulating the institution of marriage from the "changing mores of our society" was the clear impetus for our holding in that case.

To begin its analysis, the *Hewitt* court discussed at length the so-called rule of illegality. The court quoted the first Restatement of Contracts, which stated, " 'A bargain in whole or in part for or in

---

* Eds.: In the footnote referred to by the dissent, omitted here, the majority insisted that *Hewitt*'s "core reasoning and ultimate holding of the case did not rely nor was dependent on the morality of cohabiting adults".

consideration of illicit sexual intercourse or of a promise thereof is illegal.'" *Hewitt*, 394 N.E.2d [at 1208] (quoting RESTATEMENT OF CONTRACTS § 589 (1932)).... The *Hewitt* court acknowledged that "cohabitation by the parties may not prevent them from forming valid contracts about independent matters, for which it is said the sexual relations do not form part of the consideration," but rejected the "real thrust" of the argument that the rule of illegality should be abandoned. [*Id.* at 1208]. The court decried "the naivete * * * involved in the assertion that there are involved in these relationships contracts separate and independent from the sexual activity, and the assumption that those contracts would have been entered into or would continue without that activity." *Id.* [at 1209.]

Hewitt's support for the rule of illegality has disappeared. . . .

. . . [C]ourts across the country no longer perceive a conflict between the public policies of protecting and encouraging marriage and discouraging any exchange of sexual activity for value and enforcing agreements between former cohabitants.

. . .

Obviously, Illinois's common-law marriage ban is still in effect. Parallel statutes are in effect across the country,[2] but only Georgia and Louisiana have rulings similar to *Hewitt*. See *Long v. Marino*, 441 S.E.2d 475 ([Ga. Ct. App.] 1994); *Schwegmann v. Schwegmann*, 441 So.2d 316 (La. Ct. App. 1983). Courts in a vast majority of the remaining states, as well as the District of Columbia, that have chosen not to recognize common-law marriages also have chosen to recognize claims between former domestic partners like Blumenthal and Brewer.

The recognition of claims between domestic partners has not revived the doctrine of common-law marriage in jurisdictions that have abolished it. That is, "the history of common law marriage in this country"—or, more precisely, its widespread prohibition—has not prevented courts across the country from allowing such claims to proceed.

In light of this wave of authority, the Restatement (Third) of Restitution and Unjust Enrichment now contains a new section that provides former domestic partners with an avenue "to prevent unjust enrichment upon the dissolution of the relationship." RESTATEMENT (THIRD) OF RESTITUTION AND UNJUST ENRICHMENT § 28(1) (2011).

Illinois is a clear outlier on this issue. *Hewitt* must be overruled because it is outmoded and out of touch with contemporary experience and opinions on cohabitation.

---

2 According to the National Conference of State Legislatures, only Alabama, Colorado, Iowa, Kansas, Montana, New Hampshire, Oklahoma, Rhode Island, South Carolina, and Texas still recognize common-law marriage. [h]ttp://www.ncsl.org/research/human-services/common-law-marriage.aspx (updated Aug. 4, 2014).

Additionally, *Hewitt* must be overruled because the legal landscape that formed the background for our decision has changed significantly [through case-law and statutory amendments]. . . .

. . .

The majority . . . refuses to give the[ ] statutory amendments much weight. According to the majority, "[t]hese post-*Hewitt* amendments demonstrate that the legislature knows how to alter family-related statutes and does not hesitate to do so when and if it believes public policy so requires." The implication is that, in light of the many statutory changes since *Hewitt*, the legislature's silence on the rights of cohabitants somehow indicates its rejection of claims like those brought by Brewer. I interpret that silence differently. Simply because the legislature has taken some action in the domestic relations arena does not mean that this court cannot act as well. The legislature is undoubtedly well equipped to declare public policy on domestic relations. Courts, however, are better equipped than the legislature to help parties divide joint assets using familiar legal and equitable rules.

For more than a century and a half, Illinois courts have adjudicated property disputes between family members. See, *e.g., Miller v. Miller*, 16 Ill. 296, 298–99 (1855). Generally, courts have held that, when people live together in a family setting, contributions between them are presumed gratuitous and not compensable absent an express or implied contract. See *In re Estate of Milborn*, 461 N.E.2d 1075 ([Ill. App. Ct.] 1984). Thus, seen in the light of established Illinois law, claims like Brewer's claim are nothing new.

More importantly, claims like Brewer's claim do not implicate the Marriage and Dissolution of Marriage Act and, thus, do not undermine the public policy of Illinois, as expressed in the prohibition of common-law marriage, that individuals themselves cannot create marriage-like benefits. Although the parties had what the majority terms a "marriage-like relationship", Brewer does not seek "marriage-like benefits or "marriage-like rights[.]" . . . . She simply asks to bring the same common-law claims available to other people. She should be allowed to do so. The fact that Brewer and Blumenthal were once domestic partners should be no impediment. Admittedly, such claims may be difficult to plead and prove, but that is a matter for the trial court.

Hewitt's flaws, both linguistic and legal, have become more apparent with time. Our holding there is a court-made rule that this court should overrule. I believe that count III of Brewer's amended complaint should be remanded for the trial court to determine whether she has pleaded a cognizable cause of action. For these reasons, I dissent.

■ JUSTICE BURKE joins in this partial concurrence, partial dissent.

NOTES

1. As Justice Theis's separate opinion in *Blumenthal v. Brewer* indicates, *Hewitt* and *Blumenthal* are "outliers." It is now common for states to allow unmarried cohabiting adults to contract about their property relations, even when the contracts clearly aim to mimic the legal consequences of marriage—so long as the contracts are not understood as an exchange of sexual services for money. *See, e.g.*, Lawrence W. Waggoner, *With Marriage on the Decline and Cohabitation on the Rise, What About Marital Rights for Unmarried Partners?*, 41 ACTEC L.J. 49, 65–73 (2015). Minnesota and Texas require such contracts to be in writing. *Id.* at 68. According to Justice Theis's *Blumenthal* opinion, Louisiana and Georgia are the other two states besides Illinois that refuse to recognize such contracts between unmarried cohabitants. *See also* Waggoner, *supra*, at 70.

2. What role does *Obergefell* play in the majority's opinion in *Blumenthal*? Do you agree with this line of reasoning? Should a State be able to exercise its power to regulate marriage by excluding unmarried cohabitants from contracting about their property relations when those agreements aim to recreate some of the legal consequences of marriage?

3. In her dissenting opinion, Justice Theis argues that *Hewitt's* origins in a moralistic devaluation of unmarried cohabitation cannot be separated from its, and hence *Blumenthal's*, holding. Do you agree?

CHAPTER 6

ASSISTED REPRODUCTIVE TECHNOLOGIES AND THE LAW

B. ASSISTED REPRODUCTIVE TECHNOLOGIES AND PARENTAGE

1. ART AND THE SPOUSE'S PARENTAL STATUS

Page 608, Unabridged (Page 433, Concise). Insert the following case and notes at the end of the notes following *Miller-Jenkins v. Miller-Jenkins.*

Pavan v. Smith

Supreme Court of the United States, June 26, 2017.
582 U.S. ___, 137 S.Ct. 2075, 194 L.Ed.2d ___.

■ PER CURIAM.

As this Court explained in *Obergefell v. Hodges*, 576 U.S. ___ (2015), the Constitution entitles same-sex couples to civil marriage "on the same terms and conditions as opposite-sex couples." *Id.*, at ___ (slip op., at 23). In the decision below, the Arkansas Supreme Court considered the effect of that holding on the State's rules governing the issuance of birth certificates. When a married woman gives birth in Arkansas, state law generally requires the name of the mother's male spouse to appear on the child's birth certificate—regardless of his biological relationship to the child. According to the court below, however, Arkansas need not extend that rule to similarly situated same-sex couples: The State need not, in other words, issue birth certificates including the female spouses of women who give birth in the State. Because that differential treatment infringes *Obergefell*'s commitment to provide same-sex couples "the constellation of benefits that the States have linked to marriage," *id.*, at ___ (slip op., at 17), we reverse the state court's judgment.

The petitioners here are two married same-sex couples who conceived children through anonymous sperm donation. Leigh and Jana Jacobs were married in Iowa in 2010, and Terrah and Marisa Pavan were married in New Hampshire in 2011. Leigh and Terrah each gave birth to a child in Arkansas in 2015. When it came time to secure birth certificates for the newborns, each couple filled out paperwork listing both spouses as parents—Leigh and Jana in one case, Terrah and Marisa in the other. Both times, however, the Arkansas Department of Health issued certificates bearing only the birth mother's name.

The department's decision rested on a provision of Arkansas law, Ark.Code § 20–18–401 (2014), that specifies which individuals will appear as parents on a child's state-issued birth certificate. "For the purposes of birth registration," that statute says, "the mother is deemed to be the woman who gives birth to the child." § 20–18–401(e). And "[i]f the mother was married at the time of either conception or birth," the statute instructs that "the name of [her] husband shall be entered on the certificate as the father of the child." § 20–18–401(f)(1). There are some limited exceptions to the latter rule[.] . . . But as all parties agree, the requirement that a married woman's husband appear on her child's birth certificate applies in cases where the couple conceived by means of artificial insemination with the help of an anonymous sperm donor.

The Jacobses and Pavans brought this suit in Arkansas state court against the director of the Arkansas Department of Health—seeking, among other things, a declaration that the State's birth-certificate law violates the Constitution. The trial court agreed, holding that the relevant portions of § 20–18–401 are inconsistent with *Obergefell* because they "categorically prohibi[t] every same-sex married couple . . . from enjoying the same spousal benefits which are available to every opposite-sex married couple." But a divided Arkansas Supreme Court reversed that judgment, concluding that the statute "pass[es] constitutional muster." 505 S.W.3d 169, 177 [(Ark. 2016)]. In that court's view, "the statute centers on the relationship of the biological mother and the biological father to the child, not on the marital relationship of husband and wife," and so it "does not run afoul of *Obergefell*." *Id.*, at 178. Two justices dissented from that view[.] . . .

The Arkansas Supreme Court's decision, we conclude, denied married same-sex couples access to the "constellation of benefits that the Stat[e] ha[s] linked to marriage." *Obergefell*, 576 U.S., at ___ (slip op., at 17). As already explained, when a married woman in Arkansas conceives a child by means of artificial insemination, the State will—indeed, *must*—list the name of her male spouse on the child's birth certificate. See § 20–18–401(f)(1). And yet state law, as interpreted by the court below, allows Arkansas officials in those very same circumstances to omit a married woman's female spouse from her child's birth certificate. See 505 S.W.3d, at 177–178. As a result, same-sex parents in Arkansas lack the same right as opposite-sex parents to be listed on a child's birth certificate, a document often used for important transactions like making medical decisions for a child or enrolling a child in school.

Obergefell proscribes such disparate treatment. As we explained there, a State may not "exclude same-sex couples from civil marriage on the same terms and conditions as opposite-sex couples." 576 U.S., at ___ (slip op., at 23). Indeed, in listing those terms and conditions—the "rights, benefits, and responsibilities" to which same-sex couples, no less than opposite-sex couples, must have access—we expressly identified "birth and death certificates." *Id.*, at ___ (slip op., at 17). That was no accident: Several of the plaintiffs in *Obergefell* challenged a State's refusal to recognize their same-sex spouses on their children's birth certificates. See *DeBoer v. Snyder*, 772 F.3d 388, 398–399 (C.A.6 2014). In considering those challenges, we held the relevant state laws unconstitutional to the extent they treated same-sex couples differently from opposite-sex couples. See [*Obergefell*,] 576 U.S., at ___ (slip op., at 23). That holding applies with equal force to § 20–18–401.

Echoing the court below, the State defends its birth-certificate law on the ground that being named on a child's birth certificate is not a benefit that attends marriage. Instead, the State insists, a birth certificate is simply a device for recording biological parentage— regardless of whether the child's parents are married. But Arkansas law makes birth certificates about more than just genetics. As already discussed, when an opposite-sex couple conceives a child by way of anonymous sperm donation—just as the petitioners did here—state law requires the placement of the birth mother's husband on the child's birth certificate. And that is so even though (as the State concedes) the husband "is definitively not the biological father" in those circumstances.[*] Arkansas has thus chosen to make its birth certificates more than a mere marker of biological relationships: The State uses those certificates to give married parents a form of legal recognition that is not available to unmarried parents. Having made that choice, Arkansas may not, consistent with *Obergefell*, deny married same-sex couples that recognition.

The petition for a writ of certiorari and the pending motions for leave to file briefs as *amici curiae* are granted. The judgment of the Arkansas Supreme Court is reversed, and the case is remanded for further proceedings not inconsistent with this opinion.

It is so ordered.

■ JUSTICE GORSUCH, with whom JUSTICE THOMAS and JUSTICE ALITO join, dissenting.

Summary reversal is usually reserved for cases where "the law is settled and stable, the facts are not in dispute, and the decision below is clearly in error." *Schweiker v. Hansen*, 450 U.S. 785, 791 (1981) (Marshall, J., dissenting). Respectfully, I don't believe this case meets that standard.

To be sure, *Obergefell* [*v. Hodges*, 576 U.S. ___ (2015),] addressed the question whether a State must recognize same-sex marriages. But nothing in *Obergefell* spoke (let alone clearly) to the question whether § 20–18–401 of the Arkansas Code, or a state supreme court decision

---

*   As the petitioners point out, other factual scenarios (beyond those present in this case) similarly show that the State's birth certificates are about more than genetic parentage. For example, when an Arkansas child is adopted, the State places the child's original birth certificate under seal and issues a new birth certificate—unidentifiable as an amended version—listing the child's (nonbiological) adoptive parents. See Ark.Code §§ 20–18–406(a)(1), (b) (2014); Ark. Admin. Code 007.12.1–5.5(a) (Apr.2016).

upholding it, must go. The statute in question establishes a set of rules designed to ensure that the biological parents of a child are listed on the child's birth certificate. Before the state supreme court, the State argued that rational reasons exist for a biology based birth registration regime, reasons that in no way offend *Obergefell*—like ensuring government officials can identify public health trends and helping individuals determine their biological lineage, citizenship, or susceptibility to genetic disorders. In an opinion that did not in any way seek to defy but rather earnestly engage *Obergefell*, the state supreme court agreed. And it is very hard to see what is wrong with this conclusion for, just as the state court recognized, nothing in *Obergefell* indicates that a birth registration regime based on biology, one no doubt with many analogues across the country and throughout history, offends the Constitution. To the contrary, to the extent they speak to the question at all, this Court's precedents suggest just the opposite conclusion. See, *e.g.*, *Michael H. v. Gerald D.*, 491 U.S. 110, 124–125 (1989); *Tuan Anh Nguyen v. INS*, 533 U.S. 53, 73 (2001). Neither does anything in today's opinion purport to identify any constitutional problem with a biology based birth registration regime. So whatever else we might do with this case, summary reversal would not exactly seem the obvious course.

What, then, is at work here? If there isn't a problem with a biology based birth registration regime, perhaps the concern lies in this particular regime's exceptions. For it turns out that Arkansas's general rule of registration based on biology does admit of certain more specific exceptions. Most importantly for our purposes, the State acknowledges that § 9–10–201 of the Arkansas Code controls how birth certificates are completed in cases of artificial insemination like the one before us. The State acknowledges, too, that this provision, written some time ago, indicates that the mother's husband generally shall be treated as the father—and in this way seemingly anticipates only opposite-sex marital unions.

But if the artificial insemination statute is the concern, it's still hard to see how summary reversal should follow for at least a few reasons. First, petitioners didn't actually challenge § 9–10–201 in their lawsuit. Instead, petitioners sought and the trial court granted relief eliminating the State's authority under § 20–18–401 to enforce a birth registration regime generally based on biology. On appeal, the state supreme court simply held that this overbroad remedy wasn't commanded by *Obergefell* or the Constitution. And, again, nothing in today's opinion for the Court identifies anything wrong, let alone clearly wrong, in that conclusion. Second, though petitioners' lawsuit didn't challenge § 9–10–201, the State has repeatedly conceded that the benefits afforded nonbiological parents under § 9–10–201 must be afforded equally to both same-sex and opposite-sex couples. So that in this particular case and all others of its kind, the State agrees, the female spouse of the birth mother must be listed on birth certificates too. Third, further proof still of the state of the law in Arkansas today is the fact that, when it comes to adoption (a situation not present in this case but another one in which Arkansas departs from biology based registration), the State tells us that adopting parents are eligible for placement on birth certificates without respect to sexual orientation.

Given all this, it seems far from clear what here warrants the strong medicine of summary reversal. Indeed, it is not even clear what the Court expects to happen on remand that hasn't happened already. The Court does not offer any remedial suggestion, and none leaps to mind. Perhaps the state supreme court could memorialize the State's concession on § 9–10–201, even though that law wasn't fairly challenged and such a chore is hardly the usual reward for seeking faithfully to apply, not evade, this Court's mandates.

I respectfully dissent.

NOTES

1.   Mark Joseph Stern maintains that Justice Gorsuch's dissent in *Pavan v. Smith* "has it exactly backwards" when it explains that "the [C]ourt should have dismissed the appeal because 'in this particular case and all others of its kind, the state agrees, the female spouse of the birth mother must be listed on birth certificates too.'" Mark Joseph Stern, *Gorsuch's First Anti-Gay Dissent Has a Huge Factual Error—and Terrible, Dishonest Logic*, SLATE.COM, June 28, 2017, http://www.slate.com/blogs/outward/2017/06/28/gorsuch_s_first_anti_gay_dissent_has_a_huge_factual_error.html. The reason Stern offers for this position is that "Arkansas explicitly refused to list 'the female spouse of the birth mother' on birth certificates. That's how the case wound up at the Supreme Court in the first place." *Id.* Shannon Minter, the legal director for the National Center for Lesbian Rights, who "represented the two couples who were denied the right to 'legally accurate' birth certificates" in *Pavan*, agrees: "'That's just completely wrong. . . . It is patently untrue. Arkansas refused to put the female spouse of a birth mother on the birth certificate. The Arkansas Supreme Court upheld the policy, and the state would not issue birth certificates that listed both same-sex parents.'" *Id.* Did Justice Gorsuch's opinion make "a huge factual error"? Is there any way to understand Justice Gorsuch's dissent on this score that might save it from this line of criticism?

2.   In some states, like Wisconsin, the husband of a woman who has conceived via artificial insemination with donor sperm can be added to the birth certificate as a father only if the couple has complied with the requirement that the insemination be supervised by a physician and the husband give written consent. *See* WIS. STAT. § 891.40 (2016), WIS. STAT. § 69.14(1)(G) (2016). If they have not complied with these requirements, no one is listed on the birth certificate as a father. Does equal treatment for same-sex couples in these circumstances mean that the female spouse of a woman who has not complied with these requirements will not be listed as a parent on the birth certificate either? *See Torres v. Rhoades*, 317 F.R.D. 85 (W.D.Wis. 2016).

2. ART AND THE UNMARRIED PARTNER'S PARENTAL STATUS

Page 612, Unabridged (Page 437, Concise). Delete Note 4. Insert the following cases and notes after the notes following *Charisma R. v. Kristina S.*

McGaw v. McGaw

Missouri Court of Appeals, Western District, 2015.
468 S.W.3d 435.

■ ALOK AHUJA, CHIEF JUDGE.

Appellant Melissa McGaw filed a motion in the circuit court "to determine parent-child relationship, custody, and visitation" with respect to two children to whom she is not biologically related. The children were born at a time when Melissa was involved in a romantic relationship with the children's biological mother, respondent Angela McGaw. Melissa's motion alleged that she had participated in Angela's decision to become pregnant with the children, and that Melissa had acted as a parent to the children, both before and after her relationship with Angela terminated. The circuit court dismissed Melissa's motion without prejudice for lack of standing and failure to state a claim upon which relief could be granted. Melissa appeals. We affirm.

Factual Background

Taking the facts Melissa alleged as true, she and Angela started dating in 1995, and began cohabiting the following year. In 1997, the couple had a commitment ceremony in Kansas City, and in 2000 Angela legally changed her last name to McGaw. The McGaws bought a home together, and by 2002 had decided to have children.

In 2004, Angela gave birth to twins in Kansas City. The children were conceived using sperm from an anonymous donor jointly selected by Melissa and Angela. From 2004 to 2007, Angela and Melissa raised the children together as co-parents.

Angela and Melissa separated in January 2007, and Melissa moved out of the shared household. Melissa alleged that she and Angela agreed to a schedule for visitation with the children, and a division of property, through mediation. Although separated, Melissa and Angela continued to share expenses for the children and to follow a visitation schedule until June 2013. At that time, Angela stopped allowing Melissa to see the children, and sent Melissa a text message stating that "[the children] will be living at my house until the parenting plan issue is resolved. I will call the police if you try to come and get them." Melissa has not seen the children since that time.

On March 7, 2014, Melissa filed a Motion to Determine Parent-Child Relationship in the Circuit Court of Jackson County, seeking "to determine parent-child relationship, custody, and visitation" pursuant to

§ 210.826. Angela filed an application for a change of venue to Clay County, which the court granted. In addition to her answer, Angela filed a motion to dismiss, arguing that Melissa had no biological relationship to the children and therefore lacked standing to assert her claims, and that Melissa's pleading failed to state a claim for relief.

In her suggestions in opposition to Angela's motion to dismiss, Melissa argued that she had standing under Missouri's version of the Uniform Parentage Act ("MoUPA"), §§ 210.817–210.854, and that she had standing under common-law equitable doctrines defining parentage.

A commissioner recommended that the action be dismissed on the basis that Melissa lacked standing and failed to state a claim upon which relief could be granted. A circuit court judge adopted the commissioner's findings and recommendations and entered judgment dismissing Melissa's motion without prejudice. This appeal follows.

Standard of Review

Our review of a dismissal for failure to state a claim or for lack of standing is de novo. . . .

Analysis

At the outset, we note that the McGaws' relationship began, and ended, at a time when the right of same-sex couples to marry had not been recognized in Missouri. Despite their inability to marry, Melissa's motion alleges that she and Angela took multiple steps to formalize their relationship: they participated in a commitment ceremony; changed Angela's surname to match Melissa's; purchased a home together; jointly chose to conceive the children and raised the children together; and entered an agreement to govern the termination of their relationship. Nevertheless, the fact remains that Melissa and Angela were never married, and . . . Melissa's claims must therefore be addressed under the legal rules applicable to unmarried couples (heterosexual or homosexual). Following the decision of the Supreme Court of the United States in *Obergefell v. Hodges*, 576 U.S. ___, 135 S.Ct. 2584 (2015) (which was decided after this case was submitted), couples like Melissa and Angela are now able to marry if they choose. We anticipate that in the wake of *Obergefell*, situations like this one, in which important issues involving children must be decided outside the established legal framework applicable to married couples, will occur less frequently.

On appeal, Melissa does not challenge the circuit court's dismissal of her claim to have her parentage established under the MoUPA. Instead, she argues that she stated a claim for relief based on theories of breach of contract, or under common-law equitable doctrines. For the reasons discussed below, we conclude that none of those theories justifies reversal.

I.

In her first Point, Melissa argues that the circuit court erred in dismissing her motion because she stated a claim to enforce a voluntary agreement between her and Angela governing visitation. Such agreements are enforceable, Melissa contends, so long as the trial court determines that the visitation agreement serves the best interests of the children.

. . . A petition for breach of contract requires a plaintiff to "allege (1) the existence of a contract or agreement and the terms of that agreement; (2) that plaintiff performed or tendered performance; (3) that defendant did not perform; and (4) that defendant's failure to perform caused plaintiff damage." *White* [*v. White*, 293 S.W.3d 1, 23 (Mo. Ct. App. 2009)].

Melissa's motion failed to adequately plead a breach of contract theory under these standards. Our decision in *White* involved circumstances strikingly similar to those in the present case[.] . . .

. . .

Melissa's . . . motion alleged that "[f]ormal mediation determined visitation" at the time of the parties' separation, and that "until June 13, 2013, Melissa and Angela followed a set visitation schedule, Melissa paid preschool tuition costs every other week and both parents shared equally in child-rearing activities and expenses." The motion is silent, however, as to the terms of the separation agreement as they relate to visitation, or as to what the parties' "set visitation schedule" was. Moreover, the prayer of Melissa's motion did not seek to enforce any pre-existing agreement between the parties. Instead, she asked the court to determine her parentage of the children, and to "award the parties joint legal custody of their minor children, specify rights of visitation to the Plaintiff, award child support and enter such other orders as the court may deem just and necessary and in the best interests of the minor children." The motion plainly asked the court to declare that she was a parent of the children, and based on that finding to order custody, visitation, and child support on terms the court deemed appropriate. The motion did not ask the court to enforce a preexisting agreement. In addition, as in *White*, Melissa did not argue that she had stated a claim for breach of an express agreement in opposition to Angela's motion to dismiss.

Like the plaintiff in *White*, Melissa has failed to adequately plead a claim for breach of contract; as in *White*, "[i]n these circumstances, we will not reverse the trial court's dismissal of the petition" based on a breach of contract argument. 293 S.W.3d at 23. Point I is denied.

II.

In her second Point, Melissa argues that she has standing to seek custody or visitation under the doctrines of in *loco parentis* or equitable parentage.

The in *loco parentis* and equitable parentage doctrines share certain characteristics with other equitable theories which have been developed to address the parental status of third parties who are not biological parents, but who have assumed significant parental roles in children's lives. *White* refused to adopt either the *in loco parentis* or equitable parentage theories in a case factually similar to this one. 293 S.W.3d at 14–16. As background, *White* quoted the Wisconsin Supreme Court's decision in *In re Custody of H.S.H.-K.*, 193 Wis.2d 649 (1995), for a commonly used definition of the circumstances in which recognition of parental status based on equitable considerations may be appropriate:

> (1) that the biological or adoptive parent consented to, and fostered, the petitioner's formation and establishment of a parent-like relationship with the child; (2) that the petitioner and the child lived together in the same household; (3) that the petitioner assumed obligations of parenthood by taking significant responsibility for the child's care, education and development, including contributing towards the child's support, without expectation of financial compensation; and (4) that the petitioner has been in a parental role for a length of time sufficient to have established with the child a bonded, dependent relationship parental in nature.

Id. at 435–36 (quoted in *White*, 293 S.W.3d at 14).

We turn now to the two specific theories Melissa invokes in her second Point.

A.

White addressed the *in loco parentis* doctrine under Missouri law. "*In loco parentis*" is a Latin phrase meaning "in the place of a parent." BLACK'S LAW DICTIONARY at 907 (10th ed. 2014).

In *White*, Leslea argued that "she and Michelle [stood] *in loco parentis* to each other's biological child because they jointly raised the children with each other's consent, and treated each child, and held each child out to the world, as the children of both of them." 293 S.W.3d at 15. Although older Missouri cases recognized an *in loco parentis* relationship between stepparents and stepchildren, which survived the termination of the stepparent's relationship with the biological parent, *White* held that this common-law doctrine had been "displaced" by § 453.400. The statute provides that an *in loco parentis* support obligation exists only "so long as the stepchild is living in the same home as the stepparent," § 453.400.1, and that the doctrine "shall not be construed as granting to a stepparent any right to the care and custody of a stepchild." § 453.400.4; see discussion in *White*, 293 S.W.3d at 15–16. Because it concluded that § 453.400 expressed the outer limits of the *in loco parentis* doctrine, *White* held that, whether or not Leslea stood *in loco parentis* to Michelle's child while she and Michelle lived together, "that status terminated when they separated and would deprive Leslea of standing to bring her action," and could not support a claim for child custody, visitation, or support. *Id.* at 16.

Melissa argues that *White* was incorrectly decided. Unless and until it is overruled by this Court or the Missouri Supreme Court, however, we are bound to follow *White* under principles of *stare decisis.*

. . .

Particularly given that Melissa has, and is presently pursuing, an alternative remedy to seek custody and/or visitation with the children (as discussed in § II.B below), we see no justification for re-examining *White's* treatment of the *in loco parentis* doctrine.

B.

Regarding her equitable parentage claim, Melissa contends that *White* "incorrectly determined that Missouri Supreme Court precedent does not allow individuals to seek custody or visitation as equitable parents," and should be overruled. To the contrary, we conclude that the justification for rejecting an equitable parentage argument is stronger today than at the time *White* was decided.

. . .

Although *White* may be equivocal concerning the viability of the equitable parentage theory under Missouri law, we read it as rejecting the application of that theory in circumstances strikingly similar to those involved in the present case. The equitable parentage theory was raised by the appellant in *White*, and would have justified reversal and a remand for further proceedings if the equitable parentage doctrine in fact established a viable cause of action under Missouri law. Despite the appellant's invocation of the equitable parentage doctrine, *White* affirmed the trial court's dismissal of the appellant's petition, in which she sought to be recognized as a (non-biological) parent of the child of her former romantic partner.

An additional consideration, arising subsequent to the *White* decision, likewise justifies rejection of the equitable parentage theory under Missouri law. As the Missouri Supreme Court noted in *Cotton* [*v. Wise*, 977 S.W.2d 263 (Mo. 1998) (en banc)] (in which the appellant asked the Court to recognize equitable parentage), "[u]nless a statutory scheme is plainly inadequate under circumstances where a court has a duty to act, there is no need for the court to exercise its equity powers to fashion a 'better' remedy than exists in the statutes." 977 S.W.2d at 264.

In this case, Melissa has an available statutory remedy under § 452.375.5(5) to assert her claims for child custody and visitation. Section 452.375.5(5) provides in relevant part that

> Prior to awarding the appropriate custody arrangement in the best interest of the child, the court shall consider each of the following as follows:
>
> * * *

(5) Third-party custody or visitation:

(a) When the court finds that each parent is unfit, unsuitable, or unable to be a custodian, or the welfare of the child requires, and it is in the best interests of the child, then custody, temporary custody or visitation may be awarded to any other person or persons deemed by the court to be suitable and able to provide an adequate and stable environment for the child. Before the court awards custody, temporary custody or visitation to a third person under this subdivision, the court shall make that person a party to the action;

(b) Under the provisions of this subsection, any person may petition the court to intervene as a party in interest at any time as provided by supreme court rule.

"[A] significant bonding familial custody relationship with third parties can constitute a special or extraordinary reason or circumstance rendering it in a child's best interest to award third-party custody" under § 452.375.5(5)(a)'s "welfare of the child" prong. *Flathers v. Flathers*, 948 S.W.2d 463, 470 (Mo. App. W.D. 1997).

[The Court's discussion of whether custody and visitation under § 452.375.5(5) can be claimed as an independent cause of action by a third party, and its conclusion that this is possible, are omitted.]

. . .

Recognizing that Melissa may pursue an independent action to assert custody and visitation rights over children to whom she is not biologically related does not run afoul of the Supreme Court of the United States' decision in *Troxel v. Granville*, 530 U.S. 57 (2000). . . .

Section 452.375(5), as interpreted by Missouri courts, is limited in important respects that were not present in *Troxel*. First, in contrast to the Washington statute at issue in *Troxel*, § 452.375.5(5) does not authorize third-party custody or visitation merely because a court determines that it would be in a child's best interests. Instead, the court must first find that the child's parents are "unfit, unsuitable, or unable to be a custodian," or that "the welfare of the child" requires third-party custody or visitation. "Courts should not treat the term 'welfare' used in section 452.375.5(5)(a) as the equivalent of 'best interests.' Rather, the two are separate and distinct findings, and 'welfare' implicates pleading and proving special or extraordinary circumstances that make third-party custody or visitation in the child's best interest." *T.W. ex rel. R.W. v. T.H.*, 393 S.W.3d 144, 150 (Mo. App. E.D. 2013).

Further, *Troxel* held that the Washington statute "contravened the traditional presumption that a fit parent will act in the best interest of his or her child." 530 U.S. at 69, 120 S.Ct. 2054. . . . Unlike the statute in *Troxel*,

[t]he Missouri statute carries a rebuttable presumption that custody should be with the parent. . . .

Young v. Young, 59 S.W.3d 23, 28 (Mo.App.W.D. 2001). . . .

. . .

Finally, Melissa is not simply "any third party that comes along." *White*, 293 S.W.3d at 18. In this case, as in [*In re T.Q.L.*, 386 S.W.3d 135 (Mo. 2012) (en banc)] and *D.S.K.* [*ex rel. J.J.K. v. D.L.T.*, 428 S.W.3d 655 (Mo. Ct. App. 2013)], a right of action under § 452.375.5(5) is being asserted by an individual who was specifically invited by a biological parent to act as a parent of the children at issue, and in fact acted in that capacity for an extended period of time. This is not a case where custody or visitation rights are being asserted by an extended-family member, a family friend, a paid caregiver, or some other third party who was never requested by the biological parents to function as a parent of the children. *Troxel* held that "the constitutionality of any standard for awarding visitation turns on the specific manner in which that standard is applied." 530 U.S. at 73. The fact that the party seeking custody or visitation in this case previously acted as a parent to the children, at the biological parent's request, further distinguishes this case from *Troxel*.

Under *T.Q.L.*, Melissa has the right to assert her claims for child custody and visitation in an independent proceeding under § 452.375.5(5); indeed, in her briefing Melissa states that she has filed a separate petition for third-party custody under the statute concurrently with this appeal. The availability of a cause of action under § 452.375.5(5) further diminishes the need to adopt the non-statutory equitable parentage doctrine in this case.

Point II is denied.

III.

In her third Point, Melissa claims that Angela is equitably estopped from denying the parent and child relationship between Melissa and the children. In support, Melissa cites several cases discussing equitable estoppel in the family law context. Melissa acknowledges in her brief that the *White* decision determined that equitable estoppel would not provide the standing needed to seek a declaration of maternity, custody, or support. 293 S.W.3d at 16–17. Melissa attempts to draw a distinction between her case and *White* by stating that she "has standing to bring a breach of contract action to enforce the custody agreement and, independently, she has standing to bring an action as an equitable parent or person *in loco parentis*." We have rejected, however, Melissa's . . . *in loco parentis* [and equitable parentage] arguments, and have concluded that she failed to adequately plead a claim to enforce any custody agreement. The grounds on which Melissa seeks to distinguish *White* are unpersuasive. Point III is denied.

Conclusion

We affirm the judgment of the circuit court, which dismissed without prejudice appellant Melissa McGaw's Motion to Determine Parent-Child Relationship.

. . .

■ ROBERT M. CLAYTON III, SPECIAL JUDGE, concurring, in part, and dissenting, in part.

I concur with the part of the majority opinion concluding that Plaintiff has a right to pursue an independent action under section 452.375.5(5)(a) RSMo Supp. 2011 for custody and visitation of children born during her relationship with Defendant, but I would grant Plaintiff's request and remand this case for a full hearing on the merits. However, in light of the United States Supreme Court's decision in *Obergefell v. Hodges*, 576 U.S. ___, 135 S.Ct. 2584 (2015), I believe this matter should be transferred to the Missouri Supreme Court to determine whether, under the circumstances of this case, the above-referenced statutory scheme is "plainly inadequate," in accordance with *Cotton v. Wise*, 977 S.W.2d 263, 264 (Mo. 1998) [(en banc)], demonstrating a need for the court to exercise its equity powers.

I.   DISCUSSION

. . .

B. Section 452.375.5(5)(a) and an Independent Action for Custody and Visitation

In 2012, the Missouri Supreme Court issued its opinion in *In re T.Q.L.*, 386 S.W.3d 135 (Mo. 2012) [(en banc)], declaring that section 452.375.5(5)(a) RSMo Supp. 20112 could be pleaded as an independent action for custody and visitation. This case best represents the current state of the law in parentage, custody, and visitation cases where the parties never married and one party is not a biological parent of the child; however, it does not involve parentage, custody, or visitation questions of same-sex couples. . . .

. . .

Here, like in *T.Q.L.*, there has been no marriage between the parties, and Plaintiff, a party who is not a biological parent, alleges she acted as the children's parent by taking an active role in their lives, and she has filed an action to determine parentage, custody, and visitation. Therefore, I agree with the majority that "[u]nder *T.Q.L.*, [Plaintiff] has the right to assert her claims for child custody and visitation in an independent proceeding under section 452.375.5(5)[(a)]." It is important to note that such an independent proceeding initiated by Plaintiff or a similarly-situated plaintiff could clearly survive a motion to dismiss if there are allegations of unfitness as there were in *T.Q.L.* Alternatively, and less clearly, while *T.Q.L.*'s interpretation of section 452.375.5(5)(a) also allows for an independent proceeding for third-party custody and visitation in situations where "the welfare of the child requires," the petition in *T.Q.L.* did not assert any specific factual basis to support these terms, aside from the facts supporting the claim of "unfitness," and the Supreme Court's analysis focused on the facts supporting the "unfitness" prong. *T.Q.L.*, 386 S.W.3d at 137–40. Other than vague, conclusory allegations mirroring the language of the statute, which any third-party could make, potentially violating *Troxel v. Granville*, 530 U.S. 57 (2000), it is unclear what facts would need to be alleged for an independent action to stand under "the welfare of the child required" prong of section 452.375.5(5)(a).

While there are a limited number of cases defining the preceding italicized language of section 452.375.5(5)(a), "the welfare of the child requires," none have addressed the language in the context of an independent proceeding or as it applies to same-sex couples. Without specific statutory direction from the legislature, courts will continue to face difficult factual circumstances involving the parent-child relationship using these six words. It is the children of same-sex couples who will be most severely affected by being limited in their opportunity to maintain bonds with a party who is not a biological parent but who has, as was alleged in this case, "functionally behaved as the children's second parent." *See Matter of Alison D. v. Virginia M.*, 572 N.E.2d 27 (N.Y. 1991) (Kaye, J., dissenting) (indicating that when statutes are silent with respect to the rights of parties who are not biological or adoptive parents, the impact "falls hardest on the children [born into families with a gay or lesbian parent], limiting their opportunity to maintain bonds that may be crucial to their development").

Because the majority opinion is the first case to suggest the applicability of section 452.375.5(5)(a) under the unique factual circumstances as in this case, I would grant Plaintiff's request to remand. Remand would permit a full hearing on the merits and the potential of full briefing and arguments on fundamental, constitutional rights, which arose from *Obergefell* after this case was dismissed by the trial court.

C. Equitable-Parent Doctrine

Related to the impact of the unsettled law regarding the rights and remedies available to those persons involved in same-sex relationships is Plaintiff's argument that this Court should adopt what this author will refer to as "an equitable-parent doctrine." An equitable-parent doctrine, which has been set forth and adopted by a majority of the Wisconsin Supreme Court in a case involving a same-sex couple, provides a circuit court has equitable power to determine that a party has a parent-like relationship with a child and that a significant triggering event may justify court intervention in the child's relationship with a biological or adoptive parent. *In re Custody of H.S.H.-K.*, 533 N.W.2d 419, 420–21, 435–38 ([Wis.] 1995). Pursuant to an equitable-parent doctrine:

> To demonstrate the existence of the petitioner's parent-like relationship with the child, the petitioner must prove four

elements: (1) that the biological or adoptive parent consented to, and fostered, the petitioner's formation and establishment of a parent-like relationship with the child; (2) that the petitioner and the child lived together in the same household; (3) that the petitioner assumed obligations of parenthood by taking significant responsibility for the child's care, education and development, including contributing towards the child's support, without expectation of financial compensation; and (4) that the petitioner has been in a parental role for a length of time sufficient to have established with the child a bonded, dependent relationship parental in nature.

To establish a significant triggering event justifying state intervention in the child's relationship with a biological or adoptive parent, the petitioner must prove that this parent has interfered substantially with the petitioner's parent-like relationship with the child, and that the petitioner sought court ordered visitation within a reasonable time after the parent's interference.

Id. at 435–36. In addition, if those elements are sufficiently alleged and proven, a court must then determine whether visitation is in the best interests of the child.

Thus far, no Missouri case has adopted an equitable-parent doctrine. *See White v. White*, 293 S.W.3d 1, 15, 15 n.8 (Mo. App. W.D. 2009). As correctly noted by the majority, the current state of the law in Missouri, including *White*, *Cotton*, and *T.Q.L.*, justifies the rejection of an equitable-parent doctrine. In *Cotton*, the Missouri Supreme Court held the trial court erred in using a theory of equitable parentage because "[u]nless a statutory scheme is plainly inadequate under circumstances where a court has a duty to act, there is no need for the court to exercise its equity powers to fashion a 'better' remedy that exists in the statutes." 977 S.W.2d at 263–66, 264. In other words, *Cotton* could be read to indicate that Missouri courts should not adopt an equitable-parent doctrine if there is an adequate statutory scheme in place. As indicated in Section B, section 452.375.5(5)(a) may constitute an adequate statutory scheme which allows Plaintiff to assert her claims for child custody and visitation in an independent proceeding.

However, in light of the decision in *Obergefell*, in which the United States Supreme Court held same-sex couples have the constitutional, fundamental right to marry, 135 S.Ct. at 2599, it is unclear which statutory schemes can be deemed adequate or "plainly inadequate" as they relate to parentage, child custody, and visitation of children born to same-sex couples, whether married or not. Post-*Obergefell*, it is unclear whether state law adequately addresses these issues in Missouri's Uniform Parentage Act, sections 210.817 to 210.852 RSMo, or other areas of the law in Chapter 452 involving Dissolution of Marriage, not to mention the third-party custody and visitation statute section

452.375.5(5)(a) mentioned herein. While *Obergefell* addresses the right to marry, it also pronounced that "choices concerning contraception, family relationships, procreation, and childrearing" are protected by the Constitution and that " '[t]he right to marry, establish a home and bring up children is a central part of the liberty protected by the Due Process Clause.' " 135 S.Ct. at 2599, 2600 (quoting *Zablocki v. Redhail*, 434 U.S. 374, 384 (1978)) (internal quotations omitted).

The most appropriate manner of addressing these issues is with legislative action to provide the statutory direction for courts to tackle these highly sensitive and emotional cases. A legislatively-enacted statutory scheme would provide the most comprehensive path for courts to follow. However, in the absence of legislative guidance, it may be appropriate for Missouri courts to adopt an equitable-parent doctrine when a party to a same-sex marriage or attempted same-sex marriage seeks custody or visitation. Cf. *Cotton*, 977 S.W.2d at 264, 265. Unfortunately, "[t]he problem with a court-fashioned 'equitable parent' doctrine is that the court has to improvise . . . substantive standards and procedural rules about when legal custody may be modified[.] . . . " *Id.* at 265.

Because this case was filed, briefed, and argued at the trial court and at the appellate court, all prior to the decision in *Obergefell*, which establishes a related, fundamental right, I believe transfer is most appropriate for the parties to address these issues and for the Missouri Supreme Court to determine whether the current law is "plainly inadequate" in accordance with *Cotton*.

II. CONCLUSION

Based on the foregoing, I concur with the part of the majority opinion concluding that Plaintiff has a right to pursue an independent action under section 452.375.5(5)(a) for custody and visitation of the children born during her relationship with Defendant, but I would grant Plaintiff's request and remand this case for a full hearing on the merits. However, in light of *Obergefell*, I believe this matter should be transferred to the Missouri Supreme Court to determine whether the above-referenced statutory scheme is "plainly inadequate" under *Cotton*, 977 S.W.2d at 264.

NOTES

1.   Do you think the holding in *McGaw* is a victory for same-sex couples in Missouri or not? Why might it not be?

2.   Do you agree with the dissent that, after *Obergefell*, a statute with a limited ground for recognizing parentage for the unmarried, non-biologically related, same-sex partner may raise constitutional issues? If so, what are they?

Conover v. Conover

Court of Appeals of Maryland, As Corrected September 30, 2016.
141 A.3d 31.

■ ADKINS, J.

. . . This appeal arises out of a divorce between a lesbian couple, and involves a dispute over one spouse's right of access to a child conceived by artificial insemination and born before the couple was married. Petitioner calls upon us to revisit the concept of *de facto* parenthood and our previous decision in *Janice M. v. Margaret K.*, 948 A.2d 73 ([Md.] 2008).

FACTS AND LEGAL PROCEEDINGS

Michelle and Brittany Conover began a relationship in July 2002. The parties discussed having a child and agreed that Brittany would be artificially inseminated from an anonymous donor. . . . The child was conceived in 2009. The couple gave birth to a son, Jaxon William Lee Eckel Conover ("Jaxon"), in April 2010. The birth certificate listed Brittany as Jaxon's mother, but no one was identified as the father. The parties married in the District of Columbia in September 2010 when Jaxon was about six months old.

In September 2011, Michelle and Brittany separated. From the date of separation until July 2012, Michelle visited Jaxon and had overnight and weekend access. At some point in July 2012, Brittany prevented Michelle from continuing to visit Jaxon. In February 2013, Brittany filed a Complaint for Absolute Divorce, stating that there were no children shared by the couple from the marriage. Michelle filed an Answer later that month in which she requested visitation rights with respect to Jaxon. In March 2013, Michelle filed a Counter-Complaint for Absolute Divorce, in which she repeated her request for visitation rights. Michelle did not request custody.

In April 2013, the parties appeared at a hearing in the Circuit Court for Washington County to determine Michelle's standing to seek access to Jaxon. . . .

. . .

Although the Circuit Court stated that Michelle was Jaxon's *de facto* parent, it relied on *Janice M. v. Margaret*, 948 A.2d 73 ([Md.] 2008), in concluding that *de facto* parent status was not recognized in Maryland.

Next, the court found that Michelle did not have "third party" standing to contest custody or visitation. . . .

After the divorce was granted, Michelle timely appealed the Circuit Court's order on visitation to the Court of Special Appeals. The Court of Special Appeals affirmed in a reported decision. *Conover v. Conover*, 120 A.3d 874 ([Md. Ct. Spec. App.] 2015). . . .

We granted Michelle's Petition for Writ of Certiorari presenting the following . . . question[ ] for review:

> (1)   Should Maryland reconsider *Janice M. v. Margaret K.* and recognize the doctrine of *de facto* parenthood?
>
> . . .

We hold that *de facto* parenthood is a viable means to establish standing to contest custody or visitation and thus answer yes to the first question . . .

. . . Whether we should reconsider *Janice M.* and recognize the doctrine of *de facto* parenthood is a legal question, and so we review the Circuit Court's decision without deference.

DISCUSSION

. . . [W]e recognized in *McDermott v. Dougherty*, 869 A.2d 751 ([Md.] 2005), that the rights of parents to custody of their children are generally superior to those of anyone else:

> Where the dispute is between a fit parent and a private third party, however, both parties do not begin on equal footing in respect to rights to "care, custody, and control" of the children. The parent is asserting a fundamental constitutional right. The third party is not.

We have thus held that a third party seeking custody or visitation must first show unfitness of the natural parents or that extraordinary circumstances exist before a trial court could apply the best interests of the child standard. *McDermott*, 869 A.2d 751[, 754]; see *Koshko v. Haining*, 921 A.2d 171 ([Md.] 2007).

Janice M. v. Margaret K.

In *Janice M.*, we considered whether Maryland recognized *de facto* parenthood and if so, whether a *de facto* parent seeking custody or visitation had to show parental unfitness or exceptional circumstances before a trial court could apply the best interests of the child standard. . . .

. . .

But what exactly is *de facto* parenthood? The Court in *Janice M.* explained that the phrase "*de facto* parent" is "used generally to describe a party who claims custody or visitation rights based upon the party's relationship, in fact, with a non-biological, non-adopted child." 948 A.2d [at 84]. In that case, two women, Janice and Margaret, were involved in a same-sex relationship for approximately 18 years, but were not married [as same-sex marriage was not allowed in Maryland at the time]. After Janice's attempts to become pregnant by use of *in vitro* fertilization failed, Janice, but not Margaret, adopted a child. A few years after the adoption, the couple separated. After they separated, Margaret filed a complaint in the Circuit Court for Baltimore County seeking custody, or in the alternative, visitation.

Relying on *S.F. v. M.D.*, [751 A.2d 9 (Md. Ct. Spec. App. 2000)], the Circuit Court concluded that Margaret was entitled to visitation because she was a *de facto* parent and that a *de facto* parent is not required to show unfitness of the biological parent or exceptional circumstances. [*Janice M.*,] 948 A.2d [at 77–8]. The Court of Special Appeals affirmed. *See Janice M. v. Margaret K.*, 910 A.2d 1145 ([Md. Ct. Spec. App.] 2006). *Certiorari* was granted, and this Court overruled the intermediate court's eight-year-old decision in *S.F.*, holding *de facto* parent status was not a recognized legal status in Maryland. In rejecting the *S.F.* holding, the Court refused to distinguish *de facto* parents from other third parties and asserted that *de facto* parents seeking access rights must first show parental unfitness or exceptional circumstances before a trial court can apply the best interests of the child standard[.]. . .

. . .

Grounds for Decision in Janice M.

The *Janice M.* Court relied heavily on *McDermott* and *Koshko* to support its rejection of *de facto* parenthood and determination that persons meeting this status must nonetheless show parental unfitness or exceptional circumstances before a trial court can apply the best interests of the child standard.

As Judge Raker pointed out in her dissenting opinion [in *Janice M.*], *McDermott* and *Koshko* "dealt with the rights of pure third parties, and not those of *de facto* parents." *Janice M.*, 948 A.2d [at 99–100] (Raker, J. dissenting). In *McDermott*, which involved maternal grandparents seeking custody in litigation against the child's father, the Court distinguished "pure third parties" from those persons who are in a parental role. Specifically, the court differentiated "pure third parties" from psychological parents. The Court defined the phrase "psychological parents" as "third parties who have, in effect, become parents." [*Janice M.*, 948 A.2d at 99–100.] The term "psychological parent" is closely related to the "*de facto* parent" label in that these designations are used to describe persons who have assumed a parental role. 869 A.2d 751.

The Court then made clear that *McDermott* was a "pure third-party case" before it proceeded to analyze other pure third-party cases. . . .

Likewise, *Koshko* involved grandparents seeking visitation, who did not claim to be *de facto* parents. The Court in *Koshko* simply extended our holding in *McDermott*—that parental unfitness and exceptional circumstances are threshold considerations in third party custody determinations—to visitation disputes. But neither *McDermott* nor *Koshko* justified this Court's decision in *Janice M.* What the Court failed to identify was any rationale for eliminating consideration of the parent-like relationship that the plaintiff sought to protect. It seemingly ignored the bond that the child develops with a *de facto* parent.

Troxel v. Granville

The *Janice M.* Court relied in part on the United States Supreme Court's decision in *Troxel v. Granville*, 530 U.S. 57 (2000), indicating that it also undermined the intermediate appellate court's decision in *S.F.* In *Troxel*, the U.S. Supreme Court addressed an appeal from a petition to obtain visitation rights filed by the grandparents of two minor children pursuant to a Washington State visitation statute. . . . The high court determined that the state trial court's visitation order in favor of the grandparents was an unconstitutional infringement on the parent's "fundamental right to make decisions concerning the care, custody, and control" of her children under the Fourteenth Amendment's Due Process Clause. *Id.* at 72.

Troxel was an extremely narrow decision. . . .

As many courts immediately recognized, *Troxel* did not denote the end of third party visitation. . . .

In her *Janice M.* dissent, Judge Raker rightly emphasized that courts "have continued to recognize the *de facto* parenthood concept post-*Troxel*." 948 A.2d [at 97] (Raker, J., dissenting). Put simply, numerous courts have declined to treat *Troxel* as a bar to recognizing *de facto* parenthood or other designations used to describe third parties who have assumed a parental role. [citations omitted]. Indeed, no case has interpreted *Troxel* as inconsistent with parental status for nonbiological parents except Maryland. Treatment by these other courts helps to demonstrate the error made by the *Janice M.* Court in reasoning that *Troxel* undermined *S.F.* and the recognition of *de facto* parenthood.

The Wisconsin Rule—In re Custody of H.S.H.-K.

Before *Janice M.*, the intermediate appellate court's recognition of *de facto* status in *S.F.* was consistent with *McDermott*, *Koshko*, and *Troxel* because the test it used to determine *de facto* parenthood was narrowly tailored to avoid infringing upon the parental autonomy of a legal parent. The Court of Special Appeals borrowed a four-factor test enunciated by the Wisconsin Supreme Court in its seminal decision in *H.S.H.-K.*, 533 N.W.2d at 421. Under this test, a third-party seeking *de facto* parent status bears the burden of proving the following when petitioning for access to a minor child:

> (1) that the biological or adoptive parent consented to, and fostered, the petitioner's formation and establishment of a parent-like relationship with the child;

> (2) that the petitioner and the child lived together in the same household;

> (3) that the petitioner assumed obligations of parenthood by taking significant responsibility for the child's care, education and development, including contributing towards the child's support, without expectation of financial compensation; and

(4) that the petitioner has been in a parental role for a length of time sufficient to have established with the child a bonded, dependent relationship parental in nature.

H.S.H.-K., 533 N.W.2d at 435–36. As other courts adopting this test have recognized, these factors set forth a high bar for establishing *de facto* parent status, which cannot be achieved without knowing participation by the biological parent. . . . Under this strict test, a concern that recognition of *de facto* parenthood would interfere with the relationship between legal parents and their children is largely eliminated. We thus adopt the multi-part test first articulated by the Wisconsin Supreme Court in *H.S.H.-K.*

The *de facto* parent doctrine does not contravene the principle that legal parents have a fundamental right to direct and govern the care, custody, and control of their children because a legal parent does not have a right to voluntarily cultivate their child's parental-type relationship with a third party and then seek to extinguish it. As the South Carolina Supreme Court explained in *Marquez*, 656 S.E.2d at 744:

> [T]he first factor [in the *H.S.H.-K.* test] is critical because it makes the biological or adoptive parent a participant in the creation of the psychological parent's relationship with the child. This factor recognizes that when a legal parent invites a third party into a child's life, and that invitation alters a child's life by essentially providing him with another parent, the legal parent's rights to unilaterally sever that relationship are necessarily reduced.

The *H.S.H.-K.* standard for determining *de facto* parenthood is therefore consistent with the Supreme Court's reaffirmation in *Troxel*, 530 U.S. at 66, of "the fundamental right of parents to make decisions concerning the care, custody, and control of their children," as well as with *McDermott* and *Koshko*. . . .

. . .

In *Monroe* [*v. Monroe*, 621 A.2d 898 (Md. 1993),] a putative father sought custody of a child as a third party before learning from blood tests that he was not the biological father of the child. 621 A.2d 898. In discussing whether exceptional circumstances existed to rebut the presumption that the child's best interests were served by remaining with her biological mother, we concluded that "[w]hat is important, rather, is the relationship that exists between the child and each of the parties." 621 A.2d [at 906]. We further asserted that protection of a child's relationship with a non-biological parent is justified "when the relationship is developed in the context of a family unit and is fostered, facilitated and, for most of the child's life, encouraged by the biological parent." *Id*. . . .

Our previous recognition of the importance—for legal purposes—of a psychological bond between a child and non-parent confirms the notion that *de facto* parenthood is distinct from pure third party status. The *Monroe* Court's emphasis on bonding and psychological dependence reflects the longstanding judicial recognition in Maryland (and elsewhere) that children need good relationships with parental figures and they need them to be stable. The *Janice M.* Court's rejection of *de facto* parent as a status sufficient for standing in child access cases contravenes this universally accepted concept. . . .

Janice M. Has Been Undermined By Subsequent Events

The anemic grounds for the *Janice M.* decision are not the only reason we recognize the doctrine of *de facto* parenthood. Additionally, the passage of time and evolving events have rendered *Janice M.* obsolete. . . . Maryland's recognition of same-sex marriage in 2012—Civil Marriage Protection Act, Ch. 2, 2012 Md. Laws 9—undermines the precedential value of *Janice M.* Our state's recognition of same-sex marriage illustrates the greater acceptance of gays and lesbians in the family unit in society.

But gays and lesbians are particularly "ill-served by rigid definitions of parenthood." Nancy D. Polikoff, *This Child Does Have Two Mothers: Redefining Parenthood to Meet the Needs of Children in Lesbian-Mother and Other Nontraditional Families*, 78 GEO. L.J. 459, 464 (1990). As Polikoff explained, when gay or lesbian relationships end, at least one member "will find itself in a court system ill-prepared to recognize its existence and to formulate rules to resolve its disputes. . . . [t]he contestants stand as a parent and a nonparent, a legal status inconsistent with their functional status." *See id.* at 463. Thus, the General Assembly's according greater rights to same-sex couples when it recognized same-sex marriage in 2012 further undermines the value of adhering to *Janice M.*, a precedent which can be considered "archaic" because it fails to effectively address problems typical of divorce by same-sex married couples. The same problems exist even when an unmarried same-sex couple separates.

In addition, a majority of states, either by judicial decision or statute, now recognize *de facto* parent status or a similar concept. *See* Nancy D. Polikoff, *From Third Parties to Parents: The Case of Lesbian Couples and Their Children*, 77 LAW & CONTEMP. PROBS. 195, 208 (2014). Indeed, the Washington Supreme Court identified a "modern common law trend of recognizing the status of *de facto* parents" as early as 2005. *Parentage of L.B.*, 122 P.3d at 176 n. 24. A diverse array of jurisdictions, from Alaska to West Virginia, constitute this majority. In some states, legislation was enacted authorizing standing for a de facto parent to sue for either custody or visitation.

Additionally, family law scholarship and the academic literature have also endorsed the notion that a functional relationship—as well as biology or legal status—can be used to define parenthood.

The American Law Institute ("ALI") has recommended expanding the definition of parenthood to include *de facto* parents and includes a *de facto* parent as one of the parties with standing to bring an action for the determination of custody, subject to the best interests of the child analysis. ALI, PRINCIPLES OF THE LAW OF FAMILY DISSOLUTION: ANALYSIS AND RECOMMENDATIONS §§ 2.03, 2.04 (2003) (adopted May 16, 2000). Additionally, many commentators have espoused the concept of *de facto* parenthood in examining the inadequacies of recognizing only legal parenthood.

In short, *Janice M.* now deviates sharply from the decisional and statutory law of other jurisdictions. The weight of authority outside Maryland reinforces our decision to overturn *Janice M.* and recognize *de facto* parenthood.

Maryland Statutory Law

Importantly, Maryland statutory law is silent when it comes to *de facto* parenthood. At oral argument, Brittany maintained that we should not overrule *Janice M.* because *de facto* parent status should be left to the General Assembly. We disagree. The General Assembly has granted equity courts jurisdiction over the "custody or guardianship of a child." Md. Code (1984, 2012 Repl. Vol.), Family Law ("FL") Article § 1–201(b)(5). . . .

Other jurisdictions in recognizing *de facto* status have also cast aside the contention that recognition of such status should be left to the legislative branch where the relevant statutes were silent on *de facto* parenthood. . . . This reasoning is in accord with other state high courts that have recognized de facto parenthood.

Although several state courts have refused to adopt *de facto* parent status on the grounds that such decisions should be left to the legislature, we find this reasoning inapt because Maryland's statutory scheme in the area of family law is not as comprehensive as such states. Indeed, Maryland statutory law on child custody and visitation illustrates that "statutes often fail to contemplate all potential scenarios which may arise in the ever changing and evolving notion of familial relations." *Parentage of L.B.*, 122 P.3d at 176.

Maryland does not have statutory factors for courts to consider in determining whether a party's access to a child is in that child's best interests. *See* FL §§ 9–101–9–108. Rather than looking to codified rules, the factors courts consider in making a "best interests determination" are found in case law. . . .

For these reasons, we reject Brittany's contention that an equity court's ability to consider *de facto* parent status in fashioning relief pertaining to the custody or guardianship of a child lies solely within the province of the General Assembly.

Conclusion

We overrule *Janice M.* because it is "clearly wrong" and has been undermined by the passage of time. In light of our differentiation in *McDermott*, 869 A.2d 751, between "pure third parties" and those persons who are in a parental role, we now make explicit that *de facto* parents are distinct from other third parties. We hold that *de facto* parents have standing to contest custody or visitation and need not show parental unfitness or exceptional circumstances before a trial court can apply a best interests of the child analysis. The best interests of the child standard has been "firmly entrenched in Maryland and is deemed to be of transcendent importance." *Ross* [*v. Hoffman*], 372 A.2d 582[, 585 (Md. 1977)]. With this holding we fortify the best interests standard by allowing judicial consideration of the benefits a child gains when there is consistency in the child's close, nurturing relationships.

We do so carefully, adopting the multi-part test first articulated by the Wisconsin Supreme Court in *H.S.H.-K.* This test accommodates, we think, the dissonance between what is in the best interest of a child and a parent's right to direct and govern the care, custody, and control of their children.

We reverse the Court of Special Appeals, and direct that court to remand this case to the Circuit Court for determination of whether, applying the *H.S.H.-K.* standards, Michelle should be considered a *de facto* parent, and conduct further proceedings consistent with this opinion.

. . .

■ Concurring opinion by GREENE, J.

I agree with the Majority's conclusion that *de facto* parent status should be recognized in Maryland. In that regard, we are correct to recognize that this status exists, and to overrule *Janice M. v. Margaret K.*, 948 A.2d 73 ([Md.] 2008). In addition, I agree with the test enunciated in *In re Custody of H.S.H.-K.*, [533 N.W.2d 419, 421 (Wis. 1995)] and *V.C. v. M.J.B.* [748 A.2d 539, 548–50 (N.J. 2000)]. Likewise, I agree with the Majority's decision in this case to adopt and apply this test in order to establish *de facto* parentage. I disagree, however, that a person who qualifies as a *de facto* parent is not required, *per se*, to establish exceptional circumstances. Consistent with our case law, the burden was on Michelle Conover to demonstrate exceptional circumstances to justify the need for a best interest analysis. I agree that *de facto* parentage is a relevant factor but it is not the only factor for the court to consider in reaching the ultimate decision to grant child access.

In my view, *de facto* parent status can best be described as a subset of exceptional circumstances. The fact that another person has a psychological bond with the child, a bond that was fostered by the legal parent, is but one relevant factor that would warrant a finding of an exceptional circumstance, and could overcome the presumption in favor of the legal or adoptive parent to control access to the child.

Other probative factors would include:

[(a)] the length of time the child has been away from [either] the biological [and or adoptive] parent, [(b)] the age of the child when care was assumed by the [*de facto* or biological parent], [(c)] the possible emotional effect on the child [resulting from] a change of custody [or visitation], [(d)] [any] period of time which elapsed before the [*de facto* or legal] parent sought to reclaim [access to] the child, [(e)] the nature and strength of the ties between the child and the [*de facto* parent], [(f)] the intensity and genuineness of the [respective] parent's desire to have the child [for the purposes of visitation or custody], [(g)] the stability and certainty as to the child's future in the custody of [or having access to] the [*de facto*] parent.

See Ross, 372 A.2d at 593.

The existence of a *de facto* parent status, the fact that a child has a close emotional bond with the *de facto* parent and that it would be in the best interest of the child to maintain that bond, are questions for the trial judge to resolve. Thus, the trial court would decide ultimately the existence of exceptional circumstances and whether the *de facto* parent's access to a child is in that child's best interest. In its determination of the best interest of the child, the trial judge would be in the best position to consider all of the relevant factors.

For the above reasons, I concur in the judgment of the Court.

■ Concurring Opinion by WATTS, J., which BATTAGLIA, J., joins.

Respectfully, I concur. Although I agree with the Majority in the recognition of *de facto* parenthood in Maryland, in my view, the Majority, in adopting the four-factor test set forth by the Supreme Court of Wisconsin in *In re Custody of H.S.H-K.* [533 N.W.2d 419, 421 (Wis. 1995)], adopts a standard that is too broad and that could have a negative impact on children in Maryland.

By adopting the four-factor test set forth in *H.S.H.-K.*, the Majority holds that, under the first factor, when seeking *de facto* parent status, the third party must show "that the biological or adoptive parent consented to, and fostered, the [third party]'s formation and establishment of a parent-like relationship with the child[.]" In other words, the Majority holds that only one parent is needed to consent to and foster a parent-like relationship with the would-be *de facto* parent. This will work in cases such as this one, where a second biological or adoptive parent does not exist, *i.e.*, where there is only one existing parent. Where there are two existing parents, however, permitting a single parent to consent to and foster a *de facto* parent relationship could result in a second existing parent having no knowledge that a *de facto* parent, *i.e.*, a third parent, is created. Such situations may result in a child having three parents vying for custody and visitation, and being overburdened by the demands of multiple parents. Today, many children are not living in a classic nuclear family. Families include not only same-sex married parents—in which one parent had a child before marriage—but also separated or divorced parents who conceived children during a marriage, as well as two parents who have never married. The Majority has written broadly a solution for *de facto* parents that will serve couples well under circumstances similar to the parties in this case, where there is only one biological or adoptive parent. The majority opinion, however, will have greater consequences in cases for children with two existing parents because a *de facto* parent request may occur without the knowledge or consent of the second existing parent. Children who already have difficulty with visitation schedules, or experience custody issues pertaining to two parents, will not be served well by the creation of a test that does not account for the second existing parent's knowledge and consent.

. . .

Imagining the untenable situation of a child who is parented by two adults one of whom, without the knowledge or consent of the second already existing parent, creates a *de facto* parentship [sic], I cannot agree with simply adopting the four-factor test without additional limits and safeguards. Even creating a standby guardianship in Maryland has traditionally required the consent of both parents. . . .

. . .

Further, during the 2010 and 2015 legislative sessions, the General Assembly failed to pass *de facto* parent bills which were similarly or more narrowly constructed than the holding of the majority opinion. . . . [The judge discusses various details of the failed bills.]

The proposed bills from 2010 and 2015 demonstrate that there are a number of details that necessarily must accompany any decision to recognize *de facto* parenthood in Maryland—from what burden of proof an individual bears to how an action for *de facto* parentship should be pled and what criteria an individual must satisfy to be declared a *de facto* parent. . . .

To fill the obvious void left by the majority opinion, I would offer the following guidance. In every instance in which a trial court is confronted with a request for *de facto* parentship, the trial court should ascertain whether there are one or two existing biological or adoptive parents. In the case of two existing parents, the trial court should require that the second parent have notice of the *de facto* parent request and ascertain whether the second parent consents to the *de facto* parent relationship. In satisfaction of the first prong of the *H.S.H.-K.* test, an action for *de facto* parenthood may be initiated only by an existing parent or a would-be *de facto* parent by the filing of a verified complaint attesting to the consent of the establishment of *de facto* parent status. The trial court should find by clear and convincing evidence that the parent has established:

(1) that the biological or adoptive parent consented to, and fostered, the petitioner's formation and establishment of a parent-like relationship with the child, and in the event of two existing biological or adoptive parents, that both parents consented to the establishment of a *de facto* parentship;

(2) that the petitioner and the child lived together in the same household;

(3) that the petitioner assumed obligations of parenthood by taking significant responsibility for the child's care, education and development, including contributing towards the child's support, without expectation of financial compensation; and

(4) that the petitioner has been in a parental role for a length of time sufficient to have established with the child a bonded, dependent relationship parental in nature.

See H.S.H.-K., 533 N.W.2d at 435–36. The trial court should be required to issue a written opinion explaining the reasons for granting or denying the request.

. . . In addition to lacking important procedural safeguards, the majority opinion does citizens, and particularly the children, of Maryland a disservice by not including additional protections to ensure that children and families are not overburdened by the custody and visitation demands of multiple parents, and by not including the limitation that, in circumstances where there are two existing parents, both parents need to have notice of, and the opportunity to consent to, the *de facto* parentship of a third party.

For the above reasons, respectfully, I concur.

NOTES

1. The *Conover v. Conover* Court focused on an unmarried partner's parental status despite the fact that the Conovers were married, because the child was born prior to the marriage. In *McGaw*, the court refused to award the legal status of parent to the partner performing the functional role of a parent, relying instead on the already existing doctrine of "exceptional circumstances" to create a possible doctrinal pathway for third-party custody and visitation. What is the difference with what the court is doing in *Conover*? Is it important?

2. The New York State Court of Appeals also has recently reversed its rule that a partner who is not related to a child biologically or via adoption does not have standing to seek custody and visitation. The longstanding rule found in *Alison D. v. Virginia M.*, 572 N.E.2d 27 (N.Y. 1991), was reversed in *Brooke S.B. v. Elizabeth A.C.C.*, 61 N.E.3d 488 (N.Y. 2016). In *Brooke S.B.*, the court noted that the *Alison D.* rule has had a harsh effect on the children of same-sex couples. The partners of biological parents would sometimes find themselves liable for child support, as in *Shondel J. v. Mark D.*, 853 N.E.2d 610 (N.Y. 2006), but without standing to seek custody or visitation. Importantly, the *Brooke S.B.* court focused on the fact that in the case at hand the partners had entered into a pre-conception agreement to conceive and raise the child as co-parents. It explicitly refused to address cases where the parent-like relationship between a partner and a child developed after conception, noting that whether a partner without a pre-conception agreement can establish standing was a "matter left for another day, upon a different record." *Brooke S.B.*, 61 N.E.3d 488 at 501. The court explicitly considered the *Conover* functional test of de facto parenthood and declined to adopt it. *Id.* A further extension of these principles is found in *Dawn M. v. Michael M.*, 47 N.Y.S.3d 898 (Sup. Ct. 2017) (on page 181 of this Supplement).

3.   Professor Douglas NeJaime has identified a total of thirty states as having some possible path towards recognition of parenthood for unmarried, non-biological parents. *See* Douglas NeJaime, *The Nature of Parenthood*, 126 YALE L.J. 2260, 2370 (2017). Most of these states have created a path to parenthood via case law without relying on a statutory basis. Three states have statutes that make explicit reference to *de facto* parents, while courts in five states have created a path for unmarried non-biological parents by expansively interpreting their existing parentage statutes. *Id.*

CHAPTER 8

CUSTODY

Page 1001, Unabridged. Insert new section I, and change current section I to section J. Page 655, Concise. Insert new section H, and change current section H to section I.

"TRI-PARENTING"

Dawn M. v. Michael M.

Supreme Court of New York, Suffolk County, March 8, 2017.
47 N.Y.S.3d 898.

■ H. PATRICK LEIS III, JUDGE.

OPINION OF THE COURT

It is

ORDERED that plaintiff is granted shared custody of J.M.; it is further

ORDERED that plaintiff is granted visitation with J.M. every Wednesday for dinner, a week-long school recess and two weeks out of the summer as delineated in this decision and judgment.

In this matter, plaintiff Dawn M., who is the non-biological, non-adoptive parent, asks the court to grant her "tri-custody" of defendant husband Michael M.'s 10-year-old biological son J.M.[1] After denying defendant's motion for summary judgment, this court ordered a trial to determine custody and visitation rights of the parties regarding J.M.

The facts at trial established the following:

Plaintiff and defendant were married on July 9, 1994. After being unsuccessful at attempts to have a child, the parties went to a fertility doctor. The plaintiff was artificially inseminated with defendant's sperm and conceived a child. Unfortunately, that child was miscarried at 10 weeks gestation.

In April of 2001, plaintiff met Audria G. and they became close friends. Audria and her boyfriend moved into an apartment downstairs from plaintiff and defendant. When Audria's boyfriend moved out, Audria moved upstairs with plaintiff and defendant. Sometime in 2004, the relationship between plaintiff, defendant and Audria changed and the three began to engage in intimate relations.

---

[1] This decision determines only plaintiff's custody and parenting time. All other issues including child support have been settled by stipulation between the parties dated June 15, 2015.

181

As time went on, Audria, plaintiff and defendant began to consider themselves a "family" and decided to have a child together. The parties and Audria went to the fertility doctor previously utilized by plaintiff and defendant with the hope that Audria could be artificially inseminated with defendant's sperm. The fertility doctor, however, refused to artificially inseminate Audria because she was not married to defendant. Thereafter, the parties and Audria decided they would try to conceive a child naturally by defendant and Audria engaging in unprotected sexual relations. The credible evidence establishes that it was agreed, before a child was conceived, that plaintiff, Audria and defendant would all raise the child together as parents.

Audria became pregnant and J.M. was born on January 25, 2007. The evidence establishes that plaintiff's medical insurance was used to cover Audria's pregnancy and delivery, and that plaintiff accompanied Audria to most of her doctor appointments. For more than 18 months after J.M.'s birth, defendant, plaintiff and Audria continued to live together. Audria and plaintiff shared duties as J.M.'s mother including taking turns getting up during the night to feed J.M. and taking him to doctor visits.

As time went on, however, the relationship between defendant and plaintiff became strained. In October of 2008, Audria and plaintiff moved out of the marital residence with J.M. A divorce action was commenced by plaintiff against defendant in 2011. Plaintiff testified credibly that after the divorce action was commenced, defendant no longer considered her to be J.M.'s parent. Prior to this divorce, a custody case was commenced by defendant against Audria. Defendant and Audria settled their custody proceeding by agreeing to joint custody; residential custody with Audria and liberal visitation accorded to defendant.[3] The plaintiff still resides with Audria and J.M., and sees J.M. on a daily basis. She testified that she brought this action to assure continued visitation and to secure custody rights for J.M. because she fears that without court-ordered visitation and shared custody, her ability to remain in J.M.'s life would be solely dependent upon obtaining the consent of either Audria or the defendant.

The court finds plaintiff's love for J.M. evident from her actions, testimony and demeanor on the stand. Indeed, during her testimony, plaintiff beamed whenever she spoke of J.M., including her earliest involvement in his life during Audria's pregnancy. The court finds credible the testimony of Audria and plaintiff that J.M. was raised with two mothers and that he continues to the present day to call both "mommy." The court does not find credible defendant's claim that he called plaintiff by her first name and never referred to her as "mommy" in front of J.M. The court finds that in all respects, during the first 18 months of J.M.'s life when defendant, plaintiff and Audria all lived

---

[3]   There is no written parenting schedule.

together, and thereafter, plaintiff acted as a joint mother with Audria and that they all taught the child that he has two mothers. In fact, the credible evidence establishes that when J.M. had an ear operation at age two, the defendant told the nurse that both plaintiff and Audria were J.M.'s mother so that both could be with him in the recovery room.

Moreover, the in camera interview conducted by the court with J.M. clearly establishes that J.M. considers both plaintiff and Audria his mothers. When asked to distinguish them, he refers to Audria as "mommy with the orange truck" and to plaintiff as "mommy with the grey truck."[4] He makes no distinction based on biology. J.M. is a well adjusted 10-year-old boy who loves his father and his two mothers. He knows nothing about this action. He has no idea that his father opposes tri-custody and court-ordered visitation with plaintiff. The in camera with J.M. leaves no doubt that J.M. considers both plaintiff and Audria to be equal "mommies" and that he would be devastated if he were not able to see plaintiff. The interview with J.M. also clearly shows that he enjoys his present living situation and would not want it altered in any way.

Although not a biological parent or an adoptive parent, plaintiff argues that she has been allowed to act as J.M.'s mother by both Audria and defendant. She has always lived with J.M. and J.M. has known plaintiff as his mom since his birth. Plaintiff asserts that the best interest of J.M. dictates that she be given shared legal custody of J.M. and visitation with him. J.M.'s biological mother Audria strongly agrees. Plaintiff argues, along with the child's attorney, that defendant should be estopped from opposing this application because he has created and fostered this situation by voluntarily agreeing, before the child was conceived, to raise him with three parents. And, further, that the defendant has acted consistent with this agreement by allowing the child to understand that he has two mothers.

Pursuant to Domestic Relations Law § 70, a parent may apply to the court for custody based solely upon what is for the best interest of the child, and what will promote his welfare and happiness. Domestic Relations Law § 240 also requires that in any proceeding for divorce, the court "shall enter a custody order having regard to the circumstances of the case and of the respective parties and to the best interests of the child. . . ." The Court of Appeals in *Brooke S.B.* [*v. Elizabeth A.C.C.*] stressed that its decision only addressed the ability of a person who was not a biological or adoptive parent to establish standing as a parent to petition for custody and visitation, and that the ultimate determination of whether to grant those rights rests in the sound discretion of trial courts in determining the best interests of the child (61 N.E.3d 488[, 500–01] (N.Y. 2016)]).[6]

---

[4] Referring to the color of the vehicle each mother drives.

[6] Under *Brooke S.B. v. Elizabeth A.C.C.*, 61 N.E.3d 488[, 490] [(N.Y. 2016)], . . . the law states "where a partner shows by clear and convincing evidence that the parties agreed to conceive a child and to raise the child together, the non-biological, non-adoptive [parent] has

Similarly, in determining shared legal custody, J.M.'s best interests control (*see Braiman v. Braiman*, 378 N.E.2d 1019[, 1020] ([N.Y.] 1978]). Such an arrangement "reposes in both parents a shared responsibility for and control of a child's upbringing" (*id.*). As the Court in *Braiman* noted "children are entitled to the love, companionship, and concern of both parents . . . [and] a joint award affords the otherwise noncustodial parent psychological support which can be translated into a healthy environment for the child" (*id.* [at 1021]). Joint custody is usually encouraged primarily as a voluntary alternative when the parents are amicable ([*id.*]). When it is a court-ordered arrangement upon embittered parents, it only promotes familial chaos (*id.*). That is not the case here. Here, the evidence establishes that the plaintiff acts as a de [ ]facto joint custodial parent with defendant and Audria and shares in making all major decisions in J.M.'s life.

Based on the evidence adduced at trial, including the demeanor and credibility of all three witnesses, the in camera interview and the factual findings made by this court, it is clear that the best interests of J.M. will be served by granting plaintiff's application for shared legal custody with defendant. Plaintiff and defendant have raised J.M. in a loving environment as evidenced by the fact that he does not know that the defendant opposes custody and court-ordered visitation with plaintiff. They clearly do not present as so embattled and embittered that they will not work together to put J.M.'s needs first. J.M. needs a continuing relationship with the plaintiff as his mother and that relationship cannot be left to depend on the consent or whim of either his biological mother or father. Anything less will promote great hardship and suffering for J.M. This court concludes based on the evidence that plaintiff, defendant and Audria can and will get along as they have in the past, to maintain J.M.'s psychological stability and to act in his best interest, and that they will be able to cooperate in making major decisions in J.M.'s life such as health, education and welfare as they have done for his entire life.

Such joint legal custody will actually be a tri-custodial arrangement as Audria and defendant already share joint legal custody. As it appears from Audria's testimony that she wholeheartedly supports such an arrangement, this court finds no issue with regards to Audria's rights in granting this relief. Indeed, tri-custody is the logical evolution of the Court of Appeals' decision in *Brooke S.B.*, and the passage of the Marriage Equality Act and Domestic Relations Law § 10–a which permits same-sex couples to marry in New York.

Regarding visitation, plaintiff requests that she be given one weekend a month and that such weekend can be carved out of defendant's time with J.M. (he presently sees J.M. from Saturday afternoon to Sunday late afternoon, three times a month). To grant plaintiff's request at defendant's expense, however, would be inappropriate as plaintiff

---

standing to seek visitation and custody under Domestic Relations Law § 70." This case represents the logical next step.

presently lives with J.M. and sees him regularly when defendant does not have visitation. Additionally, J.M. enjoys his time with his father. Taking one of defendant's three weekends each month would significantly limit J.M.'s visitation with defendant and could have a detrimental impact on his relationship with his father. The court does recognize plaintiff's need and right to time alone with J.M. and, accordingly, will grant plaintiff Wednesday night visitation with J.M. for dinner pursuant to a schedule to be established by plaintiff with input from Audria whose time with J.M. will be impacted by this court-ordered visitation. Lastly, plaintiff also requests one week-long school recess visitation each year and two weeks of visitation each summer. The court grants this relief and directs that all parties cooperate to determine which school recess and which two weeks out of the summer will belong to plaintiff.

In sum, plaintiff, defendant and Audria created this unconventional family dynamic by agreeing to have a child together and by raising J.M. with two mothers. The court therefore finds that J.M.'s best interests cry out for an assurance that he will be allowed a continued relationship with plaintiff. No one told these three people to create this unique relationship. Nor did anyone tell defendant to conceive a child with his wife's best friend or to raise that child knowing two women as his mother. Defendant's assertion that plaintiff should not have legal visitation with J.M. is unconscionable given J.M.'s bond with plaintiff and defendant's role in creating this bond. A person simply is responsible for the natural and foreseeable consequences of his or her actions especially when the best interest of a child is involved. Reason and justice dictate that defendant should be estopped from arguing that this woman, whom he has fostered and orchestrated to be his child's mother, be denied legal visitation and custody. As a result of the choices made by all three parents, this 10-year-old child to this day considers both plaintiff and Audria his mothers. To order anything other than joint custody could potentially facilitate plaintiff's removal from J.M.'s life and that would have a devastating consequence to this child. Accordingly, plaintiff is granted shared legal tri-custody and visitation as outlined above.

This court retains jurisdiction and therefore should circumstances change, either party or Audria may make an application to modify this decision and judgment of the court.

NOTES

1. Professors June Carbone and Naomi Cahn have recently noted that "[t]he possibility of three parents has arrived. A growing chorus of law review articles favors such recognition, and several states authorize such a result either explicitly or through doctrines such as de facto parentage or third party visitation statutes." June Carbone & Naomi Cahn, *Parents, Babies, and More Parents*, 92 CHI.-KENT L. REV. 9 (2017). Recognizing that judicially-

recognized "tri-parenting" has, indeed, arrived, should it persist? Be expanded? If so, how?

2.   Various concerns about legally recognizing tri-parenting situations have been expressed from various perspectives. How should tri-parenting cases be handled? Should they proceed as case-by-case adjudications, focusing on inquiries into what, factually, is in a particular child's best interests? Or should the judicial inquiry into what will best serve a child's best interests be even more circumscribed than that? What weight should be given in these cases to how a tri-parenting ruling might disrupt the conditions under which a child is already being cared for and brought up by two other parents? *See, e.g.*, Cal. Fam. Code § 7612(c) (West 2016), *amended by* 2016 Cal. Legis. Serv. Ch. 86. (West) ("In an appropriate action, a court may find that more than two persons with a claim to parentage under this division are parents if the court finds that recognizing only two parents would be detrimental to the child. In determining detriment to the child, the court shall consider all relevant factors, including, but not limited to, the harm of removing the child from a stable placement with a parent who has fulfilled the child's physical needs and the child's psychological needs for care and affection, and who has assumed that role for a substantial period of time. A finding of detriment to the child does not require a finding of unfitness of any of the parents or persons with a claim to parentage."). Should the judgments in tri-parenting cases follow norms of shared and equal parenting? Will tri-parenting cases challenge those norms? Should they? For illuminating discussion and citations to additional sources that shed light on these questions, see Carbone & Cahn, *supra* note 1.

3.   In certain circles, tri-parenting decisions are seen as threats to the sanctity of the traditional family, and thus "the family" itself. How might you articulate these concerns in light of *Dawn M.*? Does *Dawn M.* legitimate these concerns or demonstrate how they are misplaced? Both? As you think through these questions, consider aspects of the closing argument presented by Michael M.'s lawyer in the case:

> . . .

> Often we are faced with a situation we desperately would like to solve[.] [We may want to] find an equitable solution, but sometimes there just isn't one. The [f]amily court cannot evict a tenant, the [c]riminal court cannot grant a divorce and the [state] Supreme Court cannot confer parental rights upon someone who is not a parent even if the situation cries out for such a solution. Good intentions cannot supersede the law of the land.

> These parties are involved in a divorce action in this court. They have resolved all of their issues and are about to sign a Settlement Agreement except for one issue. The plaintiff is demanding that the said agreement contain language which would confer upon her certain parental rights to a child born to the defendant/husband and another woman during the parties' marriage.

Mr. M[.], the defendant herein[,] has a simple argument: The Plaintiff was his wife when he had sexual intercourse with another woman who gave birth to a child as a result of that relationship. Plaintiff is not the biological or adoptive parent of the child and therefore is precluded by statute and case law from maintaining this custody/visitation proceeding.

The only question before this court is whether or not a New York court can confer parental rights upon a person who is not related by blood or adoption to the child. In the absence of some statutory authorization, the answer must be a resounding NO! Such a person simply lacks standing to make such a request.

CUSTODY

Plaintiff is asking this court to do something it does not have the power to do[:] make her a parent! The simple, unvarnished truth is that despite all of her qualities and the wonderful job she has done in helping to raise the child, she is a "step-parent"[—]not a parent.

This court is being asked to embark upon a journey that must take it on a most slippery slope; a slope that must lead to confusion and disaster. The step-parent wants to share in custody. This the court cannot allow. By granting her request, this court would decide that this child has **_three_** parents!

The word "[p]arent" comes from the Latin "parens", "parere" which means: "to give birth to" and remains one of the most powerful words in our language. Everyone understands what a parent is and despite the current movement to enlarge the meaning of the word, it still means only two people; the two who created the child.

The courts continue to explicitly reject any enlargement of the definition of the term "parent[.]"[ ] In *Matter of Alison D. v. Virginia M.* (572 N.E.2d 27 [N.Y. 1991]), the court refused to "read the term parent in Section 70 to include categories of nonparents who have developed a relationship with a child.[ ]" [(*Id.* at 29.)]

"Joint Custody" would become "[t]ri-custody[.]"[ ] By definition it would diminish the rights of both parents to their child. Every decision concerning this child would require three people. Which doctors, what religion? Imagine the next time someone files a relocation petition? There would be 3 parents in the [courtroom] and 3 sets of parental rights to consider.

Consider the very common situation where a woman has a child, divorces[,] and then remarries. She and the child live with the new husband for 8 years and then they decide to get divorced. Does husband number 2 have a claim of custody to the child because he helped raise the child for 8 years or they all lived together as a family for 8 years? The heart may ask that the answer be "Yes"! But the brain and the law must say ["]NO!["]

. . .

PARENTING (VISITATION) TIME

What about [the Plaintiff's] . . . request for court ordered parenting time or visitation? That too must be rejected for the same reasons as those discussed above. Although often referred to as "visitation" time, it really is "parenting" time. It is the time that a parent spends with their child. In addition, the court must ask how such an order would impact upon the parents.

. . .

Awarding visitation must diminish the father's parenting time with his son as it would to the mother. Whether or not the parents agreed to allow visitation would not make a difference; their time with their child must be impacted. Here, the biological father says that no one except the mother may try to limit his time with his son. After all, is not one of the most sacrosanct and cherished rights of a parent, the right to choose how to raise their child and with whom that child may associate . . .?

The biological mother of the child is not even a party to this divorce action. Granting the step-[ ]mother any rights to this child would create a situation where this court would [o]rder a non-party (biological mother) to give rights to someone who is not related to her child by blood or adoption. Even if the biological mother agrees now, there is no guarantee that the situation would not change in the future.[ ]

Consider the situation where two parents and their child live next door to a wonderful lady who spends hours with the young child; she provides day care and even babysits at night while the parents are out for the evening. The child loves the lady and even calls her "grammar" [sic]. When the family decides to move away, does "grammar" have standing to seek visitation?

At this time, the biological mother and step-mother get along very well. But suppose the biological mother decides to move away? Suppose she decides that she no longer wants the step-mother visiting with the child? Then what?

When questioned about just such a situation, [the] Plaintiff said she could never foresee such a thing happening. But she also testified that when the three adults lived together she never envisioned they would break up and no longer be a "family[.]"[ ]

If the Supreme Court, [m]atrimonial parts stand for anything, it is the proposition that nothing lasts forever and despite our best intentions, things and people change. "Till death we do [p]art" is a wonderful notion that many of us say and truly believe when we say it, but we know it is usually not so. Many of us part before "Death does part us[.]" Nothing lasts forever; people change. "Until death we do part" is an aspiration, not a guarantee!

. . .

Kenneth J. Molloy, Submitted Closing Argument on Behalf of Michael M.,
Dawn M. v. Michael M., 55 Misc. 3d 865 (00109/2011) (N.Y. Sup. Ct. 2017)
(on file with author).

CHAPTER 9

Property, Alimony, and Child Support Awards

A. Property Division

2. The Problem of Characterization in Equitable Distribution

b. What is Marital *Property*?

i. Pensions and Other Deferred Income

Page 1043, Unabridged (Page 697, Concise). Insert the following case and notes at the end of the notes following *Laing v. Laing*.

Howell v. Howell

Supreme Court of the United States, May 15, 2017.
581 U.S. ___, 137 S.Ct. 1400, 197 L.Ed.2d 781.

■ JUSTICE BREYER delivered the opinion of the Court.

A federal statute provides that a State may treat as community property, and divide at divorce, a military veteran's retirement pay. See 10 U.S.C. § 1408(c)(1). The statute, however, exempts from this grant of permission any amount that the Government deducts "as a result of a waiver" that the veteran must make "in order to receive" disability benefits. § 1408(a)(4)(B). We have held that a State cannot treat as community property, and divide at divorce, this portion (the waived portion) of the veteran's retirement pay. See *Mansell v. Mansell*, 490 U.S. 581, 594–595 (1989).

In this case a State treated as community property and awarded to a veteran's spouse upon divorce a portion of the veteran's total retirement pay. Long after the divorce, the veteran waived a share of the retirement pay in order to receive nontaxable disability benefits from the Federal Government instead. Can the State subsequently increase, pro rata, the amount the divorced spouse receives each month from the veteran's retirement pay in order to indemnify the divorced spouse for the loss caused by the veteran's waiver? The question is complicated, but the answer is not. Our cases and the statute make clear that the answer to the indemnification question is "no."

I

A

The Federal Government has long provided retirement pay to those veterans who have retired from the Armed Forces after serving, *e.g.*, 20 years or more. It also provides disabled members of the Armed Forces with disability benefits. In order to prevent double counting, however, federal law typically insists that, to receive disability benefits, a retired veteran must give up an equivalent amount of retirement pay. And, since retirement pay is taxable while disability benefits are not, the veteran often elects to waive retirement pay in order to receive disability benefits. See 10 U.S.C. § 3911 *et seq.* (Army retirement benefits); § 6321 *et seq.* (Navy and Marines retirement benefits); § 8911 *et seq.* (Air Force retirement benefits); 38 U.S.C. § 5305 (requiring a waiver to receive disability benefits); § 5301(a)(1) (exempting disability benefits from taxation). See generally *McCarty v. McCarty*, 453 U.S. 210, 211–215 (1981) (describing the military's nondisability retirement system).

In 1981 we considered federal military retirement pay alone, *i.e.*, not in the context of pay waived to receive disability benefits. The question was whether a State could consider any of a veteran's retirement pay to be a form of community property, divisible at divorce. The Court concluded that the States could not. See *McCarty, supra.* We noted that the relevant legislative history referred to military retirement pay as a " 'personal entitlement.' " *Id.*, at 224. We added that other language in the statute as well as its history made "clear that Congress intended that military retired pay 'actually reach the beneficiary.' " *Id.*, at 228. We found a "conflict between the terms of the federal retirement statutes and the [state-conferred] community property right." *Id.*, at 232. And we concluded that the division of military retirement pay by the States threatened to harm clear and substantial federal interests. Hence federal law pre-empted the state law. *Id.*, at 235.

In 1982 Congress responded by passing the Uniformed Services Former Spouses' Protection Act, 10 U.S.C. § 1408. Congress wrote that a State may treat veterans' "disposable retired pay" as divisible property, *i.e.*, community property divisible upon divorce. § 1408(c)(1). But the new Act expressly excluded from its definition of "disposable retired pay" amounts deducted from that pay "as a result of a waiver . . . required by law in order to receive" disability benefits. § 1408(a)(4)(B). (A recent amendment to the statute renumbered the waiver provision. It now appears at § 1408(a)(4)(A)(ii). See Pub.L. 114–328, § 641(a), 130 Stat. 2164.)

In 1989 we interpreted the new federal language in *Mansell*. Major Gerald E. Mansell and his wife had divorced in California. At the time of the divorce, they entered into a "property settlement which provided, in part, that Major Mansell would pay Mrs. Mansell 50 percent of his total military retirement pay, including that portion of retirement pay waived so that Major Mansell could receive disability benefits." *Id.*, at 586. The divorce decree incorporated this settlement and permitted the division. Major Mansell later moved to modify the decree so that it would omit the portion of the retirement pay that he had waived. The California courts refused to do so. But this Court reversed. It held that federal law forbade California from treating the waived portion as community property divisible at divorce.

Justice Thurgood Marshall, writing for the Court, pointed out that federal law, as construed in *McCarty*, "completely pre-empted the application of state community property law to military retirement pay." 490 U.S., at 588. He noted that Congress could "overcome" this pre-emption "by enacting an affirmative grant of authority giving the States the power to treat military retirement pay as community property." He recognized that Congress, with its new Act, had done that, but only to a limited extent. The Act provided a "precise and limited" grant of the power to divide federal military retirement pay. It did not "gran[t]" the States "the authority to treat total retired pay as community property." *Id.*, at 589. Rather, Congress excluded from its grant of authority the disability-related waived portion of military retirement pay. Hence, in respect to the waived portion of retirement pay, McCarty, with its rule of federal pre-emption, still applies.

B

John Howell, the petitioner, and Sandra Howell, the respondent, were divorced in 1991, while John was serving in the Air Force. Anticipating John's eventual retirement, the divorce decree treated John's future retirement pay as community property. It awarded Sandra "as her sole and separate property FIFTY PERCENT (50%) of [John's] military retirement when it begins." App. to Pet. for Cert. 41a. It also ordered John to pay child support of $585 per month and spousal maintenance of $150 per month until the time of John's retirement.

In 1992 John retired from the Air Force and began to receive military retirement pay, half of which went to Sandra. About 13 years later the Department of Veterans Affairs found that John was 20% disabled due to a service-related shoulder injury. John elected to receive disability benefits and consequently had to waive about $250 per month of the roughly $1,500 of military retirement pay he shared with Sandra. Doing so reduced the amount of retirement pay that he and Sandra received by about $125 per month each. *In re Marriage of Howell*, 361 P.3d 936, 937 ([Ariz.] 2015).

Sandra then asked the Arizona family court to enforce the original decree, in effect restoring the value of her share of John's total retirement pay. The court held that the original divorce decree had given Sandra a "vested" interest in the prewaiver amount of that pay, and ordered John to ensure that Sandra "receive her full 50% of the military retirement without regard for the disability." App. to Pet. for Cert. 28a.

The Arizona Supreme Court affirmed the family court's decision. It asked whether the family court could "order John to indemnify Sandra for the reduction" of her share of John's military retirement pay. It wrote that the family court order did not "divide" John's waived military retirement pay, the order did not require John "to rescind" his waiver, nor did the order "direct him to pay any amount to Sandra from his disability pay." Rather the family court simply ordered John to "reimburse" Sandra for "reducing . . . her share" of military retirement pay. The high court concluded that because John had made his waiver after, rather than before, the family court divided his military retirement pay, our decision in *Mansell* did not control the case, and thus federal law did not preempt the family court's reimbursement order. 361 P.3d, at 939.

Because different state courts have come to different conclusions on the matter, we granted John Howell's petition for certiorari.

II

This Court's decision in *Mansell* determines the outcome here. In *Mansell*, the Court held that federal law completely pre-empts the States from treating waived military retirement pay as divisible community property. Yet that which federal law pre-empts is just what the Arizona family court did here.

The Arizona Supreme Court, the respondent, and the Solicitor General try to distinguish *Mansell*. But we do not find their efforts convincing. The Arizona Supreme Court, like several other state courts, emphasized the fact that the veteran's waiver in *Mansell* took place before the divorce proceeding; the waiver here took place several years after the divorce proceedings. See 238 Ariz., at 410; see also *Abernethy v. Fishkin*, 699 So.2d 235, 240 (Fla. 1997) (noting that a veteran had not yet waived retirement pay at the time of the divorce and permitting indemnification in light of the parties' "intent to maintain level monthly payments pursuant to their property settlement agreement"). Hence here, as the Solicitor General emphasizes, the nonmilitary spouse and the family court were likely to have assumed that a full share of the veteran's retirement pay would remain available after the assets were distributed.

Nonetheless, the temporal difference highlights only that John's military retirement pay at the time it came to Sandra was subject to later reduction (should John exercise a waiver to receive disability benefits to which he is entitled). The state court did not extinguish (and most likely would not have had the legal power to extinguish) that future contingency. The existence of that contingency meant that the value of Sandra's share of military retirement pay was possibly worth less—perhaps less than Sandra and others thought—at the time of the divorce. So too is an ownership interest in property (say, A's property interest in Blackacre) worth less if it is subject to defeasance or termination upon the occurrence of a later event (say, B's death). See generally RESTATEMENT (THIRD) OF PROPERTY § 24.3 (2010) (describing property interests that are defeasible); *id.,* § 25.3, and Comment *a* (describing contingent future interests subject to divestment).

We see nothing in this circumstance that makes the reimbursement award to Sandra any the less an award of the portion of military retirement pay that John waived in order to obtain disability benefits. And that is the portion that Congress omitted from the Act's definition of "disposable retired pay," namely, the portion that federal law prohibits state courts from awarding to a divorced veteran's former spouse. *Mansell, supra,* at 589. That the Arizona courts referred to Sandra's interest in the waivable portion as having "vested" does not help. State courts cannot "vest" that which (under governing federal law) they lack the authority to give. Cf. 38 U.S.C. § 5301(a)(1) (providing that disability benefits are generally nonassignable). Accordingly, while the divorce decree might be said to "vest" Sandra with an immediate right to half of John's military retirement pay, that interest is, at most, contingent, depending for its amount on a subsequent condition: John's possible waiver of that pay.

Neither can the State avoid *Mansell* by describing the family court order as an order requiring John to "reimburse" or to "indemnify" Sandra, rather than an order that divides property. The difference is semantic and nothing more. The principal reason the state courts have given for ordering reimbursement or indemnification is that they wish to restore the amount previously awarded as community property, *i.e.,* to restore that portion of retirement pay lost due to the postdivorce waiver. And we note that here, the amount of indemnification mirrors the waived retirement pay, dollar for dollar. Regardless of their form, such reimbursement and indemnification orders displace the federal rule and stand as an obstacle to the accomplishment and execution of the purposes and objectives of Congress. All such orders are thus pre-empted.

The basic reasons *McCarty* gave for believing that Congress intended to exempt military retirement pay from state community property laws apply *a fortiori* to disability pay. See 453 U.S., at 232–235 (describing the federal interests in attracting and retaining military personnel). And those reasons apply with equal force to a veteran's postdivorce waiver to receive disability benefits to which he or she has become entitled.

We recognize, as we recognized in *Mansell,* the hardship that congressional pre-emption can sometimes work on divorcing spouses. But we note that a family court, when it first determines the value of a family's assets, remains free to take account of the contingency that some military retirement pay might be waived, or, as the petitioner himself recognizes, take account of reductions in value when it calculates or recalculates the need for spousal support. *See Rose v. Rose,* 481 U.S. 619, 630–634, and n. 6 (1987); 10 U.S.C. § 1408(e)(6).

We need not and do not decide these matters, for here the state courts made clear that the original divorce decree divided the whole of

John's military retirement pay, and their decisions rested entirely upon the need to restore Sandra's lost portion. Consequently, the determination of the Supreme Court of Arizona must be reversed. *See Mansell, supra*, at 594.

III

The judgment of the Supreme Court of Arizona is reversed, and the case is remanded for further proceedings not inconsistent with this opinion.

It is so ordered.

■ JUSTICE GORSUCH took no part in the consideration or decision of this case.

■ JUSTICE THOMAS, concurring in part and concurring in the judgment.

I join all of the opinion of the Court except its brief discussion of "purposes and objectives" pre-emption. As I have previously explained, "[t]hat framework is an illegitimate basis for finding the pre-emption of state law." *Hillman v. Maretta*, 569 U.S. ___, ___, 133 S.Ct. 1943, 1955 (2013) (THOMAS, J., concurring in judgment); see also *Wyeth v. Levine*, 555 U.S. 555, 583 (2009) (same). In any event, that framework is not necessary to support the Court's judgment in this case.

NOTES

1.   The *Howell v. Howell* Court recognizes that its decision might create hardship for divorcing spouses of service members who were counting on a portion of their spouse's military pension as an asset. How does the Court suggest that such hardship might be mitigated? What can a State court do in order to deal with the contingency of a possible future reduction in the pension amount available? How well do you think such remedies are likely to work?

2.   The division of military pensions at divorce is a complicated field, which entails a combination of state and federal law. As the *Howell* Court notes, the relevant statute, the Uniformed Services Former Spouses' Protection Act ("USFSPA"), made military pensions available for division at divorce, overriding the Court's earlier *McCarty v. McCarty* decision. *See McCarty v. McCarty*, 453 U.S. 210 (1981). The USFSPA contains rules on the appropriate jurisdiction for the division of pensions of military service members, as well as a mechanism for direct payout of the pension to divorced spouses through the Defense Finance and Accounting Service. For an overview of recurrent interpretive issues in military pension division Mark E. Sullivan, *Military Pension Division: Crossing the Minefield*, 31 FAM. L.Q. 19 (1997).

3.   The *Howell* decision was received positively by some Veterans' groups, while other associations working with the caregivers of disabled service members criticized the potentially harsh results, especially in cases where no other assets are available for division. *See* Amy Bushatz, *Supreme Court Ruling May Cut Spouses' Divorce Pension Payments*, MILITARY.COM, (May

18, 2017), http://www.military.com/daily-news/2017/05/18/supreme-court-ruling-may-cut-spouses-divorce-pension-payments.html.

II. HUMAN CAPITAL AND OTHER INTANGIBLE ASSETS

Page 1052, Unabridged. Replace the contents of Note 1 after *Elkus v. Elkus* with the following note.

1.   In *Elkus v. Elkus*, 572 N.Y.S.2d 901 (App. Div. 1991), the court accorded the wife's fame the status of marital property applying standard prior New York precedent, *O'Brien v. O'Brien*, 489 N.E.2d 712 (N.Y. 1985). *O'Brien* has now been overturned by an amendment to New York's Domestic Relations Statute. N.Y. DOM. REL. LAW § 236 (B)(5)(d)(7) (McKinney 2016). Effective January 2016, New York courts may no longer consider professional licenses, degrees, or professional enhancement as marital property. *Id.* Nevertheless, this statute directs courts to consider the direct or indirect contributions of a spouse to the other spouse's enhancement in earning capacity when distributing marital property that is titled only to one spouse. *Id.* What do you think the practical consequences of this doctrinal shift are going to be?

Page 703, Concise. Replace the contents of Note 1 after *Postema v. Postema* with the following note.

1.   Note that even though the *Postema* court holds the degree to be the result of concerted family effort, it does not distribute a percentage of the present value of the degree itself. Why is that? Courts in a majority of states have held that educational degrees do not constitute marital property. For example, in *In re Marriage of Graham*, 574 P.2d 75 (Colo. 1978), the court held that the husband's degree in business administration was not marital property, despite the fact that he obtained the degree while his wife was earning approximately 70 percent of the marital income. New York used to be the only jurisdiction that split degrees, licenses, and even fame as marital property. *See O'Brien v. O'Brien*, 489 N.E.2d 712 (N.Y. 1985). That has now changed pursuant to an amendment to New York's Domestic Relations Statute. As of January 2016, New York courts can no longer consider professional licenses, degrees, or professional enhancement as marital property. N.Y. DOM. REL. LAW § 236 (B)(5)(d)(7) (McKinney 2016).